The Millennial Marriage

This essential text explores the concept of "Me-Marriage"—a marital relationship that blends individualized life goals and interests—and draws from research on the current benefits and costs of marriage to consider how to achieve success, both individually and relationally.

Chapters explore the larger patterns at play and identify the trends about what a modern "healthy marriage" looks like for this new generation. Brian J. Willoughby combines a review of the latest social science research on the benefits and costs of marriage with new quantitative and qualitative data from married and single adults. The book explores how marriage has fundamentally shifted in the Western world due to the changing values and approaches to relationships by the Millennial generation that is now largely transitioning to marriage.

This book is an ideal text for clinicians and practitioners (particularly those working with young married populations) looking for guidance on how to understand the increasingly complex ways that adults are navigating their relationship landscape, as well as students and scholars in the fields of psychology, family studies, and sociology and those interested in individual development, relational development, and demographic trends on the family.

Brian J. Willoughby, Ph.D. is an associate professor in the School of Family Life at Brigham Young University and a research fellow at The Wheatley Institution, U.S.A. He has published over 80 peer-reviewed articles and book chapters on topics related to couples and marital relationships.

"This is a breakthrough book on the new world of millennial marriage. Insightful, jargon free, and clearly written, it's a must-read for anyone concerned about marriage and family life in America."

William J. Doherty, Ph.D., *Professor of Family Social Science at the University of Minnesota, USA; author of* Take Back Your Marriage

"This is a thorough and thoughtful treatment of millennial marriage, detailing the range of issues (and options) characterizing the aspirations and realities of millennials in marriage. Far beyond most scholarly treatments of marriage, Brian Willoughby writes beautifully. This book is a joy to read and an achievement in accessible scholarship."

Scott M. Stanley, *University of Denver, USA*

"*The Millennial Marriage* crafts a meaningful and comprehensive portrait of the role of marriage in the lives of millennials. Through the strategic use of narratives, Willoughby allows millennials to illuminate for the reader their personal, and varied, approaches to marriage. Supported by cutting edge research, and the voices of millennials themselves, this text indicates that among many potential relationship alternatives, marriage remains an important and influential option that continues to occupy a position of significance."

Spencer Olmstead, *University of Tennessee, USA*

The Millennial Marriage

Brian J. Willoughby, Ph.D.

NEW YORK AND LONDON

First published 2021
by Routledge
52 Vanderbilt Avenue, New York, NY 10017

and by Routledge
2 Park Square, Milton Park, Abingdon, Oxon OX14 4RN

Routledge is an imprint of the Taylor & Francis Group, an informa business

© 2021 Brian J. Willoughby

The right of Brian J. Willoughby to be identified as author of this work has been
asserted by him in accordance with sections 77 and 78 of the Copyright,
Designs and Patents Act 1988.

All rights reserved. No part of this book may be reprinted or reproduced or utilised
in any form or by any electronic, mechanical, or other means, now known or
hereafter invented, including photocopying and recording, or in any information
storage or retrieval system, without permission in writing from the publishers.

Trademark notice: Product or corporate names may be trademarks or registered trademarks,
and are used only for identification and explanation without intent to infringe.

Library of Congress Cataloging-in-Publication Data
Names: Willoughby, Brian J., author.
Title: The millennial marriage / Brian J. Willoughby, Ph.D.
Description: London; New York, NY: Routledge, 2021. |
Includes bibliographical references and index.
Identifiers: LCCN 2020029493 (print) | LCCN 2020029494 (ebook) |
ISBN 9780367262501 (hardback) | ISBN 9780367262518 (paperback) |
ISBN 9780429292217 (ebook)
Subjects: LCSH: Marriage–History–21st century. | Generation Y.
Classification: LCC HQ519 .W56 2021 (print) |
LCC HQ519 (ebook) | DDC 306.8109/0905–dc23
LC record available at https://lccn.loc.gov/2020029493
LC ebook record available at https://lccn.loc.gov/2020029494

ISBN: 978-0-367-26250-1 (hbk)
ISBN: 978-0-367-26251-8 (pbk)
ISBN: 978-0-429-29221-7 (ebk)

Typeset in Bembo
by Newgen Publishing UK

Contents

List of figures		vi
Acknowledgments		viii
1	Why Millennial Marriage?	1
2	Millennials and the New Marriage	8
3	Me-Marriage: A New Type of Marriage for Millennials	30
4	Me-Marriage and Marital Quality	50
5	Balancing Education and Career Trajectories	76
6	Mental Health and Physical Well-Being in Me-Marriage	99
7	Parenting Within a Me-Marriage	121
8	Religion and Spirituality in Me-Marriages	145
9	Gender and a Role-Less Marriage	165
10	Modern Diversity in Marriage	184
11	A New Case for Marriage	203
	Appendix	214
	Index	218

Figures

2.1	Percentage of Millennials Who Felt Ready for Marriage by Age and Current Marital Status	20
3.1	Differences in Millennial Life Satisfaction by Marital Status, With and Without Controlling for Background Factors	36
3.2	Millennial Life Satisfaction Across Domains, Percentage Who Reported Either "Mostly Satisfied" or "Very Satisfied" by Marital Status	37
3.3	Married Millennials vs. Older Married Individuals on Life Satisfaction and Happiness	38
3.4	Belief That There Are More Advantages to Being Single Than Being Married, for Married Individuals by Age and Gender	40
4.1	Estimated Means on Satisfaction and Stability by Marital Status for Millennials in their 30s	54
4.2	Percentage of Married and Cohabiting Millennials Based on Low, Medium, and High Raw Relationship Satisfaction and Stability Scores	55
4.3	Estimated Means Comparing Millennials vs. Older Newlyweds on Satisfaction and Stability	56
4.4	Number of Disagreements by Age Cohort, With and Without Controls	57
4.5	Estimated Means on Relational Aggression, by Gender and Generational Cohort	58
5.1	Percentage of Millennials in Personal Income Categories for Those Married, Divorced, and Never Married	80
5.2	Percentage of Married vs. Never Married Millennials With Access to Various Economic Benefits	81
5.3	Self-Reported Credit Score for Married and Never-Married Millennials in Their Early 30s	81
5.4	Percentage of Millennials With Educational Status Based on Being Married or Engaged	83
5.5	Age of Marriage by Educational Attainment for Married Millennials in Their Early 30s	84

List of figures vii

5.6	Percentage of Early 30-Year-Old Millennials Who Agreed With the Statement, "I Regret My Educational Decisions," by Marital Status and Gender	96
6.1	Percentage of Reported Exercise and Presence of Serious Health Problems From 18–29 by Marital Status for Millennials in Their Early 30s	104
6.2	Estimated Means for Smoking Behavior by Marital Status for Millennials in Their Early 30s	105
6.3	Percentage Satisfied With Overall Health for Millennials in Their Early 30s, by Marital Status	106
6.4	Estimated Means for Depressive Symptoms for Millennials in Their Early 30s, by Marital Status	106
6.5	BMI Category by Gender and Cohort Among Newlyweds	107
6.6	Percentage of Self-Reported Health Symptoms for Newlywed Men, by Cohort	108
7.1	Estimated Means for Relationship Stability and Satisfaction by Marital and Parenthood Status for Millennials	126
7.2	Average Relationship Satisfaction and Stability by Number of Children for Married Millennials	127
7.3	Estimated Means for Relationship Satisfaction and Stability by Parent Status and Gender for Newlywed Millennials	128
7.4	Estimated Means on Overall Conflict and Relational Aggression by Parent Status and Gender for Newlywed Millennials	129
8.1	Percentage of Self-Reported Religious Change From 18 to 29 for Millennials in Their Early 30s, by Marital Status	148
9.1	Percentage of Newlyweds Who Agreed That Their Marriages Had Power Imbalances, by Gender and Age Cohort	175
10.1	Estimated Means on Various Outcomes for Millennial Newlyweds, by Gender and Race	192
10.2	Estimated Means for Various Outcomes for Millennial Newlyweds by Gender and Racial Differences between Partners	195
10.3	Percentage of 20-22 Year Olds Who Agreed With the Statement, "Intimacy With Another Person Is Never Okay in a Relationship"	199
10.4	Percentage of 20–22 Year Olds Who Agreed With the Statement, "Relationships With More Than Two People Can Be Just As Strong"	200
11.1	Estimated Mean for Millennials In Their Early 30s on a 4-Point Scale, by Marital Status	212

Acknowledgments

Whenever a book is finished, there are countless people to thank. Most of these people never read a single line of this manuscript but were instrumental in my own education and training. So let me first provide a broad thank you to all of my mentors and teachers over the years who guided me throughout my education and early career. Specifically, let me thank my collaborators on the various data projects from which this book draws. Without the tireless efforts of Jeremy Yorgason, Spencer James, Larry Nelson, Jason Carroll, Dean Busby, and Erin Holmes, the data that formed the backbone of this book would not have existed. I would specifically like to thank all the graduate and undergraduate students who worked so hard on various elements of this book. A special shout-out is in order to the Me-Marriage team, who not only helped me interview all of the millennial couples for this book, but also were tasked with the mind-numbing responsibility of transcribing and coding over 100 hour-long interviews. These students include my graduate student, Rachel Augustus, and undergraduates Logan Nuttall, Joshua Otani, Mary Call, Charice West, Rebekah Hill, Molly Leeper, Misty Griffith, McKell Jorgensen-Wells, Lydia Lambert, Lindsey LeVitre, David Moss, Chloe Coleman, Catherine Lunt, Cassie Knight, Breanne Butler, Brianne Mu'amoholeva, and Joy Pizomo. Finally (but not least!), a special thank you goes to my wife, Cassi, and my children, who put up with Dad once again trying to write a book. The final elements of this book were written during the COVID-19 pandemic and at home. Thank you for putting up with Dad being a bit of a mess trying to put the finishing touches on this book while you were trying to do your homework.

1 Why Millennial Marriage?

My Academic Journey to Studying Millennial Marriage

Have millennials fundamentally altered the landscape of marriage forever? This question was what drove me to write this book, exploring how millennials, who have been scorned and ridiculed in the media for their unique approach to relationships, are faring now that many of them have married. I hope that through the pages and chapters of this book, you will come to appreciate the unique hopes, challenges, and pitfalls that millennials face as they strive for love and happiness. However, before we jump straight into the pool, there is some important background information to cover, not about millennials themselves but about your guide (me!).

Any book is a journey in which the author's primary job is to guide the reader through whatever narrative or subject matter the author has deemed worthy of the reader's attention. In that way, a book is an inherently biased and skewed endeavor, molded by the author's views, background, and personal opinions. While completely avoiding this bias is likely impossible, I believe in the importance of understanding the motives and background of the guide whenever beginning such a journey. After all, each guide has certain quirks, favored routes, and unique biases that change the course and nature of the journey itself. For that reason, before jumping straight into a discussion of the millennial generation and what its members may or may not be doing to the nature of marriage, I think it's important to start with a little personal history. All academic scholars who have ever attempted to study relationships have their own personal journey that took them from wandering, mostly lost, undergraduates to focused (at least most of the time) explorers seeking to uncover the secrets of love and romance.

The personal journey that would eventually lead me to write a book about how millennials may be fundamentally changing the institution of marriage began in a dark and dreary lab of a geneticist whose name I have long since forgotten. This particular lab resided on the campus of the University of Wisconsin in Madison. I was a pre-med student, majoring in genetics and planning on a long, dull, but financially lucrative career as a pathologist. As part of my major, I was tasked (likely by some wise department chair who had seen countless undergraduates embark on a career path they did not truly understand) with interviewing someone who had the career I aspired to. I honestly don't remember much about the person

2 Why Millennial Marriage?

I interviewed—including their age, gender, or really anything about them. Nor do I even recall what was said. I really only remember one specific thing from that encounter—the persistent thought that kept occurring to me about how dark, lonely, and depressing this lab seemed to be. The pathologist I interviewed was hunkered over a desk and seemed to me to be sad and alone. The lab itself, with various specimens, microscopes, and lab equipment strewn about, seemed empty and desolate. Whether my own young adult brain was projecting such thoughts or this particular researcher was merely having a bad day (trying to entertain a young freshman who was attempting to complete a course requirement probably wasn't helping), didn't change the fact that I decided that day I needed to change course in my education and career. After transferring to a university across the country, I settled into the major of many lost and confused university souls: psychology.

Psychology was fascinating to me. I enjoyed learning about cognition and emotion, sensation and perception. I was later introduced to the field of relationship and family science through an elective class that sunk me further into my fascination with romantic relationships. I found romantic relationships and marriage to be particularly fascinating at the time, likely due to my own newlywed status. What made people get married? How and why did healthy marriages last? Why did divorce happen? My own fascination with these topics, combined with some stellar and influential mentoring, made me decide to pursue a career in academics and to make the study of romantic relationships and marriage my primary goal. I elected to complete my graduate education at the University of Minnesota, where I studied under Dr. William Doherty, perhaps one of the best minds on the planet when it comes to marriage. It was during the five years of my Ph.D. program that the seeds that would eventually become this book took root.

I arrived in Minnesota determined to understand and study healthy marriage and divorce. However, while I was working through my graduate program, I began assisting on a new project that focused not on married couples but on younger, premarital couples. This project wasn't aligned with my primary interests, and, at first, my excitement level for the project was relatively low. But like many graduate students before and after me, I did what was asked with no public protest. I told myself that perhaps there was something I could glean from the young couples in the study that would help me in my future work on real marriages. The "Fragile Families Project," as it was called, was aimed at identifying young, non-married parents in the Minneapolis area who expressed an interest in marriage. The project was an intervention study, aimed at determining if project resources might help these young families build a solid foundation on which to create a healthy marriage. The project and research assistants would regularly interview the couples and then provide targeted resources and mentors for them. In the mid-2000s, this project was a part of many similar research projects around the country that were capitalizing on new federal funding under the Bush administration that was created to promote marriage across the United States.

Much to my surprise, the work I would do on this project would change the course of my professional career forever. As I worked with and interviewed these young couples, I became more and more interested in their stories. They were roughly my age but had a dizzying array of thoughts, approaches, concerns, and views of marriage. Perhaps this was one of my first true brushes with diversity, but it launched within me a fascination with not just marriage but also the premarital process itself. I wanted to learn more about these young adults and how they dated and made sense of later marriage; I wanted to understand my fellow cohort and the decisions its members were making that were different from my own. I wanted to know why some embraced marriage and relationships while others seemed petrified by it. Where did these thoughts come from, and how did they change the very relational landscape and trajectories of these people's lives?

These experiences in graduate school led me to a career focused on what would become known as the study of emerging adulthood (Arnett, 2000). I found myself in a unique niche in this field. In the years before I began my work, the study of the third decade of life had been revolutionized by Arnett's argument that a new developmental stage had emerged (pun intended). Unique educational, cultural, and relational changes (Arnett, 2000, 2007; Arnett & Tanner, 2006, p. 3) had created a unique developmental landscape for those in their 20s. Despite the variety of topics such a new field provided, most of the emerging adulthood field was composed of scholars of the adolescent stage who were taking their adolescent focus and moving later into the life course. I, along with a handful of my colleagues, were unique. We were relational and marriage scholars stepping backward in the life course—taking our unique focus on relational development and couple processes to a period in the life course where finding and sustaining love was getting more and more complex. I dove into this work and spent the better part of a decade focused squarely on what individual, cultural, and relational factors turned these emerging adults toward or away from marriage.

The Doom and Gloom Approach to Studying Millennials

I can remember, early in my career as a scholar, sitting at many academic conferences and listening to well-informed speakers tell me repeatedly how emerging adults were on the road to personal apocalypse. This message was not just relational; it also cut across many aspects of development. Young adults were selfish, flocking away from institutional pillars like religious organizations and steady blue-collar jobs to find self-fulfillment and personal edification through travel, leisure, and a unique brand of moral relativism. Though some of my colleagues took the stance that emerging adults were doomed to a future of lonely individualism, others were quick to defend this new and confusing generation. Debate raged regarding if such emerging adults were flourishing or floundering (Nelson & Padilla-Walker, 2013). Relationally, the conversation was similar. Casual sex and hook-up rates were up (Garcia et al., 2015; Grello et al., 2006), and marriage rates were down (Parker & Stepler, 2017). Not only were emerging adults changing the core ways in which they dated (more on this in Chapter 2), but they were also changing their fundamental views on relationships in general. I was on the forefront of scholars pointing out how single young adults had developed potentially harmful, and in most cases paradoxical, views of long-term relationships including marriage (Willoughby & Carroll, 2015; Willoughby & James, 2017). I would relay these

4 *Why Millennial Marriage?*

messages of doom and gloom to my college students, often joking that most scholars and presenters didn't blame them for their perceived inadequacies in life, but rather their baby-boomer parents who were too soft and too freeing in some areas and too suffocating in others.

These academic dialogues, focused as they were on a new and debated developmental area, were happening concurrently with a larger cultural dialogue about these young adults. Here, the discussion and debate was not about identity development or relational progression, it was about millennials—the term coined to describe those born roughly between 1980 and 2000. These were the same emerging adults we were studying as researchers, and the larger public had come down on them—hard. Headlines across the world noted how dysfunctional, disillusioned, and just disrespectful this supposedly self-focused generation was. Millennials were called the "Why Worry Generation" due to their care-free attitudes (Warner, 2010). They were changing the very nature of the workplace with their unique demands (Safer, 2007). They were abandoning the religion of their families in droves (Gilgoff, 2010). During the recession of the late 2000s, they were also uniquely affected by a weak and sobering job market (Samuelson, 2010), which elicited equal parts pity and snickering from their older counterparts. In 2010, *Business Insider* called millennials the "Most Broken Generation Ever" (Synder, 2010). The ridicule has spread far and wide, going so far that, just recently, millennials have even been accused of ruining Disneyland (Abell, 2019).

A quick sidenote and admission: In the interest of full disclosure, my own birthday puts me squarely on the border between the Gen X and Millennial crowds—a convenient place to be if one wished to claim the best and avoid the worst from both cohorts. Part of my own scholarly fascination with this group came about because I was, in some ways, part of it. I understood millennials' approach to the world and understood their frustrations and anxieties. As I sat in and engaged with the scholarly community, largely dominated by baby boomers at the time, I felt myself torn. Do I defend my own generational cohort? Do I acknowledge its members' unique challenges and try to help? Or do I attempt to do what many scholars do—be a robotic and detailed observer, simply driven to report the facts and figures? As a young scholar, it was the latter approach that mostly drove my early scholarship. It is and was a publish-or-perish world in academia and I felt this strategy was a necessity for survival. But over a decade later, with tenure and other academic milestones now behind me, I began to wonder if perhaps it was time to wade more into the weeds when it came to the good and bad of millennial relationships after all.

The Classroom Moment That Birthed a Book

While this background provides the context of why I decided to write a book on millennials generally, I have yet to touch on the flame that really ignited what would become my central goal for wanting to write about millennials and their marriages. As a professor, one gets into a certain cadence with teaching and talking to students. Professors often have certain jokes, stories, and examples that

Why Millennial Marriage? 5

they tell semester after semester. I believe the best professors are those who can connect with their students—to make the material come alive and make the terms and concepts applicable to them. For years when I would teach students about marriage and marital communication, I would use clips from one of the original reality television programs shown on MTV in the early 2000s, *Newlyweds*. This show chronicled the first years of the marriage between pop singer Jessica Simpson and Nick Lachey, one of the singers from the '90s boy band 98 degrees. For years, this illustration was a hit. Students loved analyzing the clips we viewed in class, dissecting the relationship between Nick and Jessica and considering why their eventual divorce might have happened. Then, a few years ago, I noticed something in my class. When I introduced the show, I was met with a room full of blank stares. I realized that the students no longer connected with the material because most of them no longer knew who Jessica and Nick were. Jessica, Britney, and Christina had been replaced by Gaga, Ariana, and Taylor. The bands 98 degrees, N' Sync, and the Backstreet Boys had been replaced by BTS and One Direction. I think teachers may get this experience—of realizing our generation has been replaced by one younger—more than others (somehow, the students stay the same age, year after year, while we keep getting older). Regardless, over the next few years I became increasingly aware that my pop culture references were becoming dated and less relevant. Millennials had moved on and were being replaced by what some are calling the rising iGen generation (Twenge, 2017). It was official: I was now part of an "older" generation.

While my interest in emerging adults continues, this experience started a train of thought in my mind. This cohort of millennial young adults I had been studying for a decade, a cohort I had written about and theorized about in dozens of papers and a previous book, were now full-grown adults. In addition, if they were in fact adults, they were likely getting married. "But wait!" I thought. Much of my theorizing had been about what would happen if and when these young adults did get married. I realized that there was no longer a need to theorize when we could see what happened. At some point along the way in my study of marriage, I had forgotten that I didn't need to just theorize about what would happen to the millennials—eventually they would show us.

And so here we are, a moment in history where we can look, with evidence, at what is happening to the institution of marriage as one of the most unique and debated generations in human history enters the fourth decade of life. For years, other researchers and I have been painting a picture of future relationship failure, largely believing that marriage would either die with the millennials as they rejected it or that their own marriages would fail to have the power of marriages in the past. We reasoned that their more individualistic and self-centered approach to life would not mesh well with what we knew was needed to sustain a long-term healthy relationship. But was this the case? At the heart of this question is one that is fairly straightforward. Would the new trends we saw among millennials that created something so unique that scholars needed to create a new development period in emerging adulthood also create a new type of adulthood and marriage? Or would such trends eventually be shown to be unique to young adulthood,

6 Why Millennial Marriage?

with the millennials eventually looking very similar to their parents once they "matured"? These questions harkened back to my early years as a scholar when I focused on marriage.

In the early 2000s, much was being made in the social sciences about the "case for marriage." Linda Waite and Maggie Gallagher's (2000) book, *The Case for Marriage*, was a touch point in social science scholarship. These scholars laid out a compelling and empirically driven argument that marriage benefited the individuals and couples involved. It has since been cited north of 2,500 times since its publication. Much of the current scholarship at the time suggested that marriage was a relationship that improved people's lives, that created the best foundation for healthy relationships. But if millennial marriage is now different, is marriage still good (for them or for society)? This became the core driving question that led me to want to write a book about millennials and marriage.

Before we really dig in, a few more disclosures are probably in order. As I hinted at earlier, I transitioned to marriage early myself, well before most of my friends and fellow millennials. I have been happily married for 18 years, and that experience shapes my views, orientation, and own beliefs about marriage as an institution. I do not doubt that many readers may find hints and glimpses of language throughout the book that carries with it a "pro-marriage" view, and I certainly attribute much of my own personal happiness and satisfaction in life to a happy and healthy marriage with my wife. However, for me this book is not for or against marriage; the question here is different. It surrounds the consideration of whether or not marriage itself has changed to the point where "marriage" itself is no longer universally good or bad for the individual or for couples. After all, if millennials have created something in marriage so unique, our entire approach to the subject needs to change. With that bit of background out of the way, pull up a chair and let's take a look at how the marriages of young millennial couples are faring.

References

Abell, B. (2019, July 25). *Angry mom thinks childless millennials should be banned from Disney World*. Inside the Magic. https://insidethemagic.net/2019/07/angry-disney-world-mom-ba1/

Arnett, J. J. (2000). Emerging adulthood: A theory of development from the late teens through the twenties. *American Psychologist, 55*, 469–480.

Arnett, J. J. (2007). Emerging adulthood: What is it, and what is it good for? *Child Development Perspectives, 1*, 68–73.

Arnett, J. J., & Tanner, J. L. (Eds.). (2006). *Emerging adults in America: Coming of age in the 21st century*. American Psychological Association.

Garcia, J. R., Seibold-Simpson, S. M., Massey, S. G., & Merriwether, A. M. (2015). Casual sex: Integrating social, behavioral, and sexual health research. In J. DeLamater & R. F. Plante (Eds.), *Handbook of the sociology of sexualities* (pp. 203–222). Springer.

Gilgoff, D. (2010, February 17). *Study: Young Americans less religious than their parents*. CNN. www.cnn.com/2010/US/02/17/report.millennials.faith/index.html

Grello, C. M., Welsh, D. P., & Harper, M. S. (2006). No strings attached: The nature of casual sex in college students. *Journal of Sex Research, 4*, 255–267.

Nelson, L. J., & Padilla-Walker, L. M. (2013). Flourishing and floundering in emerging adult college students. *Emerging Adulthood, 1,* 67–78.

Parker, K., & Stepler, R. (2017, September 14). *As U.S. marriage rate hovers at 50%, education gap in marital status widens.* Pew Research. www.pewresearch.org/fact-tank/2017/09/14/as-u-s-marriage-rate-hovers-at-50-education-gap-in-marital-status-widens/

Safer, M. (2007, November 8). *The millennials are coming.* CBS News. www.cbsnews.com/news/the-millennials-are-coming/

Samuelson, R. J. (2010, March 4). *The millennial generation is getting clobbered.* Newsweek. www.newsweek.com/millennial-generation-getting-clobbered-69309

Synder, M. (2010, April 24). *Millennials are the brokest generation ever.* Business Insider. www.businessinsider.com/millennials-are-the-brokest-generation-ever-2010-4

Twenge, J. M. (2017). *iGen: Why today's super-connected kids are growing up less rebellious, more tolerant, less happy—and completely unprepared for adulthood—and what that means for the rest of us.* Simon and Schuster.

Waite, L. J., & Gallagher, M. (2000). The case for marriage: Why married people are happier, healthier, and better off financially. Doubleday.

Warner, J. (2010, May 28). *The why-worry generation. New York Times.* www.nytimes.com/2010/05/30/magazine/30fob-wwln-t.html

Willoughby, B. J., & Carroll, J. S. (2015). On the horizon: Marriage timing, beliefs, and consequences in emerging adulthood. In J. J. Arnett (Ed.), *The Oxford handbook of emerging adulthood* (pp. 280–295). Oxford University Press.

Willoughby, B. J., & James, S. L. (2017). *The marriage paradox: Why emerging adults love marriage yet push it aside.* Oxford University Press.

2 Millennials and the New Marriage

"I think that marriage is cool. It's good." This thought was something Judy, a 30-year-old woman, said to me early in her interview about her marriage. Judy seemed enthusiastic about her relationship with Juan, a man she had met more than a decade earlier. Juan and Judy were one of the most seasoned married couples that my research team spoke to. When we sat down with them, they had been married for 10 years, marrying young compared to their peers. Their courtship was relatively quick and, surprisingly, not tied to any religious motivations. In fact, they weren't religious at all (when asked, they both labeled themselves as agnostic). They met through a friend shortly before Judy began college. The connection was instantaneous and mutual. As Judy explained,

> We both kind of wanted to [get married]. I think we knew when we first started dating that we really got along. My dad actually joked and said that he should be nice to this one because he's probably going to be his son-in-law. I think everyone kind of knew, and we were just really compatible.

This connection was so strong, they decided to move in with each other after only 3 months of dating. This move was pushed by Judy, and Juan was a bit apprehensive about the pace of their relationship, despite their connection.

This anxiety only intensified as Judy began to talk about marriage shortly after moving in together. As Juan put it, "I sort of knew early on that I would like to eventually get [married], but I wanted to wait longer." Judy also noted her husband's hesitation, saying,

> Juan didn't really want to [get married] because we had just started dating, and we just moved in together, and he thought it was too soon. But I think we both kind of knew that we wanted to get married, and then it was just kind of, at the time, a good decision.

Eventually he agreed to move forward with a quick engagement, noting in his interview, "She didn't want to wait long, so I decided it's better to do it sooner than to say no and go the opposite way." Six months later they were married, Judy at 19 and Juan at 24. They both worked and went to school, which is typical of

Millennials and the New Marriage 9

many young millennial couples. Eventually, they both landed good jobs. Shortly before they were interviewed, they had bought their first home together.

In so many ways, Juan and Judy represent the type of courtship and marriage that has been present for generations. It was a story of love, with some anxiety and hesitation but ending in eventual happiness. Juan and Judy both seemed genuinely happy, content, and satisfied in their marriage. They seemed to prioritize each other and their relationship. At one point, Juan seemed insulted by the prospect of putting his career over his marriage. As he put it, "I think that you should never put your career above your relationship. That leads you down an unhappy path." Despite these general indications that Juan and Judy's relationship was simply following the path of millions of marriages before them, their interviews slowly uncovered some unique wrinkles in their approach to their marriage—wrinkles that suggested a uniquely millennial take on matrimony.

First came Judy's admission that if she could go back in time, she'd actually prefer to have not met her husband. Let me be clear: she didn't want to never meet Juan at all; she simply wished that Juan hadn't come along for another 10 years. This took us a bit by surprise given how happy she seemed. When asked to clarify, she explained, "I always joke and wish I could have hit pause. I always tell Juan I wish I could have pushed pause and met him later on because there are a few things that I've reprioritized being married." What were those things? For Judy, they were things like simply being able to focus on herself. She felt like she had missed out on opportunities by being burdened by a spouse so early in life. When asked to elaborate, she explained what she felt she had missed out on:

> Just traveling independently, or I think, I'll be later in life when I get my Ph.D., and I was a little bit later in life when I got my master's degree than I had planned. Just being 20 and doing dumb 20-year-old things! You think you're going to go to college and you know, live like those '90s movies where there's parties and whatever. But I was married in college so I reprioritized what my college experience looked like. So instead of doing those things, I had a husband.

So did she regret her marriage? No, she was clear about that. "It's all about give and take. I don't regret it at all. But if I were single, my 20s would have looked different than if I were married."

Some other interesting details emerged that appeared to set their relationship at odds with previous generations. While they were happy and stable, Juan and Judy had no plans to become parents. When asked, Judy simply stated, "We don't have children, and we don't plan on having children." That was the only time in the interview children were mentioned. Judy also explained that marriage, despite making her happy, was maybe not the best or right choice for everyone. She explained,

> the idea of sharing your life with someone really appealed to me, but I think a lot of people are in relationships long term that don't get married, and it

10 *Millennials and the New Marriage*

works out. I know a lot of people who make it work, whether or not they're sharing each other's taxes.

She even suggested at one point that getting married was more difficult than not, arguing, "I think it's easier in our society to be in a relationship than to be married." Juan largely agreed but seemed to have an even harder time explaining why anyone would benefit from marriage. It was difficult for him to articulate why marriage was a better option than simply living together as he had done earlier in his relationship. He finally volunteered that perhaps marriage might help "to solidify the relationship."

These quick glimpses into Juan and Judy's mindset toward marriage begin to offer insights into a new approach and mentality that many millennials are taking with them into marriage. In this chapter, I will explore these new and unique approaches to marriage that set the stage for some of the specific discussions to come regarding if marriage has changed and truly still benefits millennials. The story so far seems far from conclusive. As Juan and Judy's history illustrates, millennials are approaching marriage with more hesitation and caution than ever before, even if it appears to bring happiness and fulfillment. Marriage, once the clear front-runner when it came to romantic unions, has now come under fire. There are numerous potential hypotheses as to why marriage may have lost its beneficial luster in the last few decades. For our purposes, however, we will focus on perhaps the most lingering yet important potential cause of this shift: that millennials have changed what marriage means and how it works. As I noted in the introduction, this belief was the one that I held going into this book project and one that developmental and relational theorists who study young adulthood have at least been hinting at for the last 20 years. But is it true? Are we using the term "marriage" for millennials to define a type of relationship that is fundamentally different from anything that has come before it? The only way to begin to address this question is to first discuss what marriage even means to millennials.

But before we move any further, I need to quickly address where the stories like those of Juan and Judy are coming from. From this moment forward, I will begin to share with you the stories and thoughts of millennials themselves. These illustrations and examples came from a year-long study conducted by myself and my research team that includes interviews with 100 millennial married couples from across the United States. These couples range in age, race, education, and background. Their stories are varied and complex. But over the course of these interviews, and with the help of some qualitative coding techniques, my team was able to identify common themes across several questions related to millennial marriage we were interested in. The stories and quotes to follow in this and subsequent chapters are often simply meant to illustrate and provide tangible examples of these themes. But I also hope they provide a more human touch to the struggles and triumphs of millennial marriage. I have changed the names of these couples throughout the book, along with some specific details of their experiences, to keep their data confidential and anonymous. I have also lightly edited the grammar of the quotes to make them easier to read. If you are interested in more details about these data, they can be found in the Appendix.

With that said, in this chapter I will start by outlining how the very approach to marriage, an approach that begins to take shape in the early years of millennials' lives, well before they walked down the matrimonial aisle, has shifted considerably. This exploration will be somewhat brief, as I covered such questions extensively in a previous book (see Willoughby & James, 2017) and other scholars have likewise helped illustrate and discuss these changes (see Furman, 2002; Konstam, 2019; Roberson et al., 2016; Shulman & Connolly, 2013). But, because such an understanding is vital to appreciating how millennial marriages are unique, let us dive into the question of how millennials have thought about and approached marriage differently than generations past.

The Tool Mentality

Perhaps the first issue to lay to rest is the fundamental question of if there is a different approach to how marriage is conceptualized among millennials. When I speak about "approaches" to marriage, I am referring to cognitions, attitudes, and beliefs that one holds about the broader institution of marriage and its application in one's own life. These psychological approaches have been shown in previous research to have an influence on a wide range of behaviors (Willoughby, Hall, & Luczak, 2013), from sexual decision-making (Willoughby, 2012; Willoughby & Dworkin, 2009) to decisions to engage in risk-taking behaviors, such as binge drinking and drug use (Carroll et al., 2007). More importantly, such beliefs and attitudes are also prime predictors of eventual transitioning into marriage itself (Clarkberg et al., 1995; Willoughby, 2014) and behaviors within a marriage (Willoughby et al., Forthcoming). To put it another way, an individual's expectations and beliefs about marriage generally (now or in the future), play an important role in determining both likely pathways into (or away from) marriage and actual behavior once married. This is the marriage filter through which we make our own decisions and judge the decisions of others. Most people have had moments where they offer slightly judgmental or insulting remarks about a colleague's, friend's, or family member's marriage. Often these personal frustrations result more from the fact that the target of the annoyance has taken a different approach to marriage or relationships than the other party believes is ideal.

For this reason, the most basic building block for understanding millennial marriage needs to be focused on such general marital beliefs. Are millennials as a group unique in this regard? While there is certainly some consistency between parents and their children on how they approach marital relationships (Willoughby, Carroll, Vitas, & Hill, 2012), the question here is broader. Do millennials, as a group, hold different general views of marriage compared to the baby boomers before them? A robust set of data points suggests that this is indeed the case. I helped conduct one of the first large studies to explore this question (Willoughby, Olson, Carroll, Nelson, & Miller, 2012) and the results are worth noting, as they shed some initial light on this topic. This study, conducted more than 10 years ago, when most millennials were in their late teens and early 20s, examined data from college-aged millennials across the United States. We found numerous differences between young-adult millennials and their boomer parents

12 *Millennials and the New Marriage*

on general beliefs about marriage. Many might expect that millennials would be less inclined to endorse marriage than their parents. However, we largely found the opposite! For example, we found that millennials believed that the ideal age of marriage was earlier than both their mother's and father's beliefs. Millennials were also more likely to list marriage as an important goal compared to both mothers and fathers, and were more likely to believe that marriage was a lifelong relationship compared to their mothers. They were also more likely to report wanting to get married soon, compared to their parents who both expressed a desire for their own children to marry later in life. Yet one finding bucked this trend and illustrates the increasingly complex notion of marriage that millennials were beginning to grapple with. Despite this trend toward a more "pro-marriage" approach than their parents, millennials were also, perhaps paradoxically, more likely than both their mothers and fathers to believe that there were more advantages to being single than to being married.

Such a result is, on the surface, perplexing. Why would young millennials seem to endorse the importance of marriage and show a stronger desire for marriage than their parents yet also believe that staying single held more advantages? The answer lies in what is probably the largest shift in marital approaches between the two generations. Whereas previous generations have largely held marriage as the one true culmination of the romantic relationship and dating process, millennials were the first generation to not only tolerate increased diversity in relationship trajectories but often celebrate it. Marriage remains the most common and accepted long-term relationship union (Willoughby & Carroll, 2015), but millennials, for the first time, began to articulate and embrace the benefits of *not* getting married. As I noted back in 2017 (Willoughby & James, 2017), such a shift has created interesting tensions within the minds of many millennials. But it has also opened a near-infinite road map to success in their minds. Marriage is not the singular pathway to relationship success; it is merely one of many. I call this mindset the *tool mentality* of marriage. It is a mentality that makes marriage a tool to use if one wishes but certainly not the only way to successfully construct a happy life. Cameron, a young millennial, hit this concept on the head when we asked him about marriage. He said, "For me, marriage is like a tool; [it] makes things easier for both of us to accomplish more."

This expansion of potential relational pathways has caused increasing tensions between baby boomer parents and their adult millennial children. Boomers grew up in an age of clear and direct social norms when it came to relationships and child rearing. Almost everyone got married, and almost everyone waited to have children and raise their family until after they were married. Millennials were the first generation to begin to embrace marriage as only one of several potential options. As a simple illustration from our interviews, take Trent and Becky. Becky had been previously married and divorced. Trent and Becky met each other selling pest control door-to-door and, after having a child together, were happy and content with their committed cohabiting relationship. To many millennials, Trent and Becky deserved a hardy high five. They had found happiness and stability in a relationship that worked for them and their young child. Who cared if it wasn't legally sanctioned?

Millennials and the New Marriage   13

Yet Trent and Becky's boomer parents were less thrilled with their relationship. They could not seem to get their heads around why Trent and Becky wouldn't simply tie the knot. As Trent put it, "We loved each other, we stayed together, [and] we never fought." But their parents saw things a different way. He continued, "our parents, every time we saw one or the other of them, they would give us crap about having a bastard son, or that it's not right that we're not married, and we got tired of hearing it." They would eventually cave to this pressure and get married, but it was clear in speaking to them that they viewed their relationship no differently now than they did before they received any legal sanctioning of their relationship.

But don't take this to mean that millennials no longer place any significance on marriage. Millennials appear to be holding onto something regarding marriage, but they seem, in some cases, unsure of what it is. Take Grace, who, like others, was puzzled by the question, but had this to say about the importance of marriage:

> I don't really think I ever thought [when I was younger] about getting married. I thought about having a boyfriend and stuff, but I never really thought about the whole getting married, having a family thing. I never put very much thought into it. I never wanted a typical dream wedding or whatever. I just wanted love; I didn't really think about marriage.

But she was, in fact, married. There must be something here that she felt had value, despite being unable to articulate it. What's interesting about this is not only did Grace end up marrying, but she had done it twice! Her current marriage was her second after a failed first attempt.

The best way to explain this shift across generations is to talk about it as an erosion of social norms when it comes to the timing of courtship and marriage. What was once a clear societally endorsed pathway to adulthood has splintered into a spaghetti bowl of options. As another specific example, take a common maker of normative marital timing: a belief in ideal timing, or at what age someone would ideally get married. For previous generations, such notions were clear and direct: "ideal" timing was marriage in the early to mid-20s. Aria, one of many millennials who spoke of a lack of norms when it came to the timing of marriage, expressed a common millennial sentiment when it comes to the new normal of ideal timing: there is no ideal age. She said, "Since people mature at different ages, not everyone has the same timeline. I mean, some people don't go to college, most people that we [her and her husband] know didn't go to college, [so] they got married super young." Owen, another millennial we spoke to, had a similar sentiment, sharing,

> No [there is no ideal age to marry], because everybody matures or experiences things differently. So, somebody who lives on their own or does a lot of stuff maybe at, 16, 17, 18, may be ready by 18, and there are some people who I've known that are 29, 30, and I would say they're not ready to get married. Your goal should be wanting to try to prepare and mature enough so that when you are in that relationship with the other person, you are able to deny

14　*Millennials and the New Marriage*

yourself some things or sacrifice things because you know it's for the greater good of your relationship.

Both Aria and Owen said what I consider the magic word for millennials when it comes to deciding to get married: maturity. This is the word I have noted across several interview studies that defines the parameters through which millennials evaluate marital decisions for themselves and others. There is no special age, no specific set of life circumstances to accomplish; there is simply the vague notion of being mature. These new views of dating and marital decisions connect to the general trend of increased relativism among millennials noted by scholars (Smith et al., 2011; Smith & Snell, 2009). The concept that there is no universal truth and that everyone should have the ability to carve their own path in life, free of the judgment from others, certainly bleeds into the relational arena for most millennials, including their thoughts on when someone should marry. What was once a clear age-based normative transition has become a transition of both choice and vaguely defined maturity.

Chelsea was another millennial who echoed this common sentiment. She explained,

> I think everyone matures independently of their age. I can't really say 25 is an ideal age because someone may not be ready to take on all that [marriage] entails at 25. Someone may be ready for that at 18. Someone else may be ready for that at 50. So, I feel like I can't really say there's an age that I think is ideal. It's kinda based on a factor that's bigger than that.

Again, marriage is a tool, but it's a power tool: dangerous in the wrong hands, with the potential to do long-term harm to the user if mishandled. Marriage, to millennials, appears to have a "CAUTION" sign attached to it (I imagine a sign with a bright red line on it that reads, "Do not attempt until you are *this* mature!").

As alluded to, much of this generational difference between millennials and their parents is centered on the fact that, to millennials, marriage is clearly no longer a necessary social institution. It exists to be utilized by those who see value in it. Marriage *can* be used; it no longer *must* be used. Layla, married 12 years, explained this concept like this:

> I feel like marriage matters, in my personal life, but I don't think that it's a priority for everyone to have that legal documentation . . . lots of people only see it as that. If you're in a committed relationship long term, some people don't see the need for the legal part of it, and I don't really think that is necessary. Obviously, the legal benefits are good and big, but I don't think it's necessary.

Her husband, Luke, agreed wholeheartedly. He quickly jumped on his wife's response and added this: "[For] a lot of people, it's more of a legal matter; . . . some people don't want the legalities to be involved in their relationship; they don't want the government in there." Nathan, another married millennial, was blunter in his assessment of marriage. Currently in his second marriage, he didn't understand

Millennials and the New Marriage   15

why some peers his own age even wanted to get married. He explained, "I mean, for me, it's [marriage] kinda the same as dating; it's just, ya know, legal benefits." When asked why he had gotten married, his response was telling: "I actually was opposed to getting married before we got married." He laughed at his own response; his wife looked slightly less amused. While different in tone and context, the theme in these responses is clear: marriage may be tied to legal benefits but it is connected to little else in the eyes of most millennials.

This viewpoint stands in stark contrast to previous generations. Marriage has historically been a relationship that is tied to financial and societal stability and stature (Coontz, 2006), something that appeared completely foreign to millennials. Millennials grew up in an age where almost everything, including marriage, was assumed to cater to individual needs and desires, a concept I will cover with some depth in the next chapter. For now, the main point is that the millennials that my team spoke to often seemed confused about the notion of thinking about marriage as anything more than a pragmatic and mostly legal arrangement. In some ways, marriage has lost its broader symbolic meaning for many millennials. Take this exchange during an interview with Preston and Ashley. We asked what seemed like a broad and straightforward question: What does marriage mean to you? Preston's immediate response was . . . silence. Ashley seemed flustered by the question and uttered, "I'm not sure what that question means." Preston, apparently uncomfortable with the silence and perhaps his wife's response, added a laugh and a simple, "I don't know." He doesn't know? He'd been married at this point for almost 11 years. The question itself did not seem complicated (unless I have completely lost touch with the younger generation) and was intentionally broad as to allow the interviewed couples to take the conversation in any direction they wished. But, like Preston and Ashley, many struggled coming up with anything in response. Perhaps, then, this new approach to marriage is not about some grand shift in what marriage meant to millennials, but in that it may not mean anything at all to them. Perhaps marriage now lacked any deeper meaning, or at least not one that they had ever considered before. After all, we don't give our tools much thought unless we need them. Marriage is clearly no longer a need but a want— something that may be selected on the menu of life but certainly not something that one needs to be fulfilled and happy. Returning to Chelsea from earlier, she had some strong feelings about whether or not marriage had deeper meaning. When asked if marriage was needed, she explained that it clearly wasn't. Why? "Because I feel you can fulfill your purpose in this world without being married." Despite being happy in her relationship with her husband, her own personal purpose was clearly not tied to relational or family milestones, at least none that required marriage.

Yet remember, millennials are full of contradictions in their beliefs about marriage. Marriage is not needed, and there is no clear timetable one must adhere to. Yet, the expectation of marriage has not faded, seemingly fueled by the social norms of the previous generation. Parents are reluctant to give up the expectation of marriage for their millennial children. Hunter and Zoey, married right after college, noted this high expectation they felt from their families and peers. Zoey explained,

16   *Millennials and the New Marriage*

> I always knew I wanted to get married. I think it's kind of a normal thing in life. I feel like it's almost expected. It's the normal life path that, at least in where we're living, what our family expects from us—that we should get married. My grandparents, they wanted us to get married; they didn't want us living together without being married. They helped us achieve our marriage goals, so it was nice having their support, and it feels like the right thing to do.

Zoey and Hunter, while lukewarm about the institution of marriage themselves, clearly felt generational pressure from their families. This was a similar story to that of Trent and Becky, which I shared earlier in this chapter. These two couples were just a few of several millennials who expressed similar stories, those of young couples who seemed content to simply be together but transitioned to marriage due to both negative (nagging, pressuring) and positive (financial support, emotional support) factors from their families.

The initial picture, then, appears to suggest that marriage is still very much on the minds of millennials when it comes to their relational past, present, and future; but it appears to be holding on for dear life. The tool mentality of millennials casts marriage as an optional and perhaps increasingly outdated option for relational success. Many millennial married couples appeared to be appeasing their parents rather than embarking on their own clear relational pathway. But the story of millennial marriage is not quite so simple as marriage fading away. Again, I would argue this represents a shift toward a *different* type of marriage rather than a rejection of marriage altogether. Such stories and quotes as those above suggest a rejection of their parents' marriage, not marriage in general. Marriage may have lost much of its larger meaning to millennials, but this does not mean it is meaningless or only a legal contract. To understand better what other factors may point to this new type of marriage, a few other important generational differences need to be highlighted.

Shifting Courtship Priorities

One additional recent shift in millennials' attitudes toward marriage lies in their unique approach to the courtship process that precedes marriage. While our focus here is squarely on marriage itself, a brief detour to this unique shift in courtship is in order to understand the build up toward marriage that most married millennials experienced (for a more extensive discussion and review of this shifting courtship process, see Konstam, 2019). Connected to the previously mentioned erosion of social norms, millennials take a much more practical and individual approach to courtship and dating than generations past. This new approach to dating and courtship can be summarized across several themes.

First, millennials appear to take a very pragmatic and rational approach to dating and marriage, perhaps more so than ever before. While some research has suggested little difference between age cohorts on the criteria used to select mates (Buunk et al., 2002; Schwarz & Hassebrauck, 2012), others have argued that younger cohorts are trying to process more information than ever before about potential partners in an environment that is focused on minimizing risk

(Bulcroft et al., 2000). I have already mentioned how many millennials struggled with the question of what marriage generally meant to them. Another question that elicited confusion was even more baffling.

In the interviews we conducted with millennial married couples, no question stumped them more than one that I thought would be perhaps the simplest question we asked. In fact, this question was meant to mostly ease any anxiety each couple had early in the interview and pave the way for the deeper (and seemingly more interesting) questions to come. This question was simple: Why did you decide to marry your spouse? In a world where millennials have largely become pragmatists when it comes to relationship decisions, such a question caused many of our interviewees to stumble. This is not because millennials are relational pragmatics who think through the pros and cons of a specific relationship, but rather because they are individual pragmatics, trained to consider the immediate personal gain from life decisions. Marriage happened when it made sense for them, not necessarily when it was right for the couple or based on relational process or milestones. If marriage was not hindering their personal goals or ambitions, then they didn't worry about it so much. To put it more bluntly, millennials appear to have a mentality focused on determining if their potential partner will interfere with the things they want to do; one that is more akin to "why not?" than "why?" Because of that, asking them "why" they married appears to be counterintuitive for many of them. Trevor, married for 9 years, noted his practical rationale by stating this reason for why he married his wife:

> I had some friends in high school, but I didn't date anybody until I started dating Lucy. First come, first served? Not really. I guess if you can spend 4 years dating someone then you can spend more than 4 years married to someone.

His marriage was apparently tied to the notion that he didn't see any major flaws in his relationship during their 4 years of dating, so he reasoned that his marriage was likely to succeed (I guess as long as success is only defined by stability).

Juan, our seasoned married man mentioned earlier in the chapter, likewise seemed genuinely perplexed when we asked him about why he married his wife. Remember, he had decided to marry his wife after 3 short months, and their total courtship lasted less than a year. Despite his struggle talking about why marriage mattered, surely he had a strong reason to accelerate toward marriage. Had he fallen head-over-heels in love? Had he found his perfect soul mate? He explained that, while he was hesitant, he knew he wanted to marry his wife after 3 months of dating. When asked why, he said this: "we got along well, so . . . ." We pressed a bit more, suggesting that perhaps there were things they had in common that made him consider entering what he considered a lifelong relationship with his spouse. After a pause, he concluded, "Well, we are both vegetarian, so that certainly helps . . . . That can be hard if one person is not and one person is." That's right, the best Juan could come up with on why he had married his wife was that they both avoided meat. This statement couldn't be the whole story. We pressed again, asking him a more direct question. My student interviewer wanted to know why

18 *Millennials and the New Marriage*

marriage was suddenly on the table. She asked, "So what made that change for you from just going 'this is fun, we are just going to the movies,' to saying, 'wow, this is someone that I could spend the rest of my life with?'" Juan again collected his thoughts while his wife sat silently next to him. Finally, he muttered, "Just a feeling, I guess."

It's difficult to not see shades of constraint commitment (Stanley & Markman, 1992) in the pragmatic words of these millennials. Scott Stanley and his colleagues (see Stanley et al., 2006; Rhoades et al., 2012; Stanley et al., 2019) have spent several decades documenting how some couples slide into relationship commitments due largely to barriers to leaving rather than intentional decision-making. Stanley and others have noted that such "sliding" relationships are often inherently weaker and less stable than couples who make intentional relational decisions (Rhoades, Stanley, Kelmer, & Markman, 2010; Rhoades, Stanley, & Markman, 2010). Millennials appear less likely than ever to consider the long-term implications of their marital choices, opting instead to consider the short-term and tangible experiences they are having. Am I currently happy with this person? Are we currently avoiding major fights? If so, then let's move forward! The concept of considering larger notions such as long-term life goals, projecting relational process, or considering how partner characteristics will impact the future appeared to be a foreign concept to most of the millennials we interviewed. While sliding is no longer a new relational concept, millennials may be the generation of "sliders" when it comes to relationships.

Perhaps pragmatism is not the best way to describe this new approach to dating and courtship among millennials. While it certainly has some negative connotations, I believe that a more accurate term may be this: *apathy*. Listen to Isabella and Travis talk about their 10-year marital relationship. My team started the interview by asking them to talk about their general thoughts on marriage. Travis jumped in first, saying, "I enjoy it, but I realize that it's not for everyone." Not exactly a ringing endorsement. Such a response may make sense if someone were asked about a recent movie or book, but I thought marriage might create more of a reaction. His wife's response was likewise unenthusiastic. She said,

> It's nice to have somebody around. I was single for a while, and it's nice to not come home to an empty house all the time; it's nice to have somebody around that you can talk to and do things with.

So, Travis "enjoyed" marriage and Isabella thought it was nice having someone keep her company. Their marital relationship seemed entirely dependent on their individual lives and circumstances and certainly not something that was needed or that they would encourage others to do. They would, later in the interview, become even more firm in their relativistic view of marriage, stating simply that getting married might be helpful, for certain people. Trevor explained, "I think it just depends on the people," while his wife added, "It's very individual." If you're sensing a lack of enthusiasm from these millennials, you would not be alone. As we discussed dating and marital decisions with dozens of couples, very few appeared overtly excited about their marriage. Yes, most seemed happy, and many seemed

Millennials and the New Marriage 19

to share a love and connection to their spouse. But tied to the institution of marriage? This position was where there clearly appeared to be a degree of apathy in the dating and marital process.

Perhaps some of this apathy is tied to another trend scholars have noted: the lack of marital readiness reported during the past two decades from millennials (Carroll et al., 2009). Millennials, more than any previous generation, do not feel ready to be in a lifelong committed relationship. It is here where I need to make another quick introduction. In addition to the qualitative interview data I have been showing, I will also pause at times throughout the remainder of this book and provide you with some data taken from one of two large data collection projects I have been a part of that were both partially aimed at understanding the millennial generation. One of these studies involved a national data collection effort in the United States that studied thousands of newlywed couples. Most, but not all, of these couples fit squarely in the millennial generation, and I will use these data to highlight trends in the millennial marital process and to compare married millennials to their older counterparts. The other study is a large dataset of several thousand older millennials (at the time, 30–35 years old). This project was aimed at exploring life trajectories through the 20s for these millennials and included data on both married and never-married individuals. I will mostly be using this dataset to explore the general behaviors and attitudes of millennials (both married and not) and to draw comparisons between married and never-married millennials as appropriate. Again, the details on each data collection project can be found in the appendix.

So, let's get to some of those data. Figure 2.1 clearly shows this trend of less marriage readiness based on data from several thousand millennials in their early 30s. Millennials in the sample were asked to chart if they were ready for marriage in each year, from age 18 to 29. I split the data between those who were married and those who were not. Note that this difference is meaningful. A greater percentage of married millennials in their 30s report (at least in hindsight) that they were ready for marriage earlier than those who never married. Single millennials in their early 30s appear to catch up as their 30s approached. The real story here is not in these differences but in the overall percentages of both groups. Notice that by the time these millennials were 30 years old, not even half of them (married or not) felt ready for marriage. Millennials rarely feel ready for marriage and it seems clear that their decision to marry had little to do with perception of inherent readiness. For many millennials it may be difficult to get too excited or energetic about a union for which many feel woefully unprepared.

This apathetic and individually practical approach to dating and marital decision-making, drenched in the relativism others have noted as being rampant among millennials (Smith & Snell, 2009), has created what some have argued is a capstone mentality of marriage (Cherlin, 2020; Hawkins & Vandenberghe, 2018). Marriage is no longer something people build together with a partner, intertwining their lives as they struggle through school or through a series of early jobs. It is no longer based on the recognition that marriage is a union that individuals enter understanding that they will suffer together for many years as they are moving toward a stable and happy future. Such an approach, based on the

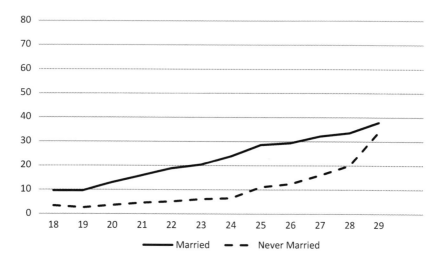

Figure 2.1 Percentage of Millennials Who Felt Ready for Marriage by Age and Current Marital Status.

perception that marriage creates the foundation on which one builds their life, is a standard of a previous generation and has largely disappeared among millennials. This approach is replaced by a capstone model that sees marriage fall into place once life has sorted itself out, and only then if it fits into each individual's own unique life puzzle. If not? Who cares, there are plenty of other routes to personal happiness. This sentiment was reflected by several young couples we interviewed. Becky and Trent, referenced earlier, were both coming from previous divorces. This gave them perhaps the most marital experience of any couple I interviewed. In their mind, these divorces occurred because they weren't yet ready or mature enough for marriage. The foundational approach to marriage had failed them. They explained that in their current marriage, they took a more cautious and capstone approach to the relationship. Becky explained,

> I think there are people that feel like it's [marriage] a milestone that they have to hurry up and get to; it's a part of making it or whatever; you definitely don't want to take that step too quick. For both of us, we were both married young, so that's why we felt like [we should] take your time, think about it.

A Cohabiting Generation

No discussion of shifting approaches to marriage among millennials would be complete without at least a short discussion of the rise of cohabitation. Again, many scholars have produced excellent books and papers on the new trends on this topic (see Brown & Wright, 2017; Eickmeyer & Manning, 2018; Sassler & Miller, 2017), and Sassler and Miller (2017) argued that the United States has become a "cohabitation nation" based on the dramatic rise in cohabitation over

Millennials and the New Marriage 21

the last few decades. The shift toward cohabitation as a dominant relational option, driven by its popularity among the millennial generation, captures many of the newer trends about what marriage and dating are or are not.

How common has cohabitation become? Several scholars have noted a large swing toward increased engagement in cohabitation among young couples (Kamp-Dush et al., 2019; Kennedy & Bumpass, 2008). In their 2019 report on marriage and cohabitation, Pew (2019) noted a striking shift toward cohabitation among millennials. From 2002 to 2017, cohabitation experienced a 5% growth in the total percentage of Americans who reported ever being in this type of union. During the same time period, marriage witnessed a 10% drop. Acceptance of cohabitation has also increased, with Pew reporting that 86% of all Americans indicated agreement with the statement that it was okay for two people to live together outside of marriage. Manning and Stykes (2015) noted that in the 25-year period between 1987 and 2013, the percentage of women who had ever cohabited doubled. They also noted that cohabitation has become the normative precursor to most marriages, showing that almost 70% of all marriages in 2013 were preceded by cohabitation. Perhaps the most telling statistics of this shift toward cohabitation are illustrated by U.S. Census data. When examining census records for young adults aged 18–24 over the last 70 years, it is clear that marriage has waned and cohabitation has risen. In 1970, almost 40% of all young adults were living with a spouse while less than 1% were living with a romantic partner. By 2010, rates were about even, with about 10% of young adults living with either a spouse or a cohabiting partner. By 2018, 10% of young adults continued to live with a partner, while only 7% reported living with a spouse. The drop in marriage is what is most dramatic here. What was once a dominant theme of young adults living with a spouse has now been replaced by a normative culture where many young adult relationships now involve cohabitation.

Like marriage, cohabitation is often tied to individual needs and pragmatic thinking. Cohabitation was considered vital by most of our millennial married couples (often only countered by those with strong religious beliefs) and most had lived with their spouse prior to their marriage. Their thought was that if marriage was going to be successful, and that a spouse always had the potential to undermine personal happiness, one needed to know everything about one's partner. Trevor identified some of the core and basic properties of the human condition one may glean from cohabiting with a romantic partner. He noted that cohabitation was "absolutely" needed before marriage. He went on to explain that such an arrangement might help you know when to end a relationship:

> If you can't stand the way they snore at night or their eating habits or just general personality. A lot of people, I think they love someone because they're not living with them, and they don't know how they are at home or at night. They could be the opposite personality when they are at home, right?

Here again we see the pragmatic and often individual focus of how millennials have approached the courtship process. Cohabitation was a way to determine if your dating partner, for lack of a better term, annoyed you. For most millennials,

22 *Millennials and the New Marriage*

cohabitation felt like the only way to peek behind the curtain and make sure that your partner's daily habits didn't irritate you or get in your way.

Circling back to Trent, he echoed the sentiment that it is impossible to really know someone without cohabitation, explaining:

> You see them when they're asleep, when they're angry, when they're disappointed. If you still love that person when they're at their worst, and they still love you and you're at your worst, and you have good financial responsibility, they work, and good things like that, then yeah there is a fair chance of getting married. But if you don't live with somebody then you don't really know them.

Trent's thoughts at least seemed to center on larger processes, like conflict and emotional regulation. For many millennials we spoke to, the issues they focused on with cohabiting partners appeared more minor. Cohabitation was an insight into the small daily life decisions of one's partner, yet millennials put a lot of stock in these minor behaviors. Let's go back to Judy from earlier. Remember, she lived with her husband prior to their marriage. She explained why cohabitation was important for her:

> I feel like you really need to know someone and how they are inside the home before you can actually decide to make a home with someone. Little things like knowing their schedules and knowing if they're compatible with your schedules, what you like to do on a Sunday morning; you know, just those things. I think I needed to know if he was on the same page. What kind of shampoo do we buy? Do we buy the high-end shampoo, or you know, save some pennies and buy the store brand? It's weird how those little things kind of amass to be important even though they are little things. So, I think for me I needed to know if I could share a space with someone before I knew if I could share a space permanently with someone.

Caleb, another young millennial who lived with his wife before marriage, explained the importance of cohabitation in this way:

> Yeah. I always felt that [cohabitation] was pretty important because, when you live with someone on a day-to-day basis, you're fighting for using the bathroom or someone's hogging the shower or, you know, "My god, you'd leave your banana peels on the floor," or whatever. Those kinds of things you don't see if you're just dating, if you just go out and you have a good time or maybe you spend a night here or there. You find out more about the nitty-gritty of a person.

Again, these potential insights about litter and showering time may seem insignificant in the grand scheme of things. But for Caleb, like so many millennials we spoke to, they mattered. He continued,

Millennials and the New Marriage 23

I think that's important if you're going to live with them the rest of your life. You can be really into a person, you can be compatible on many levels but, you can be fundamentally, just, "I can't coexist with you in the same space."

Understanding daily routines and your live-in partner's odd eccentricities is not a new relational phenomenon. Ask any married couple and they will likely have many stories of the frustrations and struggles they had with their partner when they first moved in together. However, in previous generations, this was typically done after you had already made a lifelong commitment. Oddly, millennials appear to view cohabitation as a way to sort out what has traditionally been a rite of passage for newlyweds. Millennials seemed averse to having to deal with this challenge during marriage itself and tied such day-to-day difficulties not to marital hurdles to overcome but to core concerns that may end any potential relationship.

The Enduring Appeal of Marriage

Despite a clear movement toward an approach to marriage that deemphasizes many of its traditional components, marriage does still appear to be holding on, ever so tightly, to some unique stature and importance for millennials. As noted by Omar, married for just over two years: "Yeah. I'd definitely say to really have a happy life, in my opinion, you have to be married." Millennials also appear to care about their marriages and their success. In our national study of almost 2,000 married millennial couples, 92% of them indicated that their marital relationship was among their top priorities in life. I mentioned Aria earlier when I discussed the erosion of social norms around marriage. Her husband, Carter, had some interesting thoughts on marriage. In a uniquely millennial comparison, he compared the joy of a spouse with what he felt was the artificial high that social media gave. He stated,

> Yeah. I think the whole companionship thing is something that a lot of people in today's culture don't realize that they're missing, because of how plugged in we always are with social media and things of that sort. I feel like we take that for granted sometimes. I've been gone for 4 days on a trip, and obviously miss you [referring to his wife]. Coming back, I was thinking to myself, a lot of these people that I interacted with, they don't have anybody to go to when they go home. How lucky I am to have somebody to pick me up from the airport, or just to be able to go home to see somebody is pretty cool instead of going on your phone and thinking that you have 500-and-something friends or a billion friends.

Despite these endorsements of marriage and companionship, marriage feels like it should have a larger impact to some millennials than it does, perhaps reflecting the ghosts of marriage's past. Let's return a final time to Trent and Becky, who were clear that marriage should matter and impact decisions. At first Becky seemed passionate about her marital relationship and its importance, stating,

24 *Millennials and the New Marriage*

> Your relationship has to come first, even before your relationship with, like, your kids or parents or any other family obligations you might have. That is the foundation for your life together. Like, if you don't make each other a priority, then everything else falls apart.

But when pressed for examples of this importance in their own life, both Becky and Trent struggled to identify any tangible effect. Trent went first, offering a timid response of, "Um . . . not really." Becky was likewise hesitant to come up with an example of this high importance she placed on marriage (more than anything else!). Finally, she offered, turning to her husband, "Maybe, like, when I asked you to cut your hours, when you're working at the office?" When asked for details, this example shows the type of shallow approach to we-centered marriage that many millennials have. Trent explained the situation. He said,

> Ok, yeah. When I was working many hours a day and I wasn't seeing my family as much as I would have liked to, Becky asked me to cut back on some hours so that I could spend some more time with them. So that would be an example.

So far, so good. How did this exchange happen? Trent continued,

> She [Becky] made it clear to me that she was unhappy. I asked her what I could do to make her happy. She said she wanted to see me more. So I said, how about this day? And she said, okay, that will work.

It became clear that this discussion was not a larger and more global discussion about work–family balance or work hours. This was a simple request for a bit more time, taking a day off, a request Trent fulfilled with a single day away from work.

Connor, who had been living with his girlfriend comfortably for several years, didn't seem to have much reason to transition his relationship to marriage. Yet he felt like there was some vague hint of something different that marriage might hold. He explained,

> I think for me it was just kind of doing a little bit of introspection and thinking, okay, we moved in together with the understanding that this is where it was leading [marriage]. Do I still feel that way? Yes! I just did not want to wait anymore. I understood that it was a commitment.

He felt like marriage was the next step, that marriage might change the nature of his relationship. How? He struggled with that question. At first, he seemed to suggest that marriage changed things a lot with his wife. He explained, "I don't think I understood at the time that marriage changes a lot of things." Like what? He immediately retreated, wanting to be clear it doesn't really change their relationship: "It doesn't really change who we are." Things were getting confusing. Connor tried again, "I think it probably changes who we are in the eyes of people outside the relationship." So perhaps it was just the perception of his relationship

Millennials and the New Marriage 25

from others that really shifted. After taking us on this puzzling journey of thought, he finally seemed resigned in his own confusion, stating, "I don't know, it just feels different to say my wife versus my girlfriend."

At least some millennials also still held to some general societal importance tied to marriage. But even here, this was less about greater societal good and more about the personal rewards that could be gleaned from a social institution that some millennials still felt had merit. Brock, an older millennial in his 30s who was married to Chelsea, explained,

> I think there's still some measure of having the status of wife or husband; you're viewed as cornerstones of the community. That kind of status is something that now is on me to be mindful of and conduct myself accordingly when I'm around others, particularly those that may not be married, or [among] those that are [and] may be struggling in their marriage to try to uphold that sort of ideal of being a cornerstone of the community and a leader in the community, as a husband and a leader of the family.

For Brock, marriage's societal relevance was about giving him importance and stature in the community. Madison, Caleb's wife, felt similar, stating in her interview, "I think you get more support from society if you're married versus partnered." Back to Conner; at another point in his interview, he stated something similar:

> I don't think it changed the nature of our relationship. I think a lot of benefit about it is in how society views you—the way people look at your relationship. When I say, "my wife," people automatically know that it's more serious than if I had just said, "oh, my girlfriend."

As I alluded to before, my personal sense from years of talking to and studying millennials is that their apathy and surface rejection of marriage is not complete. It is more a rejection of the old notion of marriage, the marital union their parents and grandparents entered. Millennials, with their unique approach toward both dating and marriage, appear to want to blaze a new path into a new, more flexible relationship arrangement. We may still call it marriage, but its nature and purpose appear to be shifting. For many millennials, this was a marriage focused on one enduring aspect of the old marital union: commitment. Marriage brought with it a sense of commitment that at least partially transcended other non-legally binding relationships. This was the trait that made marriage potentially different than other relationships.

Let me return to Caleb's interview. Caleb noted the important (and different) stature that marriage held for him compared to other unions, stating,

> I think that marriage is a commitment between two people. I consider it a fairly serious thing. I can almost call it sacred; it's a very special commitment. It's not just dating or even living together. It's reserved for that that one person, hopefully that one comes in.

26 *Millennials and the New Marriage*

His wife, Madison, felt similarly, although she was quick to note she was no traditionalist:

> It's hard to say it's [marriage] needed 'cause I have lots of friends who are in very serious committed relationships that haven't gotten married, but I love it. It is that extra commitment that you've made in front of other people, and to other people in your lives to try and really work things out. I think it is a little bit transformative. I'm super feminist and so there are pieces of the institution of marriage that I'm not a huge fan of, but overall, I think it is still needed. I wish there was more support for nontraditional partnerships, but I think we'll get there one day.

Aiden and Ella had been married for 2 years when we spoke to them. Aiden worked at Costco and Ella was planning on returning to school soon. When asked about why they had decided to marry, they identified an elevated sense of commitment that came with marriage. Ella explained, "I kinda see marriage as a partnership but I guess more committed." She was quick to point out this was not due to any underlying religious belief she had (she was not religious). But the idea of a committed partnership resonated with her. As she put it, "when two people get married, they decide to become partners." Her husband Aiden was a bit more abstract in his view. He followed his wife's comments up by stating, "I'm pretty much on the same page; it's not all that different than just living together, but just taking that extra step, I guess, at whatever level." What was this "next level"? Again, Ella butted in and spoke to commitment, saying, "I mean it is different because if I weren't married, I could just walk out and be done, but I'm married so that's not an option for me." Interestingly, again we see a tie to not just commitment, but constraint commitment, specifically.

This lingering focus on commitment as the one tangible benefit of marriage suggests there may still be an aspect of the fairy-tale notion of "forever" that is appealing to millennials. But while millennials appear to at least be associating marriage with elevated commitment, something they have in common with at least the last few generations, this may actually be turning many millennials away from marriage. Many married millennials reflected on the way they felt their generation was commitment-phobic. Aria and Carter explained it this way. First, Aria explained, "I think people are scared to commit to things, and obviously marriage is a huge commitment for a lifetime. I think people are scared of commitment now." Her husband elaborated on this point, adding, "If you think about people we know, we have friends who, even, like, buying a house is something that they aren't even interested in doing right now. Because it's too much of a commitment." Aria liked this example because, in her mind, marriage was even scarier than buying a home, for many of her peers. She added, "Or they feel that buying a house is an easier commitment than getting married . . . . People buy houses together, but they don't wanna be married. You can just sell a house." The implication was clear— marriage implied long-term commitment and was a relationship that would be challenging to exit. To Aria and Carter, this commitment scared many of their millennial friends away.

The bottom line appears to be this. Millennials have radically shifted their approach to dating and courtship patterns, and by extension, their marriages. Unlike previous generations for whom marriage was clearly defined by social norms, marriage for millennials, even married ones, is an oddly ambiguous entity. It's clearly a tool that could be used to solidify a relationship and achieve connection, long-term commitment, and relational stability, but only one of many such tools in the tool belt of millennials. Dating patterns, including the sudden and strong presence of cohabitation, have illustrated these shifts. But there is something deeper beneath the surface that warrants further consideration before continuing to explore if marriage does, in fact, change the lives of millennials in positive or negative ways. As I noted, these shifts in approaches, dating behavior, and beliefs about the institution of marriage have perhaps created a new type of relationship that millennials are currently experiencing. They may call it marriage, like their parents before them, but perhaps they are using the same word to mean something different. It is that potentially new and unique type of marriage that we need to explore next.

References

Brown, S. L., & Wright, M. R. (2017). Marriage, cohabitation, and divorce in later life. *Innovation in Aging, 1*, igx015.

Bulcroft, R., Bulcroft, K., Bradley, K., & Simpson, C. (2000). The management and production of risk in romantic relationships: A postmodern paradox. *Journal of Family History, 25*, 63–92.

Buunk, B. P., Dijkstra, P., Fetchenhauer, D., & Kenrick, D. T. (2002). Age and gender differences in mate selection criteria for various involvement levels. *Personal Relationships, 9*(3), 271–278. https://doi.org/10.1111/1475-6811.00018

Carroll, J. S., Badger, S., Willoughby, B. J., Nelson, L. J., Madsen, S. D., & McNamara Barry, C. (2009). Ready or not? Criteria for marriage readiness among emerging adults. *Journal of Adolescent Research, 24*, 349–375.

Carroll, J. S., Willoughby, B., Badger, S., Nelson, L. J., Barry, C. M., & Madsen, S. D. (2007). So close, yet so far away: The impact of varying marital horizons on emerging adulthood. *Journal of Adolescent Research, 22*, 219–247.

Cherlin, A. J. (2020). Degrees of change: An assessment of the deinstitutionalization of marriage thesis. *Journal of Marriage and Family, 82*, 62–80.

Clarkberg, M., Stolzenberg, R. M., & Waite, L. J. (1995). Attitudes, values and entrance into cohabitation versus marital unions. *Social Forces, 74*, 609–634.

Coontz, S. (2006). *Marriage, a history: How love conquered marriage*. Penguin.

Eickmeyer, K. J., & Manning, W. D. (2018). Serial cohabitation in young adulthood: Baby boomers to millennials. *Journal of Marriage and Family, 80*, 826–840.

Furman, W. (2002). The emerging field of adolescent romantic relationships. *Current Directions in Psychological Science, 11*, 177–180.

Hawkins, A. J. & Vandenberghe, B. (2018). *Time for fresh thinking on early marriage*. National Review. https://www.nationalreview.com/2018/11/early-marriage-cornerstone-model-for-young-adults/

Kamp Dush, C. M., Arocho, R., Mernitz, S. E., & Rhoades, G. K. (2019). Cohabitation and single mothering in the United States: A review and call for psychological research. In B. H. Fiese, M. Celano, K. Deater-Deckard, E. N. Jouriles, & M. A. Whisman (Eds.), *APA*

28 Millennials and the New Marriage

handbook of contemporary family psychology: Foundations, methods, and contemporary issues across the lifespan (pp. 667–685). American Psychological Association.

Kennedy, S., & Bumpass, L. (2008). Cohabitation and children's living arrangements: New estimates from the United States. *Demographic Research, 19*, 1663–1692.

Konstam, V. (2019). *The romantic lives of emerging adults: Getting from I to we.* Oxford University Press.

Manning, W. D., & Stykes, B. (2015). *Twenty-five years of change in cohabitation in the U.S., 1987–2013.* (FP-15-01). National Center for Family & Marriage Research. www.bgsu.edu/content/dam/BGSU/college-ofarts-and-sciences/NCFMR/documents/FP/FP-15-01-twentyfive-yrs-changecohab.pdf

Pew Research Center. (2019). Marriage and Cohabitation in the U.S. Pew Research Center. www.pewsocialtrends.org/2019/11/06/marriage-and-cohabitation-in-the-u-s/

Rhoades, G. K., Stanley, S. M., Kelmer, G., & Markman, H. J. (2010). Physical aggression in unmarried relationships: The roles of commitment and constraints. *Journal of Family Psychology, 24*, 678–687.

Rhoades, G. K., Stanley, S. M., & Markman, H. J. (2010). Should I stay or should I go? Predicting dating relationship stability from four aspects of commitment. *Journal of Family Psychology, 24*, 543–550.

Rhoades, G. K., Stanley, S. M., & Markman, H. J. (2012). The impact of the transition to cohabitation on relationship functioning: Cross-sectional and longitudinal findings. *Journal of Family Psychology, 26*, 348–358.

Roberson, P. N., Norona, J. C., Fish, J. N., Olmstead, S. B., & Fincham, F. (2017). Do differences matter? A typology of emerging adult romantic relationship. *Journal of Social and Personal Relationships, 34*, 334–355.

Sassler, S., & Miller, A. (2017). *Cohabitation nation: Gender, class, and the remaking of relationships.* University of California Press.

Schwarz, S., & Hassebrauck, M. (2012). Sex and age differences in mate-selection preferences. *Human Nature, 23*(4), 447–466. https://doi.org/10.1007/s12110-012-9152-x

Shulman, S., & Connolly, J. (2013). The challenge of romantic relationships in emerging adulthood: Reconceptualization of the field. *Emerging Adulthood, 1*, 27–39.

Smith, C., Christoffersen, K., Christoffersen, K. M., Davidson, H., & Herzog, P. S. (2011). *Lost in transition: The dark side of emerging adulthood.* Oxford University Press.

Smith, C., & Snell, P. (2009). *Souls in transition: The religious and spiritual lives of emerging adults.* Oxford University Press.

Stanley, S. M., & Markman, H. J. (1992). Assessing commitment in personal relationships. *Journal of Marriage and the Family, 54*, 595–608.

Stanley, S. M., Rhoades, G. K., Kelmer, G., Scott, S. B., Markman, H. J., & Fincham, F. D. (2019). Unequally into "us": Characteristics of individuals in asymmetrically committed relationships. *Family Process, 58*, 214–231.

Stanley, S. M., Rhoades, G. K., & Markman, H. J. (2006). Sliding versus deciding: Inertia and the premarital cohabitation effect. *Family Relations, 55*, 499–509.

Willoughby, B. J. (2012). Associations between sexual behavior, sexual attitudes and marital horizons during emerging adulthood. *Journal of Adult Development. 19*, 100–110.

Willoughby, B. J. (2014). Using marital attitudes in late adolescence to predict later union transitions. *Youth & Society, 46*, 425–440.

Willoughby, B. J. & Carroll, J. S. (2015). On the horizon: Marriage timing, beliefs, and consequences in emerging adulthood. In J. J. Arnett (Ed.), *The Oxford handbook of emerging adulthood* (pp. 280–295). Oxford University Press.

Willoughby, B. J., Carroll, J. S., Vitas, J., & Hill, L. (2012). "When are you getting married?" The intergenerational transmission of attitudes regarding marital timing and marital importance. *Journal of Family Issues, 33,* 223–245.

Willoughby, B. J., & Dworkin, J. D. (2009). The relationships between emerging adults' expressed desire to marry and frequency of participation in risk behaviors. *Youth & Society, 40,* 426–450.

Willoughby, B. J., Hall, S., & Luczak, H. (2013). Marital paradigms: A conceptual framework for marital attitudes, values and beliefs. *Journal of Family Issues. 36*(2), 188–211. https://doi.org/10.1177/0192513X13487677

Willoughby, B. J., & James, S. L. (2017). *The marriage paradox: Why emerging adults love marriage yet push it aside.* Oxford University Press.

Willoughby, B. J., Olson, C.D., Carroll, J.S., Nelson, L.J., & Miller, R. (2012). Sooner or later?: The marital horizons of parents and their emerging adult children. *Journal of Social and Personal Relationships, 29,* 967–981.

Willoughby, B. J., Yorgason, J., James, S., & Holmes, E. (Forthcoming). What does marriage mean to us? Marital centrality among newlywed couples. *Journal of Family Issues.*

3 Me-Marriage

A New Type of Marriage for Millennials

Allison and Cameron were an accomplished couple. Both had advanced college degrees and kept themselves very busy. Allison was planning on pursuing her Ph.D. in a STEM field. Cameron, who was originally from Peru, was simultaneously working, volunteering at several nonprofit organizations, and starting a few businesses (some more successful than others, he reported). They met while Allison was completing a study abroad in Peru, and they became fast friends. When she returned to the United States, they kept in contact off and on for a few years—an email here, a text message there. Years later, their friendship began to shift as they spent more time conversing online, eventually Skyping regularly. During those conversations, Allison expressed her interest in world travel. Cameron, feeling his connection with Allison growing, told her he was happy to accompany her on her travels. They decided to travel to South America together, which they did for the next year. During that time, their friendship blossomed into romance, and they became, as they put it, "partners." Eventually they were engaged and then married; they settled down in the United States and moved to Minnesota. They had been married for a few years when my research team spoke to them.

Throughout their interview, Allison and Cameron seemed like the type of people with whom just about anyone would enjoy spending an evening, if only to hear about their world travels and unique life journeys. Both were intelligent and well-spoken. They also seemed carefree and engaging. They were passionate about their interests and values and seemed to genuinely care for each other. It was clear that they gave high priority to supporting each other's goals and felt they had similar views of the world. Allison spoke of the instant connection she felt with Cameron and how, early in their relationship, she was worried that her strong and serious feelings toward Cameron would not be reciprocated. He noted that he too felt their connection grow quickly and laughed at how they had basically bypassed the dating phase and became engaged.

Despite Allison and Cameron's strong connection, the transition from single life to married life was challenging for both, especially Cameron. Both Allison and Cameron valued their independence and struggled being in a situation in which they needed to consider another person's wants and needs all the time. Cameron noted that marriage was hard work and that he initially struggled to find the desire to put effort into his marriage at the cost of his personal time. He described his early marital challenges in this way:

Me-Marriage: A New Type of Marriage 31

You got to feed it [your marriage], take care of it. I've been learning a lot. Our first years I was just being the same independent guy I was being all the time. I was waking up very early and then getting home super late because I was involved in too many things.

At the time, his wife was not thrilled that he appeared to assume he could continue his independent lifestyle now that he was married. He continued, "Allison was very clear: 'Dude, you got to be here if you want to be part of a marriage. You got to be at home at some point.'"

On the surface, such a scenario doesn't seem that odd; many newlyweds need time to find a new normal as they refocus their personal energy into their marital relationship. After all, Allison and Cameron appeared to have a strong and deep commitment for each other right from the beginning. Yet for Allison and Cameron, this situation did not appear to be an issue that resolved completely after the first few months of marriage. When we asked how they would rank their marriage compared to other life priorities, they both revealed more details about this struggle. Cameron went first, sharing the following:

Well, as I said, it's getting higher and higher on the rank. It was kind of in the middle, like after some of my other social priorities in the beginning. Now I'm constantly saying no to more stuff to leave some room or leave the weekends for us.

At this point, Allison jumped in, adding a slightly cynical "part of the weekend."

So was his marriage now, several years later, his top priority? Cameron didn't think so. He said, "Yeah, I don't know. It's getting up there. Hopefully at some point it's going to be at the top of it, very soon." Keep in mind, Cameron had been married for several years, not several months. Yet he still struggled to prioritize his marriage above personal pursuits. Before we assumed that this was due simply to a unique personality or stereotypical male avoidance of commitment, Allison reported a similar struggle. When asked the same question, she replied,

I mean my career is very important to me. Luckily, I feel like at this point there isn't a conflict between my career and my family life. I have a job where I feel like I can leave it at work and not have it take over my life. So, I feel very fortunate in that. I would probably rank my marriage and my career like one and two and I don't know which one would be top.

While Cameron was struggling to balance their marriage and his social life, Allison appeared to be struggling to balance their marriage and her career ambitions. Cameron had an opinion about which was winning between his marriage and his wife's career, and he was surprised that she couldn't decide what mattered more. He interjected, "Has that been changing? Because you were clear about having your professional life as the top at least for a while, which is fine." Allison seemed to think that, perhaps a few years down the line, she too would be able to prioritize her marriage more. She said, "We just bought a house and—I don't know. I've

32 *Me-Marriage: A New Type of Marriage*

been thinking more about two or three years from now having kids. And then, I don't know, things will change again."

Allison and Cameron's story illustrates a growing tension between the ideal of marriage held in the past and the new approach to marriage alluded to in the previous chapter. This approach involves inherent tension between one's personal ambitions and goals and the marital relationship's needs and goals. Before diving into the central question—does marriage still benefit millennials?—it is important to further discuss this unique mindset that millennials take into matrimony. In the last chapter, I outlined how millennials are approaching marriage and dating in unique ways that differ from their parents and grandparents. In this chapter, I wish to extend that discussion in one important way by addressing a core hypothesis that I believe is critical to interpreting the material in the rest of the book. As discussed in the previous chapter, millennials are not simply adjusting their broad views of marriage and how they approach it; they are changing the nature of marriage itself. While their dating and marital decision-making behaviors are certainly different than behaviors of the past, their behaviors *in* marriage are also different in meaningful and important ways. It is this different lived experience of marriage that I delve into in more detail in this chapter.

My central argument is this: Millennials have reworked the very purpose of marriage, and this reworking has changed how they act and evaluate their own marriages. Cherlin (2004) argued that, across the last 100 years, the United States and many other parts of the world have shifted from what he called companionship marriage (focused on relationship building and joint goals) to what he called individualized marriage (focused on individual pursuits and happiness). I believe millennials have taken this individualized stance of marriage one step further, crafting a marital relationship that is almost entirely self-focused and based on increasingly short-term, evaluative criteria. This new "millennial marriage" is what I refer to as "me-marriage," a handy term that can double as both shorthand for millennial marriage and the me-centered approach many millennials now take. This approach has created a unique marital environment that is critical to understand before talking about the potential health, economic, or relational benefits (or lack thereof) of marriage. It's an approach that I believe puts marriage on increasingly shaky ground for many millennials.

The Gold Standard of Personal Happiness

This discussion of the new me-marriage must begin with a focus on one of the often-debated topics among scholars who study this generational cohort: their unique self-focus. Certainly millennials have been portrayed as narcissistic in the media (see Stein & Sanburn, 2013), but do data support this hypothesis? In some ways, yes. Scholars have noted that millennials tend to score higher on standardized narcissism measures than previous generations (Stewart & Bernhardt, 2010; Twenge et al., 2008a; Twenge et al., 2008b). Various reasons have been proposed for this shift, with some pointing to the increased use of social media as the culprit (Alloway et al., 2014; Dumas et al., 2017; McKinney et al., 2012) while others have suggested it may be due to a decrease in more traditional forms of

Me-Marriage: A New Type of Marriage   33

civic engagement (Arnett, 2007). Of course, it is also important to point out that some scholars, such as Jeff Arnett (2007), have argued that self-focus among young adults and millennials is beneficial to later development. Regardless of whether such self-focus is deemed positive or negative, it does appear clear that millennials are more concerned about individual aspirations and progression than those in past generations.

As mentioned earlier, when my research team started to interview millennial married couples, we were initially shocked by the number of couples who were getting tripped up by one of the first (and presumably most straightforward) questions we asked: Why did you get married? Over time, it became clear that at least one reason for the struggle in answering the question was the fact that many of these millennial couples did not associate marriage with any higher purpose or cultural function. They had enjoyed the company of their romantic partner for long enough and, following shaky but still present societal norms, they had decided to legalize the relationship. In many cases, it seemed they were confused about why they did make the decision to marry. Perhaps the best way to summarize the new me-marriage mentality of millennials is this: Marriage—breaking free of the social norms that once strongly dictated what it was supposed to be—is now an institution that is focused completely at the couple and individual level. This new me-marriage is a very personalized experience, catering specifically to the individual needs of both partners. Every marriage is different because every couple and individual partner wants different things. Lanelle, married for 3 years, explained it simply: "No marriage is the same." This new perspective on marriage has been applauded as a new gold standard that has elevated marriage to a higher level. For example, Finkel (2018) called such marriages "all or nothing" marriages and noted that this intense focus on individual happiness and personal benefit has created the healthiest marriages in generations.

But that's getting ahead of ourselves. It is worth revisiting the dynamic of how millennials view marriage, discussed in the last chapter, from a slightly different angle. While I already illustrated how the struggle with the question of why millennials decide to marry is partially attributable to the ambiguity about what marriage means and the short-term approach to marriage many millennials take, this struggle is also an important illustration of the intense focus on personal gratification and happiness that many millennials hold as a high priority in their lives. This focus appears to translate to how they engage with their marriages. When Dustin, who met his wife in college and married shortly after graduation, was asked why he had gotten married, he stated, "I don't know, it's fun?" Marriage being fun might seem like an odd choice of words (it certainly can be fun, but seems questionable as the main criteria for selecting a marriage partner), but for a millennial focused on short-term personal gain, it might matter. Dustin's partner, Jenny, immediately connected marriage with personal happiness as well, stating,

> I think it [marriage] makes my life better knowing that I picked somebody who loves me unconditionally and makes me laugh, supports me, you know, is there for me all the time. It just makes my life better, knowing that I'm with my best friend all the time.

34   Me-Marriage: A New Type of Marriage

For Jenny, marriage made her life better because of all the things her spouse gave to her. Notice how many times she says "me" and "my" in the quote. Granted, it may feel like I'm simply putting too much emphasis on some key personal pronouns she shared. Jenny might have been simply trying to suggest that her marriage was a mutually beneficial relationship, but her husband seemed stuck on the fun factor. Dustin added that marriage was great because he appreciated "just being yourself all the time with the person that you're with. Just having fun and doing stuff together."

Embedded in the example of Dustin and Jenny is a larger theme that appeared in virtually every interview we conducted. It became increasingly clear that many millennials were placing a massive emphasis in their marriages on personal happiness. In fact, being happy seemed to be the standard on which their relationships were measured. While personal happiness has likely always been one goal for those marrying in generations past, it appeared to be *the* goal for most millennials. Many millennials spoke about how the presence or absence of personal happiness could make or break a marriage. Monique, a religious woman in her late 20s who had been married for a few years when we spoke to her, recalled seeing her siblings struggling with obtaining personal happiness in their marriages. She said,

> I saw them [her siblings] through the honeymoon phase where they're gross and all touchy. But then, when kids got introduced into the picture, I saw the stressors of marriages, and any time I hung out with my siblings as a single person, it was always like, "my wife won't let me go out 'cause we got to put the baby down," and I saw more of the ugly side of marriage.

Monique resonated with these complaints about losing "personal time" when married. To her, losing personal time was not a necessary sacrifice for the betterment of a family or even a sacrifice needed to maintain balance and focus within a marital relationship. No, to Monique, losing personal time was the "ugly side" of marriage: a relationship where one might not get to do what one wanted to at all times. Her siblings apparently felt the same way, as these complaints appeared tied to a general sense of dissatisfaction. Monique continued,

> I never really even saw them happy too often. I mean we [Monique and her husband] have a new baby now, so I see why that's always so hard, but it was very discouraging in a way because they never seemed happy.

Others described this focus on personal happiness in relationships in connection with a desire for personal growth. Marriage was a relationship that had personal benefits because it not only made each spouse happy, it also helped spouses personally grow. Ella, the young wife I mentioned in the last chapter who was very focused on the importance of commitment in marriage, felt that facilitating personal growth was one of the primary roles of a good spouse. She explained, "I think that when you're married there's a bigger commitment. It's not just, we're living together, we're having kids together, our finances are tied together. Like, our personal growth is tied together." Yet again, one of the main reasons for marriage is its potential to help create personal growth. Another example is in the case of Judy, my focal point of the previous chapter. Judy gave me one of the most direct connections between millennials and this new me-focused approach to marriage. When asked where her marriage ranked on her priority list, she first said, "I would put my marriage first." She then backtracked a bit, giving the question more thought before changing her answer. She corrected herself by saying, "I would put myself first and then my marriage." While that may seem selfish to most of us, she felt that putting herself first was needed, "because I can't be the best person in my marriage if I'm not the best person I can be."

This focus on personal happiness has created new and intensified fears for married millennials striving to reap the benefits of me-marriages. Many millennials my team spoke to were worried that marriage might not live up to their personal standard of happiness—that tying themselves to one person might force them to the ground rather than let them sprout their wings of independence. Cameron and Allison, our educated couple from the beginning of the chapter, had a unique take on this concern, considering themselves cultural rebels simply because they got married and took the risk to personal happiness that might have followed. Cameron, with his wife nodding by his side, said that he felt getting married was "being a rebel." He added,

> The easiest way to be right now is being alone—traveling the world and discovering yourself and whatever. We decided to take the rough path of just being together and trying to achieve more by being together instead of just by ourselves.

Marriage was the "rough path" because marriage made it more difficult to achieve the personal pursuits that Cameron alluded to. Chloe had been married for 11 years and already had three children when we interviewed her and her husband. She had this to say about marriage: "I think it's nice to have a partner to go through life with. I think one of the greatest things about marriage is just having a partner, to help you with your life." Notice her use of the term "your life." Very few of the married millennials we spoke to, even those who had been together for many years, spoke of their relationships in terms of "we" or "us." Me-marriage is about the *me* after all.

To be clear, not all millennials are completely on board with this shift in beliefs about marriage. Some actively expressed frustrations with their peers' self-focused approach to marriage. As Joselyn, who had been married to Jose for a few years when we spoke to her, explained,

> The institution of marriage is important. I think a lot of young people in general just stray away from commitment. Marriage is like a damper or ruining your fun time or something, and that's just sad and backwards. I think having a good view of marriage and a healthy idea of what marriage is like kind of creates just happier people, you know? I think everyone tries to fill voids of something and none of them think marriage is the answer. Some of them

36 Me-Marriage: A New Type of Marriage

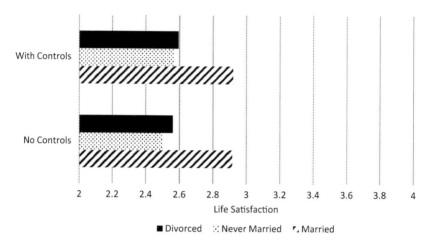

Figure 3.1 Differences in Millennial Life Satisfaction by Marital Status, With and Without Controlling for Background Factors.

think partying is, but the institution of marriage, I see it as something that is badly minimized.

Some millennials, especially more religious-minded ones that were holding on to a more traditional view of marriage, seemed frustrated or even appalled by the me-marriage popularized by their generation. They seemed to believe that such an approach would undermine the very fabric of commitment and unity that many felt was at the center of marriage.

Of course, this discussion raises the issue of whether or not millennials who do marry are achieving the personal happiness and satisfaction they are hoping for in marriage. My data suggest that there may be some evidence that they are currently achieving their goals, at least early on in their marriages. In a national sample of 30- to 35-year-olds, I compared married, divorced, and single millennials on their overall levels of life satisfaction (see Figure 3.1). The married millennials reported statistically significant higher overall life satisfaction compared to those who had never married. Of course, there is a chance that these differences are merely due to self-selection and not to marriage itself, a common argument in such social science comparisons. Perhaps happier and more satisfied millennials are the ones getting married. While there will always be merit to these arguments, Figure 3.1 also shows the same analysis of life satisfaction, this time controlling for sexual orientation, race, parents' education, and whether or not one's biological parents were married (all common selection factors tied to socioeconomic status and other potentially confounding factors). You'll note that the differences mentioned previously persist, even with these controls. In fact, accounting for these background factors made almost no difference in the results.

When I break down the life satisfaction scale into its individual elements (see Figure 3.2), the married millennials appear to be experiencing more personal

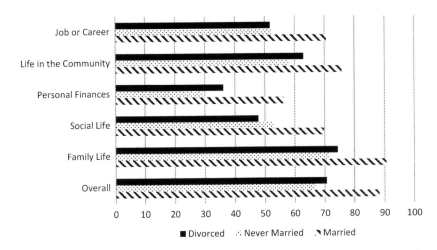

Figure 3.2 Millennial Life Satisfaction Across Domains, Percentage Who Reported Either "Mostly Satisfied" or "Very Satisfied" by Marital Status.

satisfaction across many areas of their lives when compared to those who never married. For example, most married millennials were very satisfied with their lives in categories like career satisfaction (70.5%) or satisfaction with the quality of their communities (75.7%). That's compared to only 52.1% and 58.1%, respectively, of never-married millennials. In both cases, that's around a 17-percentage-point difference in satisfaction between the groups. Even in the area of satisfaction with social life, a sphere in which one might assume that singles had the advantage, satisfaction percentages went in the same direction. Of married millennials, 69% reported being mostly or very satisfied with their social life. The never-married millennials? Only 51.7% reported being equally satisfied.

Before moving on from these data, you will notice that I included in my analysis data from divorced millennials as well. I wanted to explore if simply the act of marrying had an impact on satisfaction or, perhaps, if marrying and then divorcing not only reversed positive effects of marriage but may have actually pulled millennials lower on the satisfaction scale than their single counterparts. If true, this would suggest an additional risk to personal happiness if one were to marry. On one hand, there is a potential benefit of significantly higher personal life satisfaction. On the other hand, the potential for experiencing divorce could make life worse than before marriage. The fear of divorce may be dissuading many millennials from taking a roll of the marital dice. However, I did not find any evidence for the claim that divorce brought millennials lower on the satisfaction scale than their single counterparts. Instead, divorced millennials, at least in terms of personal satisfaction, looked very similar to never-married millennials. In fact, in all the analyses I ran, these two groups were not significantly different from each other. We might intuit from these numbers that divorced millennials took a "satisfaction hit," but that this hit was simply returning them down to where, on average, their single peers had been existing throughout their 20s and 30s.

38 *Me-Marriage: A New Type of Marriage*

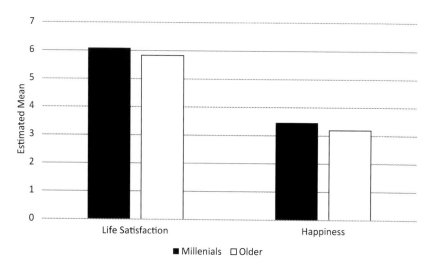

Figure 3.3 Married Millennials vs. Older Married Individuals on Life Satisfaction and Happiness.

Note: Results are estimated means after controls are accounted for.

But are married millennials happier and more satisfied in life than their parents? Using a different dataset of married couples in the United States, Figure 3.3 shows life satisfaction and happiness differences (in the week preceding the survey) between millennial married couples and older married couples. This representation is displayed with the results obtained after controlling for a range of background factors, including marriage length, racial differences between partners, education, previous marriages, and the presence of children. The difference is subtle but still statistically significant. Married millennials reported significantly more life satisfaction and overall happiness than their older counterparts and other millennials who have never married. Collectively, these data provide evidence that the me-marriage approach, at least in the short term, seems to work for millennials. This is also our first evidence of the continued benefit of marriage in our modern day. On a very general level, it would appear that the best pathway to personal happiness may indeed be through the new millennial me-marriage.

Although my previous statements may seem to paint a selfish picture of millennials, it is worth noting that the focus on personal happiness in marriage that I associate with the new me-marriage has also translated to a unique altruism among some millennials. Personal happiness was not the only goal in the millennials' marriages; it was also clear that millennials felt that the primary focus in a good marriage was to make their partner happy as well. Millennials seemed to understand that their partners were seeking to maximize their own personal happiness and that if their partners' needs were not met, they might leave. Doug, who met his wife at a local congregation and had been married for nine years, explained,

Me-Marriage: A New Type of Marriage 39

You get out of it [marriage] what you put into it. I think if you go into marriage with the right idea, that you want to make your spouse happy, and that's your main goal, then I think that's important.

Notice that making your spouse happy was not a random secondary goal for Doug but was the <u>main</u> goal one should have in marriage. Back to Cameron, he also highlighted that in a marriage, both partners should be promoting each other's personal goals. He explained how this looked in his own relationship:

It's emotionally and economically easier if, at some point, we were to pursue a professional thing. If any of us wants to [start] a project venture or start a company or something like that, the other one can be there and hold down the fort while the other one is investing in the future. That's how I see marriage.

Cameron's implication is clear: Spouses should make sure their partner's pursuits are also prioritized.

But even with this focus on one's partner, there remains the hint of self-focus. Even when talking about the importance of maintaining a spouse's personal happiness, I got the impression that, for many millennials, pandering to a spouse's wants could be tiring or perhaps even distracting from the personal happiness they valued above all else. Grace, mentioned in the previous chapter, was a good example of this point; in her interview, she first stated,

I feel like we're [she and her husband] constantly just kind of compromising, even on date nights. I don't like going to the movies, but he does. So sometimes I will just sacrifice and go, because I know he enjoys it.

While this may seem like the type of sacrifice spouses have been making for each other for many generations, Grace seemed oddly glum about these sacrifices. Rather than an opportunity to do something for her partner, she seemed to take this sort of interaction as a necessary evil of marriage. She continued, "It's just the way it is. I know he also sacrifices for my happiness." The focus here appeared to be on each partner making some effort, even begrudgingly, to make the other person happy. This valuation of personal happiness seemed to be the central component of marriage for Grace, who would later explain that, to her, the whole point of marriage was, "in a sense, just compromising and making each other happy."

In the previous chapter I noted that millennials no longer believe marriage is a necessity but that it is an instrument to be used as needed, based on individual circumstance. It would appear that personal happiness is the key ingredient in many millennials' minds about when such an arrangement may be beneficial. In some ways, this me-marriage focus on personal happiness has elevated the potential that marriage has in the eyes of millennials. After all, who wouldn't want a relationship that is centered on your personal happiness? Rather than institutional norms or family pressure, marriage is now—as mentioned in the last chapter—a tool. But it isn't just any tool, it's a personalized tool used to help attain happiness. And this makes marriage appealing, even in an era where it seems less needed.

40   Me-Marriage: A New Type of Marriage

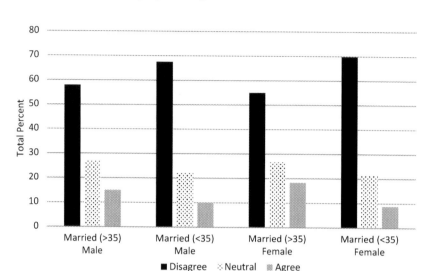

Figure 3.4 Belief That There Are More Advantages to Being Single Than Being Married, for Married Individuals by Age and Gender.

To some degree, the data support the idea that married millennials place more, not less, value on marriage than previous generations have. I noted in the previous chapter that millennials as a whole were less likely to think that marriage had advantages over being single when compared to their parents. But this comparison was done for all millennials. What about if the analysis was focused just on those millennials who actually do get married? Figure 3.4 shows the percent of married individuals (male and female) who agreed that being single has more advantages than being married. It's not surprising that most of those individuals who are married disagree with such a statement. But notice that, for those younger than 35, male and female, there is a sharp increase in the percentage who disagreed. For both men and women, this difference between the older and younger generations was statistically significant, suggesting that married millennials appear to be less likely to believe that being single is better than being married, even more so than their older counterparts. When added to the broader comparison from the last chapter, it would appear that at least some millennials, particularly those who do get married, may in fact be putting more, not less, significance on the marital relationship than the previous generation.

While such an importance in personalized me-marriage would seem to lead married millennials to be happy about their relationships, I found many reservations and hesitations about their own marriages in our interviews. As illustrated by Allison and Cameron's story, married millennials seem to struggle in their marriages to maintain the personal fulfillment they hope for. Me-marriages that maximize or at least contribute to personal happiness appear to be elusive entities to millennials, despite their own self-reported satisfaction with life. While many millennials I spoke to discussed the importance of personal happiness in marriage, they also discussed their concerns about marriages in which happiness was not achieved. Digging deeper into what me-marriage was really about, I uncovered several caveats to the personalized version of marriage that millennials aspire to and some of the unique challenges their me-marriage approach creates. The rest of this chapter is dedicated to some of these additional unique challenges.

Trying to Have It All

One struggle millennials appear to be having in their me-marriage arrangement is dealing with the fact that personal happiness is a multifaceted construct. Happiness is not derived from just one, but multiple, facets of life. I may be passionate about and enjoy a hobby, but spending all of my time doing that hobby will be unlikely to maximize my happiness in the absence of other successes or achievements. Personal happiness is most likely to be achieved when an individual is making progress in every role and goal they have in life. Yet, we all understand that being perfect in everything is unreasonable. Similarly, finding time for every pet project or hobby is also unreasonable. The focus on personal happiness that millennials have when it comes to marriage is no different. Despite similar time constraints, millennials seem to strive for a more global personal success and happiness than in the past. They truly do "want it all." In this context, marriage is meant to promote or help facilitate happiness in all areas of life: careers, friendships, personal interests, etc. The focus of me-marriage goes beyond simply being a way for them to evaluate if marriage is providing relational happiness; it is tied to a larger sense among millennials of wanting to have it all in life. For millennials, trying to achieve success in all aspects of life is often crucial to happiness and a sense of overall self-worth. This leads to a delicate balancing act of trying to juggle multiple priorities at once in the hope of achieving the multi-tiered happiness that millennials crave. Having this form of personal happiness seems at odds with a long-term marital relationship that may necessitate time and energy dedicated solely to maintaining one's relationship, energy that could otherwise be spent on personal pursuits. Yet millennials seem determined to find this elusive balance, even if that means engaging in some mental gymnastics that allow them to say their marriage is important while not actually prioritizing it.

In Monique and her husband Justin's interview, they were clear that marriage was just one of many priorities in their lives that they were attempting to balance. Monique noted, "I may not be the top priority though [for her husband]. The most important one but not the first one, I think that's how we say it sometimes." This was an interesting choice of words, suggesting that one's spouse was the most important yet not the "first" priority. She went on to give an example:

> Sometimes, it's his schooling because this is a big semester, or his work because he's going through training, or it's our son. So, there can be other first priorities, but I know I'm the most important one, and our marriage is . . . . You give the flexibility where things can be first priority, second priority as long as you don't lose sight of what's the most important ones.

42 Me-Marriage: A New Type of Marriage

Monique and her husband were attempting an interesting balancing act. They wanted to give each other space to prioritize other things while not diminishing the value of their relationship. To them, "first" priority was clearly measured by time. They acknowledged that there were periods in which each of them wanted or needed to put more time and energy into other areas of their life, but neither wanted to sacrifice the importance of their marriage. Other millennials were even more straightforward about how marriage may need to play second fiddle to other life priorities. Tiffany, a young millennial with three children, had this to say about how marriage ranked in her life:

> It's [marriage] at the bottom. As horrible as it sounds. We have a lot of things going on with our kids. All three of our kids have health issues, so that all comes first. And then finances to keep the house running and bills and stuff like that. And work because without work, you don't have money to keep a roof over your head . . . and then it's our relationship.

While Tiffany's case may be more about personal time constraints rather than personal fulfillment, the theme of marriage taking a backseat to other life roles was a constant focus in our interviews.

This juggling of priorities was common among millennials we spoke to. We asked each person in our interviews if they felt that having a good marriage meant sacrificing in other areas of their life. We return to Dustin, who had been married for 9 years and had a young daughter with his wife, whom he married right after graduating college. He responded to this question by saying,

> Nah . . . I don't think so. You just have to make sure you know what the priorities are that day. Because one day it could be family that you need, maybe the next day the business or your work. It's a juggling act—you have to make sure everything is smooth.

All marriages require this juggling act that Dustin references. In fact, in the scholarship on work–family balance, these instances of shifting priorities are called interdomain transitions (Matthews et al., 2014) and are common in most families. The unique spin millennials put on this balancing act—to succeed in each area of one's life equally without limiting one's ability to succeed in others—seems to stem from the desire to have it all. Traditionally, interdomain transitions, or transitions of resources from one domain of life to another, come with an understanding that whatever is not being prioritized will suffer. This correlates with the classic idea of an opportunity cost. Millennials seem determined to avoid this, desperate to not miss out on one opportunity for another. Dustin continued:

> You have to take care of *everything*. It might not be all at the same time but throughout. I don't feel like my work's more important than my wife, my kids; I feel like they're all important, because without one I don't have the other.

Me-Marriage: A New Type of Marriage 43

Trent, from the previous chapter, also spoke about the need and desire to have all aspects of life functioning well. Otherwise, he assumed, the whole structure of one's life may collapse. He stated,

> You have to be understanding of certain realities. You can't have a guarantee of food if you don't make your career a priority. I mean, if you decide you need to stay home more, you won't have a job; you won't be able to support a family. If you don't talk and have fun with your partner, and you don't have a partner to help you, then it doesn't matter if you have a family to support. I mean, it is all circular.

For Trent, all aspects of his life were connected, and success in all areas was needed to bolster the others. The concept of prioritizing one area over the other—for example, being willing to be less successful at work to place a higher priority on family—didn't occur to him. He felt he had the right to work as much as he wanted, not because it was a selfish pursuit, but because he felt he needed to work more to succeed and be happy. If he was personally fulfilled and happy, his spouse should understand that she would reap personal benefits as well. But what if a spouse wasn't on board with this personal plan for happiness? Remember, the pursuit of personal goals was a major factor in a happy marriage for millennials; this was certainly true for Trent, who said the following when asked what would happen if his spouse needed him to prioritize their marriage over his career or didn't help him achieve his personal goals: "If your partner doesn't understand that you have to work or doesn't understand that you need more attention, then you need a different partner."

Millennials seemed undeterred by the complexities of attempting to navigate so many roles and responsibilities to achieve total personal fulfillment. Keep in mind that most of the millennials we spoke to were comfortably residing in the middle class, perhaps leading to a slightly more optimistic view than if we were to have spent more time talking to married millennials in poverty. But for the couples we spoke to, there was a clear sense that having it all was possible, not just a pipe dream, with enough hard work. After all, all these millennials we spoke to had already decided to make the leap to marriage. They clearly thought that successfully navigating such a transition and the balancing act to follow was possible. Kevin, a recent graduate of medical school who was just starting his residency, seemed unconcerned about his ability to be successful in all areas of his life, even if time was a scarce resource, stating,

> I think it's important to recognize that success doesn't necessarily mean that everything is getting in the same amount of time, because that's impossible. But I think that all things can be going well as long as you give everything the correct focus when it's time to focus on each individual aspect of those things.

There is a trend in many of these quotes: millennials understood they had limited time and resources; again though, rather than prioritizing some life goals

44 Me-Marriage: A New Type of Marriage

over others, millennials seemed to be of the opinion that they would just need to shift their focus and energy to keep attending to each role before any one fell too far behind. One way to understand this is to think about a row of basketballs spinning atop a series of poles. To keep them spinning, one would need to quickly move from pole to pole, focusing on each ball to keep it moving but quickly advancing to the next pole before the ball fell off of it. Many millennials view their marriage as one of these balls—a ball that is not elevated or diminished compared to the balls that represent careers, friends, or personal hobbies; it is simply one of many balls to keep spinning.

Other millennials felt less positively about this balancing act. They wanted the multifaceted success we've spoken about but acknowledged that it would take sacrifice. Many found that a good compromise was not to pick one role or goal over the other, but to put them in a sequence—to find the correct order of attending to the spinning balls to make the effort of running back and forth the most efficient. This is similar to what Allison believed: she was clear that she felt she could accomplish all the things she wanted in life with some proper rebalancing and life sequencing. For her, it was largely about career and, eventually, kids. She explained:

> There are times where you really need to invest more in your career if you want to succeed. Take medical residency. You can't really have a robust, healthy marriage and have kids and be in residency. It just doesn't work. You have to realize there's a time in your life when you're going to be dedicating more time to your career development.

She felt that if goals were properly sequenced in life, success was more likely. Marriage simply became one of those roles that may need to be placed farther down in the sequence depending on personal ambition and goals. She used her own desire to return to school in the near future as an example:

> I'm going to be doing that [going back to school], but it's a choice to maintain our income and our lifestyle while I also pursue a degree. I'm choosing to do that before we have kids so that I don't have to then balance school, and work, and kids, and marriage. I think at some point it is too much. Depending on how flexible your professional life is, you can balance it in a more or less attainable way, but I think circumstances do kind of create a situation where you are having to prioritize one or more of the priorities in your life.

Other millennials found that me-marriages necessitated outside help in the difficult task of having it all. In the challenging world of today's relationships, millennials often feel like it is impossible to keep up with the tasks life places in front of them, even in a marriage with two people hard at work. Katie, a young stay-at-home mom who had been married for 5 years, contrasted the reality of modern marriage with needing to juggle more than their parents' generation did. She first talked about her parents, explaining, "My mom was a stay-at-home mom. My dad worked and brought home the income, and she took care of the home. That division of labor was equitable." This described a typical baby boomer,

Me-Marriage: A New Type of Marriage 45

gendered arrangement. Katie noted that things have changed and that part of that change was tied to dual careers and the individual ambitions of each partner. While Katie had mostly stayed at home with her kids, she had recently decided to take up some work from home, working for a crisis hotline. She continued, "It is, it's very different [today] suddenly when both of us need to be working. When both of us are working, and we're also trying to maintain a home, it's hard." While the simple solution may be to prioritize one career or carefully divide tasks between spouses, Katie did not see these as options. This separation of tasks and careers would suggest that one spouse's personal career goals were less important. As she has begun working again, she and her husband had struggled while trying to find a balance between careers and life tasks and had eventually resorted to outside help, even with Katie being at home all day. She said,

> I've been a stay-at-home wife, and there were more things that I was able to do, and there are things we just have to outsource, because we just don't have as much time. We've paid people to do our laundry, because it's very difficult to maintain a home and a family, as well as everything that needs to be done for the home. I think that's a struggle in modern marriage. And it's not a struggle my mom or my grandmother had!

Certainly, her parents and grandparents had laundry that needed to be done, but for this millennial, the personal goals that needed her attention took priority over tasks like the laundry. Mundane daily or weekly domestic tasks simply got in the way. Marriage provided extra resources to help maintain these tasks, but, in Katie's case, even those resources fell short.

Many of the examples I have given have come from more educated and middle-class millennials, those with perhaps more options at their disposal when it comes to attempting to balance all aspects of personal fulfillment. Those with less education and less opportunity with whom my team spoke often still desired personal happiness in all areas of life. However, this balancing act was even more difficult with less education. Cole and Serenity, who had one young child together and children from previous relationships, were struggling to keep up with the day-to-day grind of their life. Yet, throughout their interview, they clearly wanted to not only "get by" but also succeed in all areas of their life, like many of their peers. Like their more educated counterparts, they acknowledged that this ambition meant that sometimes their marriage had to a take a backseat. Serenity explained:

> We don't get enough time to dedicate to it [their marriage] because he works so much. We don't have anyone to babysit, so we really don't have time to dedicate [to the marriage]. We communicate, you know, we address issues that we have, and we try and make it as good as we can right now.

Interestingly, as we discussed this need to have it all in marriage, the millennials we interviewed became more altruistic in their tone. They appeared to understand that it is difficult to balance multiple roles and that their spouse was likewise

46   *Me-Marriage: A New Type of Marriage*

attempting this difficult balance in pursuit of personal happiness. It was during this discussion that millennials talked about a sense of partnership in marriage in ways similar to generations past. Trevor and Lucy from the previous chapter gave short and succinct answers throughout their interview, and when they were asked about what marriage meant to them, their answer was simple—it was a partnership. This partnership was necessary to accomplish all they wanted to in life. Lucy said, "It's [marriage] a partnership, you have to work together to get things done and to make it work." Her husband agreed, stating, "I agree with what she said; it's definitely a partnership. You can't get through it without both parties."

Leaning on Your Spouse

The final unique challenge concerning the personal happiness millennials hope to achieve in modern me-marriages is linked to the elevated stress hinted at in the quotes throughout the current and previous chapters. Stress and anxiety are viewed as the enemy of personal happiness. And millennials appear to be, more than ever before, overly stressed, at least in terms of their rates of mental health problems. Recent studies have documented an acute increase in depression and other mood disorders among millennials and younger cohorts (Mojtabai et al., 2016; Olfson et al., 2002; Twenge et al., 2019). Examining a national survey of U.S. teens and young adults, Twenge and colleagues (2019) found that there may be an even greater increase in reported health problems among millennials and younger generations. Presumably because of the frequency that depression, anxiety, and other health problems pervade the lives of those who are millennial age or younger, millennials appear to be sensitive to the fact that a spouse may, occasionally, add stress to their life. However, millennials also appear to hold a strong desire to be in a marriage (or really any romantic relationship) where one's partner is a source of stress relief, not stress creation.

Elise had a long history of mental health struggles that she shared with us during her interview. At the time my team spoke with her, Elise was seeing two therapists: one personally and one with her husband of 3 years. She had a lot of stress in her life and many personal struggles. Marriage, to her, was meant to alleviate some of these personal struggles. She illustrated this principle as she described what was initially attractive to her about her husband: "I wanted somebody that I didn't have to deal with constantly." For Elise, this idea of not having to deal with her husband constantly seemed tied to needing to give her attention to personal problems, things like "overdosing or relapsing or anything like that." Elise had a personal history of addiction. She explained,

> I've been clean for 5 years. I didn't want that life. Brandon [her husband] was the one that was there through that whole thing and helped me. As soon I saw that I could lean on him for everything that was going on, I automatically knew this is the person that I wanted to spend the rest of my life with. That's what I wanted, somebody that I could go to and lean on.

This concept of "leaning on" a spouse captures a common theme in our interviews. While anyone with a history of addiction needs support from those around them, Elise translated this example in her life into a general principal of marriage. She went on to explain that she could lean on her husband "if something's going on, or I had a bad day at work or had a bad day as a mom; that was the type of person that I wanted, and that was the type of person he was." To Elise, this kind of support was meant to be reciprocal. She noted that she also needed to help relieve the stress from her husband's life:

> I helped him through stuff. We lost his mother in 2017. I was there through that . . . . That's what our marriage is, we can lean on each other for the littlest things. That's the reason why I got married. That's what I wanted.

Ben had been married for 3 years and his wife was expecting their second child when we spoke to him. He had a similar thought when he suggested that the ability to depend on his spouse for support was the reason he was married:

> I feel safe in being able to voice opinions or being able to bounce some ideas that I'm not necessarily comfortable with bouncing off of other people, because I know that she [his wife] is committed to helping me grow as a person; she's agreed to help me do that.

Here we see another example of the me-marriage view that each spouse is there to help the other, as Ben put it, "grow as a person." In Ben's interview, he elaborated on this point and noted that having a sounding board available helped reduce anxiety in his life.

This expectation of mutual support puts a lot of pressure on spouses. Not only do millennials believe that marriage is and should be about helping your partner fulfill and maintain their personal goals and pursuits, it also seems important to them that spouses minimize both interference with one's daily schedule and anxiety they cause by disrupting one's life. Perhaps the fact that many of these married millennials were childless or only had small children reflects their ability to maintain such beliefs. Parenthood, after all, is notorious for both creating stress and disrupting family and relational patterns (Doss et al., 2009; Lawrence et al., 2008).

So, what is the bottom line when it comes to the reality of the new me-marriages that millennials are establishing? While the previous chapter outlined the hesitations and unique approaches to the premarital process and marriage that millennials have, this self-focused me-marriage is more about how millennials appear to conduct themselves in their day-to-day lives and how they evaluate their relationships and partners. Marriage, for most, is now squarely about personal benefit. Spouses are judged largely based on their additive or subtractive merits to personal happiness. The me-marriage itself seems to be primarily evaluated on the rate at which it creates and sustains one's personal happiness. Spouses are meant to balance their own happiness with the happiness and goals of their spouses while providing stress relief in their partner's life. At the same time, millennials are attempting to delicately balance a new shift toward holistic personal fulfillment—satisfaction that is derived not from prioritizing some goals over others but by trying to succeed in multiple facets of life. Marriage and relationships are merely one of many roles millennials are attempting to maximize in their life.

48   *Me-Marriage: A New Type of Marriage*

The early data suggest that, at least at the individual level, some of the me-marriage shift has succeeded in achieving its goals. My own data suggest that married millennials are happier and more satisfied in almost every aspect of their life than their single peers and older married counterparts. But this only begins to address the question of, is millennial marriage indeed benefiting these individuals in the same (or different) ways than the marriages of generations past? Having provided an overview of how millennials are approaching and acting in marriage differently, it is now time to tackle the core question of this book: Is marriage still a net good in the lives of millennials? The following chapters (Chapters 4–10) will explore this question by examining millennial marriage across a range of traditional outcomes and focal areas.

References

Alloway, T., Runac, R., Qureshi, M., & Kemp, G. (2014). Is Facebook linked to selfishness? Investigating the relationships among social media use, empathy, and narcissism. *Social Networking, 3,* 150–158. https://doi.org/10.4236/sn.2014.33020

Arnett, J. J. (2007). Suffering, selfish, slackers? Myths and reality about emerging adults. *Journal of Youth and Adolescence, 36,* 23–29. https://doi.org/10.1007/s10964-006-9157-z

Cherlin, A. J. (2004). The deinstitutionalization of American marriage. *Journal of Marriage and Family, 66,* 848–861.

Doss, B. D., Rhoades, G. K., Stanley, S. M., & Markman, H. J. (2009). The effect of the transition to parenthood on relationship quality: An 8-year prospective study. *Journal of Personality and Social Psychology, 96,* 601–619. https://doi.org/10.1037/a0013969

Dumas, T. M., Maxwell-Smith, M., Davis, J. P., & Giulietti, P. A. (2017). Lying or longing for likes? Narcissism, peer belonging, loneliness and normative versus deceptive like-seeking on Instagram in emerging adulthood. *Computers in Human Behavior, 71,* 1–10. https://doi.org/10.1016/j.chb.2017.01.037

Finkel, E. J. (2017). *The all-or-nothing marriage: How the best marriages work.* New York, NY: Dutton.

Lawrence, E., Rothman, A. D., Cobb, R. J., Rothman, M. T., & Bradbury, T. N. (2008). Marital satisfaction across the transition to parenthood. *Journal of Family Psychology, 22,* 41–50. https://doi.org/10.1037/0893-3200.22.1.41

Matthews, R. A., Winkel, D. E., & Wayne, J. H. (2014). A longitudinal examination of role overload and work–family conflict: The mediating role of interdomain transitions. *Journal of Organizational Behavior, 35,* 72–91. https://doi.org/10.1002/job.1855

McKinney, B. C., Kelly, L., & Duran, R. L. (2012). Narcissism or openness?: College students' use of Facebook and Twitter. *Communication Research Reports, 29,* 108–118. https://doi.org/10.1080/08824096.2012.666919

Mojtabai, R., Olfson, M., & Han, B. (2016). National trends in the prevalence and treatment of depression in adolescents and young adults. *Pediatrics, 138,* e20161878. https://doi.org/10.1542/peds.2016-1878

Olfson, M., Marcus, S. C., Druss, B., Elinson, L., Tanielian, T., & Pincus, H. A. (2002). National trends in the outpatient treatment of depression. *Jama, 287,* 203–209. https://doi.org/10.1001/jama.287.2.203

Stein, J., & Sanburn, J. (2013). The new greatest generation. *Time, 181,* 26.

Stewart, K. D., & Bernhardt, P. C. (2010). Comparing millennials to pre-1987 students and with one another. *North American Journal of Psychology, 12,* 579–602.

Twenge, J. M., Cooper, A. B., Joiner, T. E., Duffy, M. E., & Binau, S. G. (2019). Age, period, and cohort trends in mood disorder indicators and suicide-related outcomes in a nationally representative dataset, 2005–2017. *Journal of Abnormal Psychology, 128*, 185–199. https://doi.org/10.1037/abn0000410

Twenge, J. M., Konrath, S., Foster, J. D., Campbell, W. K., & Bushman, B. J. (2008a). Egos inflating over time: A cross-temporal meta-analysis of the narcissistic personality inventory. *Journal of Personality, 76*, 875–902. https://doi.org/10.1111/j.1467-6494.2008.00507.x

Twenge, J. M., Konrath, S., Foster, J. D., Campbell, W. K., & Bushman, B. J. (2008b). Further evidence of an increase in narcissism among college students. *Journal of Personality, 76*, 919–928. https://doi.org/10.1111/j.1467-6494.2008.00509.x

4 Me-Marriage and Marital Quality

While most of the millennial couples we interviewed reported generally happy and healthy marriages, many also mentioned common conflicts and frustrations that any married couple experiences. Cyrus and Heather were one such couple and were up front in their interview about their marital struggles. They shared that these issues emerged while they were still dating. While these conflicts and disagreements did not seem to amount to anything major, they both felt they would benefit from counseling and sought out a therapist prior to marriage. Cyrus first brought this up during their interview when asked about what he felt made his relationship unique. This prompted him to share the following: "We've gone to counseling, briefly at one point . . . . We bounced things off a friend of mine." It was a bit unclear if this counselor friend was offering formal paid therapy sessions or had clinical experience and was just willing to sit down and help a friend get his relationship on track. Either way, Cyrus and Heather noted that having a successful marriage in the modern world was difficult and that any outside support would be beneficial.

After they got married, they decided to try counseling again after conflicts continued to crop up. As Cyrus reported, "After we got married and we moved, we did another short stint of counseling." But this stint didn't last long either, something they both attributed to their busy lives. Cyrus explained,

> I don't know; we probably didn't try hard enough to continue with that kind of counseling. But life really has honestly been so busy. . . . It really is hard to fit in even an evening of counseling with somebody and do that every week.

That did not mean that everything was going perfectly in his relationship with Heather. At times, Cyrus felt like his new marriage was a burden, something that weighed him down. He seemed to think part of this was not just due to overall busyness but rather to a clash of their individual tendencies. He explained his marital difficulties in this way:

> I think our personalities don't mesh a lot. Sometimes there's the tendency to think, "it's not going to take tons of counseling if you would just do this, this way, everything should be cool." And, we don't do that. And then we hope that it happens, and it still doesn't happen.

You could feel his frustration; he wanted marriage to be easy and to work, yet he knew it would probably take more effort—effort he felt he and his wife had yet to put into it.

If you're curious if his wife felt the same, she seemed to largely agree. Here was her perspective on their early marital struggles: "We still had that childlike mind where we both want the other person to change. Which I think that happens in 99% of marriages. You always want the other person to change." While their therapy sessions had waned, Heather did mention a new social-based intervention she felt might be helping. She explained,

> One of the steps we are taking now is that we do try to hang out with people from church. We spend time in church every week. So, at least we do see very positive examples of marriages, and it is a push to be better. Even though it may be not an active way to do it, it's still modeled for us. So, that's kind of a positive I would say.

Like her husband, Heather seemed frustrated that neither one of them could muster enough effort or energy to really invest in their marriage.

While Cyrus was generally optimistic about the future of his marriage, he also acknowledged that things were not magically going to get easier. One thing both he and his wife had clearly learned was that marriage required work. He added this:

> It's like nothing's going to be good enough until I have a good enough job. It's concerning; we're going to be on our second kid, and so there is a concern there with work and money. We have to realize that the marriage is the priority. . . . And if that core relationship isn't strong enough, then our circumstances are just going to tear apart and slip.

Freedom, personal choice, and individual happiness are at the center of the me-marriages of millennials that I have laid out in the previous chapters. As we begin to explore the implications and realities of marriage for millennials, it makes sense to begin where the rubber meets the road: relationship quality. Over the course of their marriage, Cyrus and Heather had realized that marriage was not purely connected to the individual pursuit of happiness. Rather, there were and would be bumps in the road, along with needed sacrifices that would be required of both partners. Despite the stated desires of millennials to create marriages based on individual happiness that seem to be succeeding, are millennial marriages actually healthy when it comes to relational quality? Have they learned to reconcile their individual wants with the needs of their partners? And perhaps most fundamentally, is marriage still linked to better relationship outcomes compared to other types of relationships that millennials are increasingly creating space to explore? I examine these questions in this chapter, looking at outcomes associated with millennial me-marriages. In this and each of the chapters to come that are focused on the outcomes associated with me-marriages, I begin by first reviewing the historic evidence linking marriage to the outcomes focused on in that particular

52   Me-Marriage and Marital Quality

chapter before exploring whether or not these outcomes are replicated in my data on millennial couples. After that, I focus on my qualitative interview data to draw out additional themes and insights on how millennials themselves see connections between their marriage and the main topic of the chapter—the relational health and well-being of their relationship.

The Historical Evidence

For decades, the assumption that marital relationships were healthier and more stable than other forms of romantic relationships was the bedrock of most relational science. Indeed, at the heart of Waite and Gallagher's (2000) *Case for Marriage* argument was the large amount of evidence suggesting that marital relationships were the most likely type of romantic union to produce long-term success. Dozens of studies through the '80s and '90s (for examples, see Brown & Booth, 1996; Nock, 1995; Waite, 1995) suggested that this was the case. Research in the early 2000s likewise continued to find that married individuals appeared happier (Lee & Ono, 2012) and more satisfied (Moore et al., 2001) than those who were not married.

Then, roughly 10 years after *The Case for Marriage* was published, Kelly Musick and Larry Bumpass (2012) published a thorough critique of the central argument that marriage was the ideal form of romantic union, titling their paper "Reexamining the Case for Marriage." Rather than argue that decades of previous scholarship were faulty, these scholars posited that trends had merely shifted, particularly when it came to comparing the relationship quality of married couples to cohabiting couples. Cohabitation rates at the time had skyrocketed, something I noted in Chapter 2. The argument was simply that perhaps the benefits of marriage had been overstated when it came to relationship quality, especially when cohabiting became both more socially acceptable and more institutionally supported. If cohabiting was more normative and supported, perhaps differences between cohabiting and married couples would diminish. Using national U.S. data from the National Surveys of Families and Households dataset, they found that marriage was not always superior to cohabitation, particularly when considering individual outcomes, such as happiness and self-esteem.

This created an open question for scholars: Was marriage still the benchmark on which other relationships should be judged? Many of these research findings, largely centered on the marriages of the baby boomers and Generation Xers in the early 2000s, have been mixed. On one hand, some scholars have continued to find that marriage appears to benefit couples in terms of relationship quality. Using data from four countries, Tai et al. (2014) found that married couples reported significantly higher relationship satisfaction compared to cohabiting couples and couples who were dating but living apart from each other. Others have continued to find some differences in relationship quality between cohabiters, especially those without plans to marry, and married couples (Brown et al., 2017; Willoughby et al., 2012), with outcomes typically favoring those in marital relationships.

Some scholars, however, have continued to find evidence that previous links between marriage and relationship quality are potentially diminishing or at least more nuanced than previously thought. Only a few years after the Case for

Marriage was published, scholars were noting that, in some ways, non-married couples were showing superior relational outcomes compared to married couples (Punyanunt-Carter, 2004). Several scholars have shown that, when background factors are controlled for, cohabiting and married couples no longer look different in terms of relationship quality (Botha & Booysen, 2013; Willetts, 2006). Shafer and colleagues (2014) found evidence that cohabiters may be more satisfied than married couples, although they largely chalked these findings up to subgroup differences in age and relationship length. Gatzeva and Paik (2011) found that emotional and physical satisfaction in relationships was generally higher among married couples but that such satisfaction was more conditional in marriages based on jealousy, a factor that could easily erase any reported benefits among married couples.

Again, my aim here is not to bore you with a lengthy and detailed review of this scholarship comparing married couples to other relationship types. The bottom line is simply this: It was once largely assumed that marriage would provide the best environment to nurture and sustain a happy and healthy relationship. However, in the last two decades, that assumption has been challenged with good data suggesting that, as marriage becomes deinstitutionalized and other relationship forms become more normalized, these benefits may be shifting or disappearing.

But again, most of this is based on data collection efforts in the early 2000s, when only the youngest married millennials would have been included. As millennials have reshaped the nature of the marital relationship, the questions remain: Are the marriages of millennials healthy? Are they continuing the trend of seeing fewer benefits to tying the knot? Are they better off just moving in together? Let's look at the data.

The Millennial Data

There's a lot to unpack here, given that the question of how me-marriages look in terms of relationship quality is core to the central question of this book. Of course, the main outcome of interest in these types of explorations is often general relationship satisfaction. In the sample of 3,000 millennials in committed relationships in their early 30s, married and never-married millennials did, in fact, significantly differ on their reports of relationship satisfaction after controlling for gender, race, parents' education, sexual orientation, and parents' marital status. Unfortunately, relationship length, a potentially important differentiator between married and unmarried relationships, was not available in the dataset, so I was not able to control for it. With that in mind, and like previous research has suggested, married millennials reported significantly more satisfaction, after controls, than their never-married peers. A similar result was found for stability, where married millennials reported significantly higher relationship stability after controls than the never-married millennials in committed relationships. Figure 4.1 illustrates these differences, which were not monumental. Still, it suggests at least some preliminary evidence that me-marriages do appear more satisfying and stable than dating relationships among millennials.

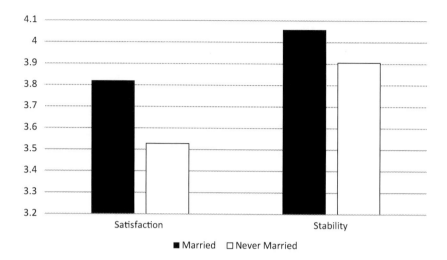

Figure 4.1 Estimated Means on Satisfaction and Stability by Marital Status for Millennials in their 30s.

One of the more specific elements of relationship quality lies in questions about millennials' sexual lives. With the increases in casual sex and a dominant hook-up culture (Heldman & Wade, 2010; Owen et al., 2010) among millennials, it's possible that they are placing increased importance on the physical chemistry of their relationships. Traditionally, married couples have experienced more satisfying (Laumann et al., 1994) sex than their non-married peers, although these findings have also been recently debated (Birnie-Porter & Hunt, 2015; Galinsky, & Sonenstein, 2013). Is that still the case? Data from our sample of over 3,000 millennials who were in a committed relationship suggests it is not, at least in terms of frequency of and satisfaction with sex. When comparing married and never-married millennials on their sexual frequency, orgasm frequency, and sexual satisfaction, no significant differences emerged after demographic controls ($p = .767$, $p = .514$, and $p = .142$, respectively).

A difference did emerge when it came to thoughts (but not acts) of infidelity. Here, married millennials and never-married millennials significantly differed ($p < .001$) after controls. Never-married millennials were significantly more likely to report thinking about having sex with someone other than their partner compared to their married peers. This finding has been found previously, especially among cohabiting individuals (Treas & Giesen, 2000), and may simply be due to the more unstable nature of non-marital dating relationships.

While this literature provides some context for comparing married millennials with all other types of non-marital relationships, what about differences when compared to specific types of non-marital relationships, especially those in cohabiting relationships? After all, cohabiting relationships are where many relationship experts have focused their attention given that they are often assumed to be more long-term and stable than early dating relationships. I focused my

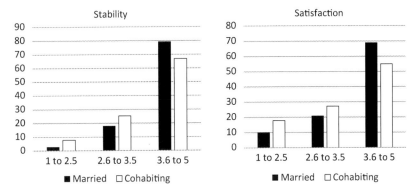

Figure 4.2 Percentage of Married and Cohabiting Millennials Based on Low, Medium, and High Raw Relationship Satisfaction and Stability Scores.

analyses on comparing married millennials with cohabiting millennials. Here, controlling for the same crop of demographic factors as before, I found that married millennials reported significantly higher relationship satisfaction compared to cohabiting millennials. After controls were factored in, the mean difference between the two groups was roughly two-tenths of one point—the differences were not huge. I found almost the exact same thing when it came to stability, with married millennials significantly but narrowly edging out cohabiting millennials in reporting more stability in their relationships. Figure 4.2 displays the raw numbers for both stability and satisfaction for cohabiting and married millennials. Both stability and satisfaction were measured on a 5-point scale (1–5), and to help visualize the differences, I broke the sample into three groups based on their satisfaction and stability scores: a low stability/satisfaction group, a moderate satisfaction/stability group, and a high stability/satisfaction group. In both graphs, you can see a similar story emerge. While cohabiting millennials were more likely to report both low and moderate stability and satisfaction, married millennials were more likely to report high satisfaction and stability.

Interestingly, one area where I did not find a difference was in their intimacy. Across almost every measure, millennials' sex lives appeared very similar, regardless of being in a married or cohabiting relationship. I found no significant differences after controls in the frequency of sex, rates of infidelity, or the frequency of orgasm. I did find one significant difference in that millennial cohabiters were significantly more likely to report thinking or fantasizing about having sex with someone other than their partner compared to married millennials.

My data also provided another type of comparison. Rather than comparing millennials based on the type of relationship they were in, the other national U.S. dataset of newlywed couples allowed me to compare the marital relationship of millennials to those who were older. This permitted me to answer a different type of question. Instead of exploring whether married millennials had differing relational quality compared to millennials who were not married, these data allowed me to examine whether millennial marriages were in fact different than

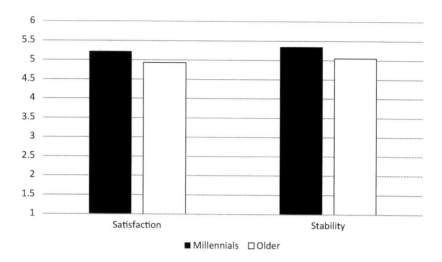

Figure 4.3 Estimated Means Comparing Millennials vs. Older Newlyweds on Satisfaction and Stability.

the marriages of an older cohort. Given that these data were collected at the same point in each group's marriages, when all couples were newlyweds, I could compare new current marriages that differed only by the age of the spouses rather than needing to compare current data with historical comparison data.

I first looked at the tried and true relationship-quality markers of stability and satisfaction (see Figure 4.3). These models controlled for relationship length, the education of both partners, racial differences between partners, the presence of children, if their parents had been married, and if each partner had been previously married. Here I found some consistent differences between millennials and their older counterparts. Married millennials, after controls, reported significantly higher relationship satisfaction for both male and female partners. Further, they reported significantly more stable relationships based on both male and female responses. Figure 4.3 displays the estimated means (which account for controls) for both outcomes comparing the older and younger couples in the dataset. As you'll see, the differences were again not large, but they were consistent. While such results may be tied to research suggesting some risk in simply getting married at older ages (Wolfinger, 2015), these findings may also suggest the presence of some cohort effects as well.

What if we go beyond more general markers of relationship quality to process outcomes, such as conflict and communication? While these outcomes were not available in my dataset comparing me-marriages to other millennial relationships, I was once again able to compare across cohorts on these process outcomes in the data on newlyweds. Conflict scores appeared to be mostly the same between millennials and older married couples. Overall ratings of conflict resolution were also essentially identical between the two age cohorts in our data. The one slight difference I found was that millennials reported slightly fewer overall disagreements

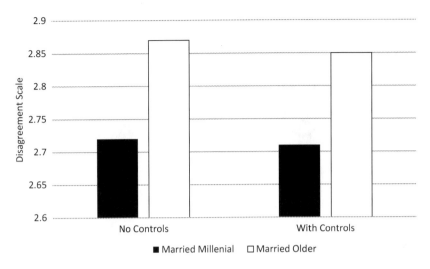

Figure 4.4 Number of Disagreements by Age Cohort, With and Without Controls.

than older married couples did, but this difference was barely statistically significant. In fact, once I accounted for background factors (Figure 4.4), these differences slightly diminished and became statistically insignificant. On the other hand, older newlyweds reported significantly more hours attending professional counseling for relationship problems over the course of their marriage, at a rate almost double that of millennials (millennials averaged about three hours of counseling while older couples averaged a total of almost seven hours of counseling).

One other process outcome stuck out to me. Aggression and aggressive behavior is another important element in any relationship. One specific area this can manifest is related to what scholars call relational aggression (Goldstein, 2011; Prather et al., 2012). Basically, this type of behavior is characterized by classic passive-aggressive behaviors that are largely meant to establish power and exert control over a partner. When I explored relational aggression generally in the sample, I found that married men reported significantly higher relational aggression than did married women. However, when I split the newlywed sample by generational cohort (Figure 4.5), this difference was only statistically significant for millennials, despite the gap in the raw numbers appearing larger for older couples. Curiously, when I compared overall relational aggression levels for men in millennial and older married couples, millennial men reported significantly less relational aggression than their older peers. How is that possible? The answer appears to lie in variation. Older men were much more diverse in their reports of relational aggression. Older men in our sample had a standard deviation (a measure of how spread out the responses of the questions were) of 1.31. Millennial men had a much smaller spread of only .94. To illustrate this result in a less statistical way, 10% of older men reported high relational aggression (scores above 4) while only about 3% of millennial men reported the same levels. Because of these

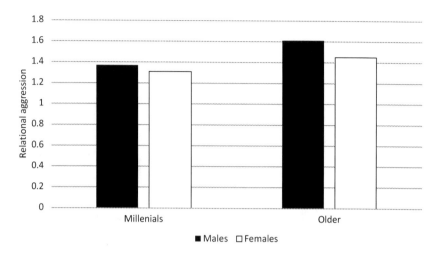

Figure 4.5 Estimated Means on Relational Aggression, by Gender and Generational Cohort.

interesting data issues, I ran the same analysis, this time creating groups based on whether men reported high levels of relational aggressive behaviors. When I isolated highly relational aggressive men, I again found clear differences. Married millennial men were significantly less likely (6%) than older married men (13%) to report high levels of relational aggression. This complicated matters more. This new analysis showed that women, not men, were reporting differences across age cohorts. Millennial women (23%) were less likely than older women (34%) to report any relational aggression in their marital relationship. What does it all mean? It probably means that millennials, as a whole, appear to be using relationally aggressive behaviors less than their older peers.

So, what is the takeaway from all these data? It appears that millennial married couples are self-reporting better satisfaction and stability scores than older couples, despite the fact that conflict levels and other indicators of couple processes are largely the same. In other words, I do not find much evidence that the relationship processes between millennials and older couples are drastically different, but the millennial couples are *reporting* better relationship quality, nonetheless. While there is not tangible evidence that millennial me-marriages are of better quality than older couples, millennials sure seem to think their marriages are, on average, better.

The national dataset of newlywed couples allowed me to explore one final question when it came to cohabitation. As I reported earlier, my national millennials dataset suggested that married millennials were reporting slightly more stable and satisfying relationships compared to their cohabiting counterparts. But was this really a marriage benefit or a finding due more, perhaps, to the unique nature of cohabiting relationships in the United States, most of which are still precursors to eventual marriages? With my newlywed data, I could examine one more thing that would provide some additional evidence for a "marriage bump" by examining whether any relationship differences emerged between millennial newlyweds who had or had not cohabited prior to marriage. While differences may exist between the groups before marriage, are cohabiting couples who eventually marry receiving the same "bump" in outcomes and becoming like their married peers in the other sample? Using the same set of controls as before, I found no differences between the newlyweds who had cohabited and those who did not on levels of reported conflict, stability, satisfaction, or relational aggression for both partners.

While the national dataset of all millennials provides at least some evidence that marriage was still an advantageous relationship for millennials, the newlywed data suggest that perhaps such differences are based on relationship stage, rather than context. Cohabiters who eventually transition to marriage appear to enjoy most, if not all, of the same benefits as couples who transition directly into marriage. To me the bottom line is two-fold. First, there is still some evidence that millennials are receiving some bump in relational quality by being married that scholars have historically noted. I use the word "bump" here intentionally. Marriage does not appear to elevate a relationship to a higher plane or provide an exponential increase in relationship quality. The bump is there, but it appears small, likely at the mercy of several underlying contextual factors that vary across couples such as economic resources, personality, and family background. But the second takeaway for me may be more important. That is, me-marriages and the uniquely individualized approach to marriage that millennials are increasingly taking does not appear to be hurting the quality of their relationships. These marriages still appear, on average, to be happy and satisfying.

Making Sense of the Unique Relational Challenges of Me-Marriages

I will be honest with you at this point in our exploration. Given some of the themes I noted in previous chapters about the individualistic nature of me-marriages, I truly did not think I would find many relational quality benefits among their relationships. Open science and the preregistration of hypotheses are a growing trend in the social sciences (essentially meaning that we, as researchers, need to clearly articulate our educated guesses before we do a study, rather than attempting to restructure those guesses after we already see what the data show). In this case, I would have registered the hypothesis that millennial marriages would likely look no different than other non-marital relationships and certainly would not look healthier than the marriages of older adults. Yet, as I noted, the data seem to support the conclusion that me-marriages are, at least in their early stages, havens of relational health for many millennials. Despite their unique challenges and shifting circumstances, millennials appear to be navigating the sometimes turbulent waters of marriage.

So, I turn next to my qualitative interviews to provide some guidance on how and why this is happening. How are married millennials talking about the health and quality of their relationships, and how are they responding to some of the unique challenges posed in previous chapters to beat the odds and

60   *Me-Marriage and Marital Quality*

create marriages of generally high quality? Perhaps the simplest solution is that millennials understand that if their marriage is failing, their personal pursuits will be hampered. There was a sense from many millennials that the health of their relationship did impact their daily life. As Naomi, who had been married to her husband for several years, put it,

> If you're unhappy in your marriage, I feel like that affects your surroundings. Meanin' when I go to work, if we get into an argument I may be in a bad mood, and I may jeopardize my job because I am in a bad mood. Or I may jeopardize some friendships because I am going through things with [my husband]. I may cut off some people because I'm going through issues with him. Marriage should be a top priority, just because he's somebody I'm with the majority of the time and it effects my surroundings.

Yet I believe the quality of me-marriages goes beyond a simple desire to avoid negative interactions due to the fear that they may undermine personal happiness. There's more going on in these marriages that is still creating that marriage bump I referenced before. As I explored my interview data, a few themes emerged that are worth discussing in more depth. The first two speak to potential mechanisms that are benefiting millennials in their pursuit of a happy marriage: the strong and perhaps increased emphasis they put on communication, and their acknowledgment and desire to seek out relational resources more than ever before. Let me provide some context for both.

The Growing Importance of Healthy Communication

It is not news that healthy communication is an important part of any marriage. However, due to the flexibility desired in me-marriages and the challenges such flexibility creates, negotiating openly between partners is perhaps a more important aspect of these marriages than in those of the past. When asked about how they overcame challenges and obstacles in their marriages, communication was at the top of their minds for many millennials. Avery was one of many millennials who specifically brought up the role of communication during her interview, although it was unprompted in our questions. Avery's marriage had struggled through many hardships, including addiction. She noted the important role communication had played in her marriage, saying,

> I think open communication is what really helped our marriage. If I felt unsure of myself, I could say that to him. I could say, "Hey, I don't know if I feel like I'm doing this right," or, "Is this something you think you'd handle better or differently?" Communication is so important in just figuring out yourself as you change and grow.

Communication was, to Avery, an essential element of what had allowed her marriage to survive. Aubrey, a millennial who had seen her husband's parents and her own parents divorce, immediately identified communication as the problem in both cases. She shared that she had learned from "all the examples of [my parents] and his parents and all the things we don't want to emulate. Just that lack of communication and letting things go on for years and never addressing them." Aubrey felt the lack of open communication was what doomed both of their parents' relationships—something she was determined to fix in her current marriage to her husband.

Brielle and Carson, married for a few years and living with several children at home (one of their own and a few from Carson's previous relationships), were also clear that communication was the key to their marriage. Brielle shared their daily communication ritual that she felt was one of the glues of their marriage. She believed their secret was simple, yet effective: "We talk before we go to bed." This talking happened even if they had conflict or disagreements during the day. For both, such frustrations made the nightly communication ritual even more vital. Carson tied this to some age-old marital advice, adding, "We shouldn't be able to go to bed mad. We just talk and talk it out." They both identified that sometimes this communication made things worse in the short term and that Brielle had a tendency to leave the bedroom and escape into another room of the house if she was feeling overwhelmed. Brielle was clear that, even if she went to cool off,

> we come back and talk. Every time we have an argument, I go to a room upstairs and lock the door. But, he follows me fast and gets the keys up in the door, . . . then he talks to me and, yeah, the problem is solved after that. We talk.

While I know several couples therapists who may not be thrilled by Carson and Brielle's conflict resolution pattern, the emphasis on "talking it out" for both this couple and Avery was illustrative of almost every millennial couple my team spoke to.

Like other couples, Evan and Cora credited strong communication as a key element for the success in their young marriage. They had been married for almost three years, and Cora tied her focus on good communication to watching the success of her parents. She shared,

> I think you just need to communicate and be on the same page. I don't even know if Evan knows this. My dad didn't work for a while; there was a strike, and he chose to go without pay. Watching [my parents] talk through that and figuring things out . . . . I watched them make decisions together.

Evan agreed and felt they had been able to incorporate healthy communication skills into their own marriage. He had this to add:

> Speaking about Cora and me, I don't think we've ever really hit a really down period yet, in our marriage. We have very acute arguments, disagreements, things like that. But we work through it because it doesn't change how I feel about her on a broader scale. How would we deal with a more major issue should it crop up in our marriage? I don't know, but I'm not really concerned,

62 Me-Marriage and Marital Quality

to be honest with you. Because I know that she's got a good head on her shoulders.

As noted by Evan in his comment about the potential for more serious issues in his marriage down the road, "talking it out" in a rational and open way was simply what millennials felt was the solution to just about any problem marriage could throw at them—past, present, or future.

For many millennials, this open communication was critical, not just to improve and maintain the quality of one's relationship but also to balance marriage with all of life's other family and personal duties (something I will return to in the next chapter). For example, Jaxson and Peyton had been married for about five years and were juggling kids, careers, and hobbies. In their minds, communication was the key to making this complex life work. Jaxson gave the example of what would happen if one of their kids was sick and required a parent at home:

> Sometimes Peyton has to take off work, like if our kid's sick. Sometimes I do [take off work]. We'll just communicate with each other, like, "what do you have going on, what do I have going on?" [Figuring out] who's got the best opportunity to take this day, and we just communicate more through it.

Another couple, Axel and Mia, were balancing two busy and complicated careers. Mia was very clear about what helped them through it daily: "Communication is probably our biggest way that we handle those things." Good open communication for millennials was not just about resolving conflict but also about navigating the increased complexity of modern life.

Addy and Sawyer, a young couple who had struggled with poverty, mental illness, and a host of relationship problems in their marriage, were another couple that talked about the ways communication helped them navigate the complexity of modern married life. Communication was the constant that made things feel more manageable. When asked how her marriage would continue to survive the many trials they had described in their interview, Addy said,

> I think we need to have very strong communication in order to manage that. It's not going to be easy; it's going to be super hard. But I think that we've been through a lot. Health issues, job issues, money struggles. I think we've been through the mill and back. . . . Having a strong understanding about who you each are as people as well as a couple [is important].

Of course, millennials put their own unique spin on open communication. Remember, me-marriage is largely self-focused, and open communication was often seen as a way to openly and clearly express one thing to a partner: personal needs and wants. Sadie and Kayden had been married for 6 years when they were interviewed. They had one little girl and another baby on the way. They were both clear that communication was once again at the heart of their successful marriage but noted that the key to this communication was the freedom to express one's

Me-Marriage and Marital Quality   63

personal needs openly to each other. Sadie said that communication was critical to a good marriage because it gave you the option of

> being able to be yourself around somebody and for them to accept you for who you are. And being on the same page because that's gonna make a marriage last. You have to have the same wavelengths, and you understand each other, and you support each other, and you're open, and you're communicating all the time with each other. You're really there for the other person, no matter what.

This unconditional support of one's partner was seen as vital to Sadie, who wanted her husband to support her in whatever endeavor she felt she needed to embark on.

Her husband agreed, tying this openness to the critical area of career and educational decisions. Kayden shared:

> I think both people in the marriage need to be themselves and need to be honest with who they are and what's important to them and what they're all about. If it's very important to one person to pursue some kind of graduate program or something and the other person truly isn't supportive of it, then that will probably add stress to your marriage. That was one thing when me and Sadie were married, and when I started dating her I told her, I'm not going to be available physically the first few years. I didn't get her really nice stuff for her birthday or Christmas. I really wasn't that romantic because I couldn't be. I guess to sum it up, you have to be real with what you're doing and what's important to you.

Kayden sums up what I heard from many millennials when he said, "you have to be real." The concept of being real with a spouse, being clear about what you want early in a relationship, was key to millennials who, remember, want marriage to be a relationship that supplements and enriches their personal goals.

This concept of relational honesty being tied to the ability to communicate seemed very important to many millennials. Whether it be the constant need to portray a perfect image on social media or just the increased social connection of millennials, many married millennials we spoke to noted the importance of marriage being a haven of honest communication about who you really are and what you really want to be. Emery, married for 6 years to her husband, noted that it was the moment she realized she could do this with her boyfriend that she knew she had met the one she wanted to marry. She shared:

> I have really curly hair, and I straighten it, and I remember the first time we were in a fight and I had just blow dried my hair. I hadn't flat ironed it yet and I didn't have any makeup on and I still wanted to go work out this fight with him. It was just a really big turning point with me. I felt so comfortable with him and I could be myself, which I think is really important. It's huge.

64 Me-Marriage and Marital Quality

> I have a little sister who's married. They've been married for 2 years now, and she feels like she can't quite be herself in front of her husband. That's just a huge scary red flag to me. I am totally comfortable with him [her husband] and have been since the beginning. That was huge for me.

As I mentioned, open communication is not a new concept in healthy marriages. But millennials certainly seem preoccupied by it. It was mentioned by almost every person my team interviewed, even though we never asked about it. It was a concept that helped millennials navigate a marital landscape that was more complex than ever before and also seen as a key way in which to make sure each partner was clear about the personal needs and desires of the other. It was the mechanism through which it appeared most millennials felt they had already conquered, or would in the future conquer, the challenges of modern marriage.

Seeking Out Additional Relational Resources

Another answer to this question of how married millennials may be actively seeking to improve their relationship quality may be in the fact that millennials are accessing more resources than previous generations. Whether this means they have real access to more resources than in the past, or simply perceive more resources as available, many couples my team spoke to identified a variety of resources they had tapped into that they felt helped them navigate difficulties in their marriages. Perhaps as a result of growing up in the modern area of technology and instant information access, millennials are simply much more capable of and comfortable with accessing outside resources to help them solve problems. In past generations, marital struggles and problems were often taboo, the type of issues that most couples hid from the outside world and rarely sought help with until it was almost too late. This isn't to say that I believe millennials are more likely to air their relational dirty laundry out to the public. However, given the amenity afforded by most modern technology, perhaps they feel more capable than ever before in seeking out resources in discreet ways. Hundreds of online resources are at the fingertips of millennials when it comes to relationship and marriage advice. However, these resources were not always positive. A content analysis of relationship advice published in the ever-popular *Cosmo* magazine revealed that much of the advice was both sexist and counter to what most relationship scholars would often recommend (Gupta et al., 2008), a problem also found in many men's magazines (Spalding et al., 2010). Even Reddit has been studied as a platform where many people turn for relationship advice (Collisson et al., 2018).

One example of this perceived increased access to resources that came up in our interviews was access to mental health and counseling professionals, resources that many millennials felt very comfortable both accessing and talking about, even if their marital difficulties did not seem too severe. Perhaps one benefit of our modern society is the destigmatization of mental health resources. While couples of the past may have been hesitant to seek out professional counseling until their relationship was essentially falling apart, millennial couples appeared to have much more open minds about such help. Katie and Jeremy, whom I introduced in the

Me-Marriage and Marital Quality 65

last chapter, had a seemingly strong and happy marriage of 5 years. They noted that they had regularly been to a marriage counselor during their marriage. Katie joked in their interview that the key to their happy marriage was, "We have a marriage counselor that we pay very handsomely!" Jeremy added, "I joke that she's named her boat after us!"

Katie and Jeremy's road to therapy started with a job loss and significant reduction in income for Jeremy. As Katie explained,

> About a year ago, Jeremy experienced a job loss. We had to move out of our home. We lived in my cousin's spare bedroom for about six months. That was really hard. We were trying to figure out how to assign roles as far as maintaining family structure because at the time I wasn't working. He had gotten a part-time job with UPS. So our income was drastically diminished. We struggled, we were both really lost in that situation. It was definitely a struggle. That's actually when we first started seeing our current marriage counselor because my needs from what I expected from my spouse were so drastically not being met that it really shook our marriage to its foundation.

Things were so rocky at the time that Katie and Jeremy decided to separate, something that lasted for 4 months. Katie struggled with the lack of stability in their relationship and struggled to see what the future would hold. Eventually, and with the help of a therapist, she was able to rebuild her trust in their marriage. She noted that therapy gave them a sense of clarity in terms of their goals and roles. She said, "just knowing how your roles are supposed to be in your family was really integral in having any stability! I'm really grateful we were able to get through that."

Mental health professionals were not the only relational resource millennials appeared to be tapping into to help improve their marriages. This was another area of life where millennials identified the importance of technology. Social media, for example, offered an almost infinite supply of resources in the minds of many millennials we spoke to. Of course, millennials often recognized that these resources might both hinder and help young marriages. Alexis had met her husband when she was 13 years old and married very young compared to most millennials. When she struggled in her marriage, she found empowerment from a social media group she joined. As she put it,

> I think it's helped things, in good ways. For me at least. Because they make me start being more vocal about my needs instead of just pushing them to the backburner all the time just to avoid confrontation. Now, I don't worry about confrontation anymore because I don't think of it in that same way anymore.

Alexis felt that her social media interaction had given her specific skills, in this case related to open communication, that had benefited her marriage. This created a synergy between the millennial themes of seeking resources and the need for open and honest communication. She did, however, note that this positive influence

66 *Me-Marriage and Marital Quality*

had not always been there and that she had also seen social media be a negative resource for her marriage. She noted,

> There was a point in time where social media did not affect our marriage well at all. Because I did have other friend groups that I would talk to about [our marriage], and it's really easy for other people who don't have physical eyes on your marriage to give opinions. You know, one-sided things.

This example helps illustrate the double-edged sword that online resources afford millennials. While their access to information and resources may be exponentially larger than previous generations, the need for millennials to have strong digital literacy and discernment in this process of resource gathering is key. Millennials are forced to try to discern what resources will help or hurt their growing relationship.

Sometimes the resources millennials were accessing were more mundane. Aubrey, whom I mentioned earlier, and Jordan had been married for several years but felt their relationship had waned in priority recently. They were a busy couple, both with full-time and hectic jobs. They had also recently moved and had a young child, adding more chaos to their lives. Therapy, or other forms of formal relationship education, seemed out of reach with their busy schedules. Aubrey reported that they had gotten creative with their resources, turning to a relationship enhancement game they had purchased online. She shared,

> A couple years ago, we bought this deck of cards. You choose one, and it's, like, for every week in the year, and you pull it out, and there's a manual that tells you what the card means. You're supposed to do that action throughout that week. It just gets you to get out of your comfort zone, and it keeps things exciting and you're doing different things. So we started that again last week, actually. We're doing that again. We started that a couple years ago and then never followed through with it, so we're trying to do it again through the whole deck this time.

Even with their lives increasingly hectic, many married millennials appeared to turn to a diversifying (and growing) business of relational resources, many of them digital.

Peers were a final resource mentioned for several millennials we spoke to, and technology often allowed millennial married couples to stay connected and interact with peers more consistently than in years past, making these peers a more numerous and perhaps accessible resource. Continuing to discuss resources Jordan mentioned that he had very few good marriage examples in his life. His parents and most of his family members had divorced. He worked in the mental health field and dealt with struggling families on a daily basis. For him, getting negative about marriage was easy—almost second nature. He reported that having a positive view of marriage largely came from his peers. He shared this:

> A couple of friends [are] a sounding board for me. Just seeing what they were dealing with and how they were dealing with it. What they were doing right

and wrong and what was working and what wasn't working . . . just seeing them interact. Just seeing them come together; they were really doing well.

These positive examples and the advice he drew from these peers motivated Jordan to keep working on his own marriage. Whether peers, counselors, social media, or other relationship enhancement tools, millennials appear to be turning to a variety of resource to both sustain and improve their marital quality.

What If It Starts Falling Apart?

No discussion of relational quality would be complete, however, without at least some consideration of major relational hurdles and divorce. While all the couples my team interviewed were currently together, that does not mean that they had not dealt with, considered, or contemplated the realities of divorce. It's clear that millennials still very tangibly feel the fear of divorce from their parents' generation, despite declining divorce rates. Allison, from the previous chapters, mentioned this as a major fear of her cohort, noting, "Oh my God, that's [divorce] such a bad joke. I feel like there's this fear of this. I've seen how it [marriage] can end badly and so I'd rather just not take the risk that it'll end badly."

While divorce has always been a part of marriage, do millennials approach the decision to end a marriage any differently than generations past? While divorce rates are down, they remain at relatively high levels. In our national dataset of millennial newlyweds, 31% of all couples reported they had actively discussed divorce or break-up at some point in their young relationship. Attitudes in favor of divorce are also becoming more neutral, with a recent study suggesting that only about half of young adults believed that divorces should be harder to get (Stokes & Ellison, 2010), and another study suggesting that divorce permissiveness is high in many industrialized countries (Sieben & Verbakel, 2013). This suggests that many millennials are open to and aware of the possibility of divorce in their marriage. This interesting dynamic of continuing to want their marriages to succeed while acknowledging the realities of divorce has created a rather pragmatic approach to the divorcing process among many millennials my team spoke to. They seemed much more open and accepting of divorce than previous generations. Take Sam and Avery as an example. Despite having a happy and fulfilling young marriage, at one point in the interview, Avery jumped in with a rather casual statement about divorce. As they talked about some of the small arguments they have had, Avery threw in this, "If this [marriage] doesn't work, I'm never doing it again. I'll tell you that much." She laughed this off quickly, but notice that Avery's comment acknowledges the possibility that this "might not work out." Perhaps to some this is simply being more realistic than previous generations.

I mentioned Elise in the last chapter as one of the many married millennials who had sought out therapy with her husband, Brandon. Elise and Brandon offered another interesting illustration of this modern and more nuanced thinking process. Their interview took place a mere 2 months after Brandon had given his wife an ultimatum: get help or get out. He felt that she had a "bad attitude" about their relationship and her life in general and was frustrated with the negativity

68 *Me-Marriage and Marital Quality*

she was bringing to the table. These issues were compounded by his wife's mental health struggles—problems that had recently flared up. A veteran who had already ended his first marriage due to his own mental health issues, Brandon was willing to give his wife an opportunity for redemption, but only one. He said,

> I didn't know what the hell I was getting myself into because she has two mental diagnosed problems that were leading her life and leading her. I didn't know what I was in for. We eventually got to that point, within the last couple months where I said, "I'm, done. I'm done with this bullshit."

Elise responded to this by starting individual counseling, a resource I have already mentioned as common tool among millennials. Brandon reported,

> she sought help, so she's on a slowly changing path. I've already gone through the slow changing path, and I strive ever forward from there. There's no going back. Everything is about growth and change in my opinion, and you can never stop doing that, and I did a lot of my big changes already, so I'm on the slow path now. She's just beginning.

Remember, Brandon had been in a similar situation himself with his first marriage. The irony was not lost on him as he explained,

> Basically it just feels like I'm going full circle because my first wife gave me that ultimatum years ago, and I left and have changed, and when she [Elise] was going through this, I knew that there was a possibility that she could do that to me, too, but that was a chance I had to take.

Brandon did not seem to bat an eye at the possibility of divorce, despite already going through one. Divorce was merely another tool, a resource one could utilize if marriage was jeopardizing one's personal happiness. Cooper is another young millennial we interviewed who had been married three times and was initially skeptical about marrying his current wife. He said this when asked how his previous marriages impacted his current marriage of 3 years and why he had decided to marry again. He said,

> I was just worried about getting hurt or wasting everyone's time because I wasn't ready to settle down, or wasting my time. I'd already done it twice, and I knew what worked and what didn't work, and I just wanted to make sure that it was going to work before I made that commitment.

Again, Cooper took a very pragmatic approach to both marriage and divorce. While he alluded to "being hurt," his main concern was "wasting time." He knew he could simply pull the trigger on another divorce if needed, but wanted to avoid the hassle if possible.

Millennials appear to be much more open to divorce than in the past. For many, perhaps divorce is an alluring and tempting option. In fact, Whitney and Claire, married now for several years, noted that the unique nature of their same-sex relationship actually benefited them by reducing this divorce temptation due to the legal hurdles it would have taken to divorce when they got married at a time when same-sex marriage was rarely recognized. Claire explained,

> We went to Massachusetts to get married, and to be divorced you have to be living in the state, but we were living in Georgia, so our marriage wasn't recognized. So to get divorced, you'd have to move to Massachusetts. Which has been really helpful to be like, "Is it so bad you want to move to Massachusetts?"

For Whitney, this institutional barrier was key early in their marriage. As she put it, "It got us through our first year."

Carson, from earlier in the chapter, was another interesting case study in the somewhat casual attitudes some millennials have created around divorce. He was in his fourth marriage (he was only in his early 30s when he was interviewed). He noted that he had made some mistakes in the past, noting,

> I was very young, and I shouldn't of did it [gotten married young]. I don't know what I was thinking about. I was too young. I was just going into the military and, trying to think ahead, and thought I was going to be with the woman that is my ex now. It never worked out, . . . but I do have a son with her.

While Carson certainly had some regret about his past marital decisions, these experiences had never dissuaded him from remarrying. He did not appear to view his divorces as a personal stigma or any sign that perhaps he just wasn't the marrying type. Divorce was a tool, like marriage is for many millennials, and a tool he had often utilized.

His current wife, Brielle, had a different tolerance for this tool and a fairly high threshold for divorce: At one point in her interview, she explained, "As long as he don't hit me and he don't cheat on me, I'm good with that." Yet her strong views against divorce did not seem to translate to her husband. At no point in the interview did she even hint at the fact that she disagreed with her husband's decision to end his previous marriages. That was his right and his choice. Curiously, it also never seemed to occur to Brielle that his quick divorce trigger might someday have quite the impact on her own marriage, despite her stated intention to stay married in virtually any circumstance.

There was certainly less stigma about divorce manifested in the comments of many of the millennials I interviewed. But I also need to be careful to not leave you with the impression that all millennials had such a whimsical view of divorce. Other millennials continued to talk about the gravity and seriousness of the divorcing process and the toll it would take. Brent, a tow truck driver, was one of the shortest interviews my team conducted. He was to the point and rarely expanded on his answers. He had been married once before his current spouse and didn't seem to think his previous marriage had much connection to

70 Me-Marriage and Marital Quality

his current situation. As he put it, "the first one I think was just a mistake. The second [marriage], at the beginning I thought I learned from my mistakes. So I think that's why this one is a lot better than the last one." When asked to elaborate on the differences between his two marriages, he got right to the point, "I'm still with her."

Brent's wife Tiffany was interviewed separately from Brent due to scheduling conflicts. While Brent rarely disclosed any details of their relationship, Tiffany provided more context for the struggles they had been through. She explained that Brent had cheated on her in the past before they were married, something he did not disclose in his interview. Why did she stay with him after that? She explained,

> To be completely honest, one of the reasons I stayed after he cheated was I didn't think I could do it on my own. Especially with two kids. . . . We planned to get married before I had our first son when I was like 20, and then I found out he cheated so I called off the wedding. But then there was a custody battle going on with my stepson a year later when I was 21. And the judge literally looked at us and said it would look better if we were married. So 2 weeks later we got married.

Tiffany was clearly describing the constraint commitment I mentioned in a previous chapter. But she illustrates that, while some millennials feel like divorce is an easy tool and option to use if needed, many others may feel stuck in marriages they don't feel they can leave.

Some millennials seemed aware but frustrated with this new casual perspective about divorce from others in their cohort. Victoria, a religious millennial whom I mentioned a few chapters ago, said,

> It's individual-centered. If it's not working out, then just kick it to the curb; try it out for a little bit, if it works out, great, if it doesn't, no big deal or whatever. I think a casual approach to that brings a level of uneasiness, not just from a religious standpoint but from a security standpoint. How would I know if my spouse is ever really gonna stay with me, because obviously hard times are gonna come.

As I noted, many of the couples we interviewed had strong marriages. But even if their own marriage was not suffering, many had seen the marriages of their peers already fall apart and were aware of the consequences of a slightly more laid-back approach to divorce that many millennials observed in their peers. Charles and Ruby, married for 3 years, had seen many marriages around them collapse. Ruby shared,

> I think in watching that [her friend's divorce], it just makes me realize how seriously you should take being married because when you get married to someone that you are not compatible with, and you cannot make it work, for

whatever reason it is, it just kinda made me realize that, like, marriage really is a big deal. And although it's easy—well, I wouldn't say easy, but it's not difficult for us on a daily basis—doesn't necessarily mean that it's not difficult in general. I guess it's just made me think, in watching other people get divorced, and knowing the reasons that they're getting divorced, that I did a good job and picked a good, compatible person for me. Watching marriages fall apart because people couldn't accept faults or had unknown faults or whatever, [it's tough].

Ruby took this opportunity to pat herself on the back for a job well done in the marriage market, but her identification of a millennial pattern of divorce tied to "incompatibility" echoed what many of her peers also mentioned.

Her husband, Charles, agreed with most of what his wife said. He added one more nuance, perhaps unveiling another wrinkle to how millennials approach divorce as yet another individual choice. He wanted to make it clear that, just because many of their friends had ended their marriages, that did not mean they felt general negativity toward marriage. Remember, me-marriage is an individual choice and something that may fit some, but not others. Charles wanted it clear that his divorced friends still thought it was great that he was happy and stable in his own marriage, noting,

Our friends have always been supportive of our relationship and our marriage. So while our friends have done things differently, and they usually have their own lives, they end up getting divorced or not being in long-term relationships, everybody in our social group or social circle has never once tried to discourage us from marriage or anything like that. They've always encouraged us to stay together or get married or wished us well and things like that.

When millennials talked about divorce around them, they often tied it back to the me-marriage ideals I have mentioned in previous chapters. Many millennials appeared to believe that most divorces occurred when their peers were not being true to the millennial ideal of marriage being a relationship that helped support and lift up individual pursuits and happiness. If someone was not "genuine" or honest about their personal needs, divorce was almost seen as inevitable. Kayden, one of the millennials who emphasized open communication in his marriage, provided a good illustration of this idea. He shared this in terms of his thoughts regarding why marriages around him failed:

I think a big thing is you just have to be yourself. I see some people that are actually already getting divorced that are our age. They got married years ago and it's not working out, and I feel they are trying to be someone they're not or fit in or maybe they're trying to fit in somewhere where they're not fully themselves. That is one thing for me in my marriage, we are totally 100 percent ourselves and totally honest about that and I think that's the big important thing I have about marriage.

72 Me-Marriage and Marital Quality

Clearly, the prospect of divorce is still on the minds of married millennials. But their attitudes toward divorce may becoming increasingly casual and permissive, something that is creating another unique wrinkle to the marriages of millennials.

The Ease of Alternative Seeking

One final tangent is worth a brief mention. While much of this chapter may paint a rosy picture of me-marriages and the ways in which they are still creating healthy and stable unions, interviews also suggested that there were some indications of potential pitfalls and problems that may be uniquely millennial when it comes to maintaining marital well-being. One such stumbling block that was identified by several individuals and couples was related to the concept of alternative seeking (Leik & Leik, 1977). Alternative seeking refers to thinking about potential partners other than your current partner or engaging in behaviors that directly put you in contact with other available partners. Research suggests that the availability of attractive alternative partners may undermine healthy relationship processes and make healthy relationships harder to maintain (Sabatelli & Cecil-Pigo, 1985).

There was a belief among some millennials that alternative seeking had increased and become easier in their generation. Some scholars would agree, arguing that online access to a wide range of potential alternatives may increase the likelihood of such seeking behavior (see Abbasi, 2019). My own data may support this, although I did not have historical data to compare it to. Regardless, I found among the married millennials in my dataset that 20% believed they would have found a better partner if they kept looking and thought that their life would be better if they married someone else. Some millennials we spoke to highlighted how technology has allowed increased alternative seeking behavior. For example, Austin, married to Naomi from earlier, felt that many his age feared marriage because they felt the temptations would be too high. Austin felt that this temptation, as he put it, could be accessed anywhere. He shared, "I feel like a lot of people are scared of marriage. It's the temptation toward their old life or what they used to do while they were single, ya know? It seems like it would be hard to adjust to it."

Ben, from the last chapter, provides another example of this line of thinking. Ben had recently returned to school when we interviewed him, and he explained that comparing your spouse to others was something he felt a lot of his peers struggled with. He noted that he felt this was the case because he lived "in an era where it's so easy to compare." He felt this put extra pressure on his relationship, explaining, "if we don't invest into our marriage and make it something that we love and are excited to work together on, then it'll just naturally fall apart." Notice that Ben touches on some of the me-marriage ideals here. Marriage should be exciting and something you "love" (notice he didn't say that they needed to be in love; only that you needed to love the relationship). If not, if marriage somehow lost its luster, Ben worried that there were simply too many other alternatives available in a culture that encourages comparison.

This phenomenon went both ways. Not only did millennials believe that they lived in a culture where seeking out comparison points was easier, but this same

Me-Marriage and Marital Quality   73

culture also meant that they needed to take extra precautions against others putting them in uncomfortable situations. While a wedding ring may have stopped many potential romantic partners in the past, millennials seemed especially wary that many of their peers may not see such an outward expression of commitment as an obstacle. Many felt they needed to take proactive steps to avoid situations where they might be pursued. Millennials seemed aware that, in a world of increasing technology, they had a larger social presence that might attract unwanted (or perhaps in some cases wanted) attention from others. Brooklyn and Ryan met through friends and had been married for just a few years. They mentioned this concern in their interview, saying that one of the biggest things that had changed since being married was how they presented themselves online. Ryan mentioned that he changed a lot when he got married: "I mean even in the way that I dress [changed]. The way that I post on social media. I really try to think about literally every decision that I make during the day even if it is very small." While Ryan remained a little vague on why he felt the need to change his appearance or social media posting, his wife, Brooklyn, was more to the point. She added that her changing online behavior was based on this: "I guess I would just say that I try to honor my husband with every choice. That's the best way I could put it." There was a sense that Ryan and Brooklyn understood that their online presence was a potential tension point if their online interaction suggested anything but complete fidelity to their spouse.

There are likely other uniquely millennial barriers to healthy marriage, but this potential to access more available partners seemed an important one to mention, given both that it was frequently mentioned by millennials themselves and because of its potential implications for future scholarship. While some scholars have begun to explore internet-related and other forms of technological infidelity (see Henline et al., 2007; Martins et al., 2016), this area may be an important avenue for exploring the health of me-marriages in the future.

References

Abbasi, I. S. (2019). Falling prey to online romantic alternatives: Evaluating social media alternative partners in committed versus dating relationships. *Social Science Computer Review, 37*(6), 723–733.

Birnie-Porter, C., & Hunt, M. (2015). Does relationship status matter for sexual satisfaction? The roles of intimacy and attachment avoidance in sexual satisfaction across five types of ongoing sexual relationships. *Canadian Journal of Human Sexuality, 24*, 174–183.

Botha, F., & Booysen, F. (2013). The gold of one's ring is not far more precious than the gold of one's heart: Reported life satisfaction among married and cohabiting South African adults. *Journal of Happiness Studies, 14*, 433–456.

Brown, S. L., & Booth, A. (1996). Cohabitation versus marriage: A comparison of relationship quality. *Journal of Marriage and the Family, 58*, 668–678.

Brown, S. L., Manning, W. D., & Payne, K. K. (2017). Relationship quality among cohabiting versus married couples. *Journal of Family Issues, 38*, 1730–1753.

Collisson, B., Cordoviz, P., Ponce de Leon, L., Guillen, S., Shier, J., & Xiao, Z. (2018). "Should I break up or make up?" A text analysis of online relationship advice. *North American Journal of Psychology, 20*, 301–310.

74 Me-Marriage and Marital Quality

Galinsky, A. M., & Sonenstein, F. L. (2013). Relationship commitment, perceived equity, and sexual enjoyment among young adults in the United States. *Archives of Sexual Behavior, 42*, 93–104.

Gatzeva, M., & Paik, A. (2011). Emotional and physical satisfaction in noncohabiting, cohabiting, and marital relationships: The importance of jealous conflict. *Journal of Sex Research, 48*(1), 29–42.

Goldstein, S. E. (2011). Relational aggression in young adults' friendships and romantic relationships. *Personal Relationships, 18*, 645–656.

Gupta, A. E., Zimmerman, T. S., & Fruhauf, C. A. (2008). Relationship advice in the top selling women's magazine, Cosmopolitan: A content analysis. *Journal of Couple & Relationship Therapy, 7*, 248–266.

Heldman, C., & Wade, L. (2010). Hook-up culture: Setting a new research agenda. *Sexuality Research and Social Policy, 7*, 323–333.

Henline, B. H., Lamke, L. K., & Howard, M. D. (2007). Exploring perceptions of online infidelity. *Personal Relationships, 14*, 113–128.

Laumann, E. O., Gangnon, J. H., Michael, R. T., & Michaels, S. (1994). *The social organization of sexuality: Sexual practices in the United States.* University of Chicago Press.

Lee, K. S., & Ono, H. (2012). Marriage, cohabitation, and happiness: A cross-national analysis of 27 countries. *Journal of Marriage and Family, 74*, 953–972.

Leik, R. K., & Leik, S. A. (1977). Transition to inter-personal commitment. In R. L. Hamblin & J. H. Kunkel (Eds.), *Behavioral theory in sociology* (pp. 299–322). Transaction Books.

Martins, A., Pereira, M., Andrade, R., Dattilio, F. M., Narciso, I., & Canavarro, M. C. (2016). Infidelity in dating relationships: Gender-specific correlates of face-to-face and online extradyadic involvement. *Archives of Sexual Behavior, 45*, 193–205.

Moore, K. A., McCabe, M. P., & Brink, R. B. (2001). Are married couples happier in their relationships than cohabiting couples? Intimacy and relationship factors. *Sexual and Relationship Therapy, 16*, 35–46.

Musick, K., & Bumpass, L. (2012). Reexamining the case for marriage: Union formation and changes in well-being. *Journal of Marriage and Family, 74*, 1–18.

Nock, S. L. (1995). A comparison of marriages and cohabiting relationships. *Journal of Family Issues, 16*, 53–76.

Owen, J. J., Rhoades, G. K., Stanley, S. M., & Fincham, F. D. (2010). "Hooking up" among college students: Demographic and psychosocial correlates. *Archives of Sexual Behavior, 39*, 653–663.

Prather, E., Dahlen, E. R., Nicholson, B. C., & Bullock-Yowell, E. (2012). Relational aggression in college students' dating relationships. *Journal of Aggression, Maltreatment & Trauma, 21*, 705–720.

Punyanunt-Carter, N. M. (2004). Reported affectionate communication and satisfaction in marital and dating relationships. *Psychological Reports, 95*, 1154–1160.

Sabatelli, R. M., & Cecil-Pigo, E. F. (1985). Relational interdependence and commitment in marriage. *Journal of Marriage and the Family, 47*, 931–937.

Shafer, K., Jensen, T. M., & Larson, J. H. (2014). Relationship effort, satisfaction, and stability: Differences across union type. *Journal of Marital and Family Therapy, 40*, 212–232.

Sieben, I., & Verbakel, E. (2013). Permissiveness toward divorce: The influence of divorce experiences in three social contexts. *European Sociological Review, 29*, 1175–1188.

Spalding, R., Zimmerman, T. S., Fruhauf, C. A., Banning, J. H., & Pepin, J. (2010). Relationship advice in top-selling men's magazines: A qualitative document analysis. *Journal of Feminist Family Therapy, 22*, 203–224.

Stokes, C. E., & Ellison, C. G. (2010). Religion and attitudes toward divorce laws among US adults. *Journal of Family Issues, 31*, 1279–1304.

Tai, T. O., Baxter, J., & Hewitt, B. (2014). Do co-residence and intentions make a difference? Relationship satisfaction in married, cohabiting, and living apart together couples in four countries. *Demographic Research, 31*, 71–104.

Treas, J., & Giesen, D. (2000). Sexual infidelity among married and cohabiting Americans. *Journal of Marriage and Family, 62*, 48–60.

Waite, L. J. (1995). Does marriage matter? *Demography, 32*, 483–507.

Waite, L. J., & Gallagher, M. (2000). *The case for marriage: Why married people are happier, healthier, and better off financially.* Doubleday.

Willetts, M. C. (2006). Union quality comparisons between long-term heterosexual cohabitation and legal marriage. *Journal of Family Issues, 27*, 110–127.

Willoughby, B. J., Carroll, J. S., & Busby, D. M. (2012). The different effects of "living together": Determining and comparing types of cohabiting couples. *Journal of Social and Personal Relationships, 29*, 397–419.

Wolfinger, N. H. (2015, Jul 16). *Want to avoid divorce? Wait to get married, but not too long.* Institute for Family Studies. https://ifstudies.org/blog/want-to-avoid-divorce-wait-to-get-married-but-not-too-long/

5 Balancing Education and Career Trajectories

Jaxson and Peyton, a couple I introduced in the last chapter, were one of the more educated couples my team spoke to. They had three master's degrees between them—Peyton had two and Jaxson had one—and Jaxson was working on a doctorate degree while teaching high school on the side. Peyton was working in the medical field, and they had two young boys, with a third child on the way. They were, as Peyton put it, "a busy young family." They were both college athletes who started dating after spending a spring break trip together. They dated throughout college and then, after college, moved in together. A few years later, they married.

Their story and relationship trajectory mirrors that of many millennials. They are also a prime example of the ever-evolving balancing act demanded of married millennials: finding individual career success while also prioritizing marriage and family. For both Peyton and Jaxson, marriage was a sequential step that was tied into their personal education and career trajectories. Jaxson explained that he felt that cultural expectations ordered marriage, education, and career in a "linear fashion":

> You go through and graduate high school, and then you go to college and find a job, and sometime after that comes your socially normal time to get married. I think most people fall into that, but it doesn't mean everyone has to. We actually probably did fall into that.

I will note that what Jaxson is describing as a very linear sequence of life transitions is nestled very much in his white, upper-middle-class upbringing. Regardless, the concept that marriage comes *after* one has settled into a profession is something I referenced earlier when I outlined the unique attributes of me-marriages. For both Jaxson and Peyton, having a good career foundation was central before they were willing to get married, despite their dating relationship being strong and committed. As Peyton added,

> We had gone through college together, and then we were living at home for a little while after that as we got our careers in place and things like that. We kind of knew for a while that we wanted to get married, and it was kind of about timing.

Balancing Education and Career 77

That timing was important: Embedded in their conversation was the assumption that marriage may interrupt their careers or make establishing them problematic.

Of course, getting married did not mean they no longer had to strike a balance between their busy work lives and their marriage. They were both dedicated to their individual career trajectories and wanted to make them both work. As Peyton went on to say,

> We both work full time, and we both supported each other through going back to school, so we've had the same values about work and getting a higher education. We haven't had that thought that one of us should stay home with the kids. We just kind of worked together to find a good balance for our family.

This balance between their two careers was a challenge, but one that they both felt held value. The decisions were never tied to income or resources; they would have done just fine with only one income. Instead it was connected to their own individual desires and personal career goals. Yes, it made things tricky, but they were willing to make some individual sacrifices to make each other's career success possible. As Jaxson noted later in the interview,

> It's kind of just survival. With two little kids, a dog, two jobs, coaching, school, our Google calendar really helps out. As long as we're able to organize ourselves and plan ahead, it just gets done. That's kind of that teamwork aspect of it.

It is this teamwork mentality, perhaps tied to their athletic days, that has made things work so far. That doesn't mean that they haven't both made sacrifices to maintain some semblance of sanity around the home. Sometimes these sacrifices even extended to other family members. As Peyton explained,

> I think every day we make sacrifices in our relationship. I mean, speaking of last spring, I was finishing grad school and working, so our families helped a lot with watching the kids so that I could complete my master's degree. So those kind of sacrifices. I mean, obviously I wanted to be home with our kids, but also I wanted to graduate with my master's degree.

Despite being able to find a general balance between her education and her family, there was a tinge of worry in Peyton's voice as she spoke about maintaining this balance in the future as her kids got older. She said,

> I really hope we can [maintain this balance] 'cause we're kind of banking on that. If not, we're setting ourselves up for failure. I mean, so far I'd like to say our boys are pretty awesome little guys and are both doing well, and our jobs [are great], and we're really happy in our families. So I'd like to say it's possible.

She'd like to say that, but she can't guarantee it. This is the concern of many millennial married couples. In the growing number of dual-income households,

78   *Balancing Education and Career*

where incomes in middle-class and higher families are often based less on the desire for personal wealth and more on personal fulfillment, work–family balance is at the heart of many me-marriages. Changes in both millennials' mentality toward employment and the structure thereof has created some unique challenges and opportunities. While the last chapter established that me-marriages appear relatively healthy, how are they managing the unique educational and employment landscape that was altered for most of them during the global recession of 2009? In this chapter I explore these unique intersections, first studying whether marriage still offers any financial or educational benefits to millennials before discussing some of the challenges and patterns found within me-marriages regarding educational and career decisions. There is a lot to unpack here, as I believe that this balance between marriage and individual ambitions among millennials may be one of the biggest areas of cultural shift from the previous generation.

The Historical Evidence

So how has being married traditionally been tied to educational and career outcomes and trajectories? Like in the previous chapter, my goal here is to give you a sense of the literature rather than an exhaustive review. Just as there is a connection between marriage and relational outcomes, there are clear and consistent links between educational decisions, career decisions, and marriage. For example, pursuing higher education tends to increase the likelihood of marriage, although this association varies by culture (Kalmijn, 2013; McClendon et al., 2014). Other economic factors also appear to influence the decision to marry: the accumulation of debt decreases the likelihood of marriage (Addo, 2014; Gicheva, 2016), while the accumulation of wealth increases it (see Zissimopoulos et al., 2015). Other scholars have argued that marriage impacts wealth not only on the individual level, but also on the societal level. Lerman and colleagues (2018) provided evidence that marriage in the United States is linked to not only positive economic benefits at the individual level, but also economic growth at the state level. About ten years ago, the Pew Research Center published a report on education, income, and marriage (Fry, 2010) and noted several important trends at the time. First, they observed that marriage was now more likely among the most educated segments of society, a reversal of previous decades when marriage was most common among the least educated. They also replicated a long-standing finding that married men tend to make more than unmarried men, finding the median income of married men was $77,000 per year compared to only $54,000 for unmarried men. Historically, marriage is often associated with similar economic benefits for families.

That marriage is associated with better economic and educational outcomes for men is one of the most robust historical findings in this area of scholarship. Even recently, married men have been found to report significantly higher wages than unmarried men (de Linde Leonard & Stanley, 2015; Ludwig & Brüderl, 2018), although there is some debate about whether or not these associations are real (Killewald & Lundberg, 2017). Many potential explanations for this so-called "marriage wage premium" have been proposed. These have ranged from theories

Balancing Education and Career   79

suggesting that married men may act differently in the workplace than unmarried men (Gorman, 1999; Killewald & Gough, 2013) to evidence that employers may view married men in a more favorable light (Jordan & Zitek, 2012), creating institutional biases that benefit married working men. Regardless of the specific mechanisms and whether they are causal, selective, or stereotyped, marriage is clearly linked to better economic well-being in the workplace for men.

This research does have a gendered flavor to it. While married men reap the benefits of their unions, research on married women is mixed. For example, while married men are often viewed in a favorable light, married women who work are sometimes viewed less favorably than their unmarried peers (Jordan & Zitek, 2012). Hymowitz and colleagues (2013) noted that marrying early may have a negative impact on women's income-earning potential, finding that women who delayed marriage tended to earn more than women who married early. They also found that never-married women tended to earn a higher average income than married women, a finding that is likely partially offset by the larger share of married women who are staying at home and raising children, hence bringing in little to no personal income.

Despite the robustness of these findings over time, some scholars have argued that the potential economic benefits of marriage have been slipping away. For example, one team of legal scholars recently noted that the growing income inequality in the United States has created very different marriage markets and incentives to marry, potentially undermining some of these historical effects for millennials (Akers & Kohm, 2018). While marriage may still provide economic benefits to the less educated, finding suitable marriage partners is often challenging. On the higher end of the socioeconomic spectrum, these same scholars noted that marriage has little economic benefit for the educated when compared to generations past. Tapping into the essence of me-marriage, these scholars concluded, "Millennial prerogative on the high end of the income inequality gap has decreased the incentives of marriage for any other function than personal happiness" (Akers & Kohm, 2018, p. 390). Despite fairly consistent research suggesting that marriage remains the best economic choice for most individuals, such arguments have raised the question of if millennials are still enjoying the economic success of marriages in the past.

The Millennial Data

Since one of the most consistent findings in previous research has been the economic benefit afforded to the married, I was curious to see if, in an age of shifting and diversifying educational and career opportunities, such benefits are still apparent. As I explored the data on a variety of economic outcomes, I found that millennials do indeed continue to receive this marital benefit. Let's start with the gold standard of economic outcomes, at least inasmuch as it is a good proxy of financial resources: personal income. It is important to note that I use personal income level in my analyses rather than household income, which would be unfairly skewed toward dual-income, married couples. In the dataset of 30-something millennials, when comparing personal income levels and adjusting

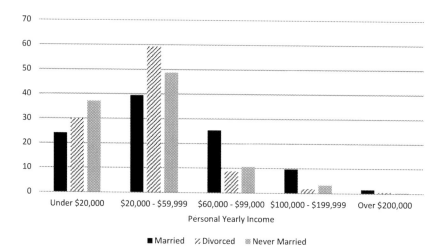

Figure 5.1 Percentage of Millennials in Personal Income Categories for Those Married, Divorced, and Never Married.

for race, sexual orientation, parents' education, and whether they lived with their parents all 18 years of their childhood, married millennials were significantly ($p < .001$) more likely to report a higher personal income than those who had never married. Consider Figure 5.1 for an idea of the scale of these differences—married millennials are often two or three times more likely to be earning higher incomes than their never-married peers. I added millennials who had been divorced to this table to show that simply the act of marrying is not a magic pathway to personal financial success. Rather, *staying* married appears to be what is linked to higher personal income. I have already noted that this link between marriage and incomes has been found in the past (see de Linde Leonard & Stanley, 2015), and research on divorce also shows that divorce often takes a financial toll on all individuals involved (Amato, 2010; De Vaus et al., 2017).

Let us turn our attention to economic outcomes beyond personal income. In the same national study of 30-to-35-year-old millennials, I explored a number of other outcomes tied to economic well-being and resources (see Figure 5.2). What I found was not only consistent with research on past generations but also painted a clear picture regarding the connections between marriage and economic outcomes for millennials. I found that married millennials were significantly more likely than unmarried millennials to have medical insurance, dental insurance, vision insurance, life insurance, and homeowners insurance. They were also more likely to have money invested in a 401K, a Roth IRA, and a health savings plan. Other than being an insurance agent's dream, married millennials appear to have significantly more benefits and financial resources than their single counterparts.

Married millennials also report significantly better credit (at least by their own report) than their single counterparts. Figure 5.3 shows the difference in credit rating by marital status in the national dataset I helped collect on millennials. Note

Balancing Education and Career 81

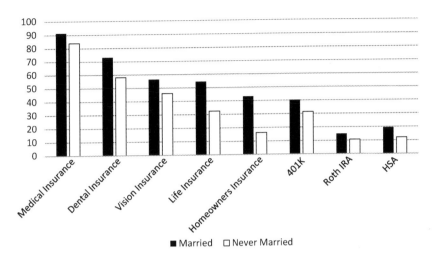

Figure 5.2 Percentage of Married vs. Never Married Millennials With Access to Various Economic Benefits.

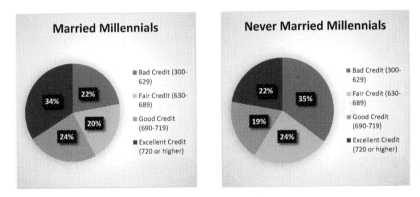

Figure 5.3 Self-Reported Credit Score for Married and Never-Married Millennials in Their Early 30s.

that while a third (33.9%) of married millennials report excellent credit, less than a fourth (22.1%) of their unmarried peers report the same.

These data do not mean that the economic picture is completely rosy for married millennials. Some economic indicators require a bit more nuance to understand. Debt is a good example here. In our national sample of early-30s millennials, the average debt for those who were married was just over $131,000. That's compared to an average debt level of just under $37,000 for their single counterparts. While married millennials seem to have access to more income and more economic resources, they are also carrying significantly more debt. It is important to note that this difference, while it may seem larger, was not statistically

82 *Balancing Education and Career*

significant due to large variations among both groups within the data. In that way, it is unclear if this difference is meaningful or simply an artifact of this dataset. But taken at face value, despite their economic success, many married millennials may be carrying a large amount of debt and this may be an important area of well-being to continue to explore with more conclusive data.

Two caveats are important here regarding debt. First, married millennials are much more likely to own a home, something that likely accounts for most, if not all, of this raw difference. Home ownership is an interesting debt in that it is one of the only forms of debt that has been linked to positive individual and family outcomes (Hu, 2013; Zumbro, 2014). The other important note is that married participants are likely accounting for the debt of their entire household in our survey, including their partner's personal debt. That's the potential for twice as much student debt, additional auto loans, and more. This debt burden is partially offset by the increase in household income.

With the debt aspect of the equation noted, it is still interesting that, despite so many changes to the nature and culture of marriage, marriage is still almost universally connected to positive economic well-being and increased economic resources. Of course, much of this difference may be due to selection, with more educated and financially well-off individuals more likely to marry. Scholars have noted the general retreat from marriage among the less educated (Harknett & Kuperberg, 2011; Lee & Payne, 2010), with less-educated women often citing the lack of available and marriageable men as a primary barrier to marriage (Edin & Kefalas, 2011). Other research has suggested that the financial burden of weddings and the potential loss of welfare access (Edin & Reed, 2005) are other reasons why economic situations may have a selection effect on marriage, rather than a causal relationship. But it would be narrow-minded to write off these consistent associations as simply the byproduct of cultural selection and the growing income divide in most modern economies. There are likely some causal factors at play. For example, part of this benefit may come from the increased focus and determination to succeed that marital relationships give to some millennials. As one quick illustration, Natalie, married for about five years, was clear in her interview that she owed much of her career success to her husband. She had just completed school with a degree in social work, and Natalie felt that having a long-term and committed partner kept her focused during her education. She shared,

> I think that being in a relationship with Lucas has impacted . . . every single thing about my day. . . . We're really different in a lot of ways, and I think that I have been able to find a lot of balance in my life because of his influence on me. I do think that the stability of our relationship allows me to focus on things like school and my career in a more focused way. If I was single, I'd probably be doing other things. That would be distracting from my school and career.

In my data, education was clearly connected to the likelihood of marriage among millennials. Figure 5.4 shows the raw percentages in our study of older

Balancing Education and Career 83

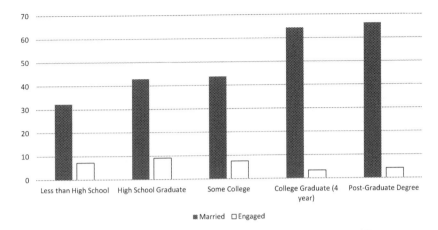

Figure 5.4 Percentage of Millennials With Educational Status Based on Being Married or Engaged.

millennials in their early 30s in terms of proportion married and engaged millennials who had obtained various educational levels. You can clearly see that higher education was associated with an increased likelihood of marriage, with large percentage jumps in our sample between the group not graduating high school and those having at least a high school education or some college, and then an even larger jump from those with some college/high school graduation to those graduating with a college degree.

Like other scholars have noted, however, educational attainment has an interesting relationship with marriage. While having more education may now make millennials more likely to marry, it also may make them delay the transition to marriage. Figure 5.5 shows, in that same sample, the average age of marriage based on educational attainment. Here, an interesting U-shaped curve appears: The average age of marriage generally declines among millennials who have less than a high school degree up to those with "some college" education, but the average age then increased from that point through having a post-graduate degree. Bear in mind, this dataset did not have a large sample of those with less than a high school degree (fewer than 50 out of several thousand in the dataset), so those numbers would need further replication. Still, it appears that, while millennials with the most education may become the most likely to eventually marry, they may also delay that transition longer than their peers.

The example of Natalie, combined with the quantitative findings I have presented, suggests that the marriages of millennials continue to follow many of the trends of the past, with some unique caveats. But as we move our analysis beyond the simple associations between marriage and economic trajectories and well-being, additional questions arise, including: How are millennials tackling the unique challenges of a workplace environment and job market that have changed dramatically in the last 20 years? While the economic benefits of marriage may

84 *Balancing Education and Career*

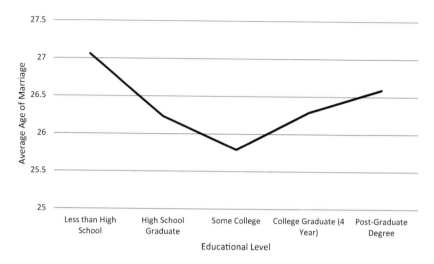

Figure 5.5 Age of Marriage by Educational Attainment for Married Millennials in Their Early 30s.

remain for these millennials, their interviews shed light on unique challenges and opportunities that marriage affords them.

Can You Really Have It All?

One of the themes that I mentioned in earlier chapters as I outlined the unique elements of millennial marriages was their desire to succeed in all aspects of life. Rather than prioritizing one role over another, millennials seem to increasingly want to "have it all."Yet I noted in Chapter 3 that some millennials were struggling with this balance and had fears about their ability to adequately juggle each area of their life successfully. Decisions centered on careers and educational trajectories form perhaps the most salient priority conflicts in millennials' lives. Dedicating personal resources and time to career or educational pursuits may often directly compete with fostering and developing healthy marital relationships. This raised several questions for me: Are millennials feeling pressure to choose education and career over marriage, or vice versa? Despite their stated desire in me-marriages to have it all, does reality force them to select one path over the other? Does marriage dramatically alter the educational and career decisions of millennials as they make these hard decisions?

On the surface, these links seem inevitable. With their close ties to lifestyle and economic resources, career decisions will always be interconnected with family trajectories. Research across several decades has verified this. Marriage has been increasingly linked to those with higher educations in most segments of the population, something that some scholars have argued is enhancing the "marriage gap" in overall wealth (Siassi, 2019). Data suggest this connection between marriage and education continues into the millennial generation. In our national study of

Balancing Education and Career   85

30-something millennials, married millennials were significantly more likely to report higher education than those who never married. This result was after controlling for race, family origin factors, sexual orientation, and parents' educational level. As just one specific illustration of this general fact, in this same sample, 35.7% of married millennials reported holding at least a 4-year college degree, while only 29.8% of their never-married counterparts held a similar level of degree. While there is likely a fair amount of selection going on in these numbers (i.e., those with more education are much more likely to get married), they do clearly demonstrate the interconnection between marriage and career trajectories that is still salient for millennials.

Of course, the question of education is always gendered. Once men and women are separated, a slightly different picture emerges. Historically, the educational bump appeared to mostly be available to men. In their national study of young adults in the United States, Hymowitz and colleagues (2013) found that women who delayed marriage were more likely to continue to pursue their education. However, in our more recent data focused on millennials, we found that married men *and* women were significantly more likely to have a higher education than those who had never married. Almost 53% of married men reported a 4-year degree or higher, compared to just 27% of those men who were never married. While less dramatic, the same effect was seen for women, where 40.8% of married women reported achieving a 4-year degree or higher, compared to 32% of never-married women.

So perhaps we are seeing a general trend where either (a) married millennials are more motivated to complete higher education or (b) educated individuals of both genders are more likely to marry than in the past. Other scholars have noted that the latter explanation appears to be the case: Marriage is becoming more and more the preferred relationship goal of the college-educated crowd (Kuo & Raley, 2016). But these trends only give us a broad look at the general relationship between education, career, and marriage. What are the actual dynamics and lived experiences of millennials as they attempt to juggle these aspects of their lives, in which both partners often wish to have independent careers? Here, we can find several important insights into how millennials are navigating these decisions.

Reformatting Career Priorities

One of the first things that stood out to me in my interviews with millennial couples was the disconnect between their broad ideals and their actual educational and career decisions. As I have previously asserted, millennials broadly desire an idealized world where education, career, and family life all intertwine in a way that allows them to be successful and happy in every area. Yet the reality was often quite different. Millennial couples, often forced to navigate careers that pull both partners in separate directions, have to make hard decisions about their personal ambitions. Though options for education and careers have increased in this era, millennials sense that certain career choices will make family life, including marriage, much more challenging. Dylan, a young millennial who had completed a Ph.D. and had a well-paying job, thought that the modern workplace is almost

86 *Balancing Education and Career*

hostile to marriage. He described a workplace environment that emphasizes dedication to one's employer so much that having a balanced homelife would be essentially impossible. He explained,

> You can try and prioritize family and marriage, but you can't do it. They expect too much of you as a person. Most people [at his workplace] aren't married and certainly don't have kids so the expectation of you is that you will give 100 percent.

Dylan didn't identify what specific careers he felt fell into this category, but it was clear he felt some tension between his employment environment and his desire to put at least some emphasis on his marriage.

Many couples my team interviewed had faced clear decision points in their lives where they needed to choose between what would be best for their own careers or what would be best for their partner or marriage. Some millennials expressed fear about trying to make this choice. Madison, about to start a new career as a therapist, expressed some of this anxiety when she related,

> I think fear definitely jumps in there at times. I just started a new career and [my husband is] about to start a new career. So, I think there are days that are just focused on getting these new careers launched; whatever's left is what we have.

That "whatever's left" that she references was in relation to time, a resource she worried would quickly dwindle in her marriage.

Syed had been married for 4 years after meeting his wife online. He was working as a truck driver when he was interviewed and was adamant in his interview that marriage should be put off until the late 20s or early 30s because of the possible career disruption a spouse might create. To him, this strong belief in delayed marriage had everything to do with the fear of losing out on career opportunities. He explained that he did not think it was reasonable for anyone to marry in their early 20s: "I don't think you know exactly what you want at that time and age." He connected this disruption specifically to education, noting that one spouse might be far along in college and already working on their career, while the other has just started. This lack of sync, in Syed's mind, could create even more problems as time went on, as each partner tried to figure out "who do you want to work for, where do you want to work, where you're going to live." He concluded that this complication simply made marriage too complex for those still in school or starting out their career, saying, "I don't think you're ready to bring somebody else into your life, because marriage is work." Another millennial I've mentioned before, Isabelle, agreed and reflected in her interview that when considering marriage, you should be asking questions like, "Is the timing right when you met the right person? Are you both in a good place to tie your life together? Or is your career dragging you all over the place?"

So how do millennials who have gotten married navigate the problems that Syed and Isabelle mentioned? For many, sacrificing career ambitions on the altar

Balancing Education and Career 87

of marriage appears to be a common strategy. Jenny, a stay-at-home mother, felt like she sacrificed at least the potential for certain careers when she opted to be married and have kids. She admitted that when she had considered employment opportunities after marriage, she often was forced to consider the larger context of her family situation. She eventually settled on what she considered a slightly less-engaging position, one that was only part-time. She justified this decision because it made the most sense with her current family context, reframing the infrequent hours as a positive. Here's how she explained why she took the position:

> I was thinking that the hours will be great because I'll be [at work] when the kids are in school. I never really looked at it like marriage would be an issue with that. I mean, maybe if I saw myself being a lawyer or something where I would be away for hours and hours and hours, and stuff.

Jenny freely admitted that having a career that would demand more time and resources was likely not in the cards for her, or at least would cause major disruptions to her family life.

Justin and Monique, a religious couple, are another example of couples faced with difficult decisions in this area. In their case, Monique also opted to sacrifice her career trajectory in the pursuit of a strong marriage. Justin noted during his interview, "Monique decided not to work after we got married, and that was a big sacrifice on her part because she put in a lot of work and time to have her degree." Justin noted that he too had made career sacrifices in their marriage. He continued, "When we got married, I was in a pre-med program and had plans to become a doctor. . . . As I re-prioritized my life, I realized that was not where I wanted to spend my time." To Justin, the time away from home that he would experience as a doctor felt at odds with his new focus on his wife and family after becoming married. He was clear that he still had the desire to become a doctor; he simply thought that this personal goal would interfere with something he now felt was more important. He explained that,

> while [becoming a doctor] was a worthy goal and a good goal—there's nothing wrong with it—we opted for a shorter education track. Monique very early on was prepared to make the sacrifices that were necessary for me to go to med school and everything to finish that program. But I recognized that my happiness was going to be at home and not at work. And so, we reformatted.

I like the concept of *reformatting* that Justin uses here. This resonates with a lot of what I heard from millennials as they spoke of navigating their careers in the context of marriage. While they may have entered marriage believing that it would interfere in only minor ways with their personal ambitions, many realized shortly after marriage that a lifelong commitment to another person involves an intertwining of lives and forces a reevaluation of personal goals. Allison, whom I have referenced several times, was working in a well-paying government job when she was interviewed. She put the concept of a need for reformatting in broader terms,

88 *Balancing Education and Career*

illustrating how she felt that having conflicting career goals was a major disadvantage to marriage. She felt this conflict may be one of the main reasons millennials avoid marriage, saying,

> Educational and professional opportunities are so much more global. Nationally, people move a lot, especially people who are really motivated by their careers. I think that's hard to do with a partner because usually one person's professional goals are going to have to take a backseat to the other one's at some point. Because it's rare. I mean it happens. Where both of you have the same level of professional opportunity in the place that you want to go. So, I think that's one reason people don't want to commit to a person and then be like, oh well I got this great job across the country, and I don't want this relationship with this person to stop me from following that dream.

Prioritizing One Career

Of course, the concept of sacrifice looks different in each millennial marriage. Like any decision involving two partners, this decision to sacrifice or compromise one's education or career is not up to one individual. Remember, both partners in most millennial couples have their own individual goals and career plans. When sacrifice is needed, millennial couples need to consider both partners' plans and goals before deciding where sacrifices might be made. The solution to this dilemma might involve a variety of options. While some couples opt to each make small sacrifices, as noted, other couples are willing to fully prioritize one spouse's career over the other's. This decision to focus on one partner's career while the other's takes a backseat appears to be the most common solution to the career dilemma that the millennials in our study faced.

Ashley, a conservative and religious stay-at-home mother, explained that she and her husband had made the deliberate decision to prioritize his career and education after marriage. Despite graduating from college herself, Ashley had opted to fully support her husband, who worked as a production manager, while minimizing her career aspirations. In her mind, this was a simple and pragmatic decision because her husband's career demanded a lot of location flexibility. She explained,

> [My husband] is the main breadwinner. Every time that we move, it's for his job. So, that's fine, I don't mind it. . . . His career is pivotal. I will never make near as much money as he does. . . . So it would just be pointless not to support him.

The demands of her husband's job, plus the higher salary she perceived he would make, made Ashley feel that trying to pursue any kind of independent career was fruitless.

At the end of the day, many of the millennials we interviewed found it difficult, if not impossible, to equally balance two careers. Prioritizing one career over another was something that many felt was more reasonable than equally supporting two careers and would help keep their lives at a manageable level of

Balancing Education and Career 89

sanity. For Denzel and Lanelle, it was Denzel's career in human resources that mattered the most for them. Though Lanelle worked, she worked part-time and mostly from home. They had jointly made this decision based on Denzel's larger income, with a similar rationale to Ashley. They felt that by focusing on the career with the best financial prospects, they would reduce any potential tensions in their marriage down the road because they had already decided to prioritize one career. Lanelle explained,

> This just goes back to balance; I'm more flexible, so if his job was to be, "Hey, we need you to move to California," it wouldn't really be an issue with me because I can do what I do anywhere. You can't really fight with the fact that it's important, because we need finances, because I need him, because he's the breadwinner. Without him I really wouldn't have much to stand on.

Sometimes this prioritization of one partner's career was so vital that it was listed as almost an ultimatum or prerequisite of the relationship early on. In the case of Natalie and her husband, Lucas, Lucas had been clear with her that if they were ever to marry, he was not willing to deviate from his educational and career plan. He had always planned on going to school, working, and living in Vermont. He knew that this would likely limit the career prospects of any future spouse, but he was unwilling to budge. Natalie shared that she knew exactly what would happen if she did indeed decide to marry Lucas. She said,

> I wouldn't even be in Vermont if it weren't for our relationship. I didn't know anything about the state; I had no personal connection. I always said, when I married Lucas I understood I'd be marrying the state of Vermont. He was going to come live here, with or without me.

While Lucas was not restrictive of his wife's career beyond location, his stubbornness about their location clearly weighed on her mind. She shared one clear example of this, when a friend encouraged her to apply to graduate school in social work in Massachusetts. Lucas was supportive and willing to be in a long-distance marriage while she attended school. But, despite the personal appeal, the decision no longer made sense for Natalie. As she explained,

> I didn't want to be that far away from Lucas because [the school] is in Massachusetts. I knew that we would be living here [Vermont], and if I went to grad school here, I would learn about the specific skills you need to work here. That college wasn't going to teach you about being a social worker in rural Vermont. So yeah, I'd say our relationship has influenced every aspect of my education and my career choices.

There were tangible and real sacrifices that Natalie was forced to make to prioritize Lucas's career, sacrifices she was willing to make that had been a clear priority for Lucas from the beginning of their dating relationship.

90 *Balancing Education and Career*

In some cases, this prioritizing of one career was seen not only as a compromise but as a positive decision, a way to enhance personal flexibility in the workplace and, despite its traditional gendered overtones (you have likely noticed it is often the wife who sacrificed her career), a benefit of me-marriage that aligned with personal discovery. For example, Aria from Chapter 2 was a schoolteacher who was feeling burned out. She noted that, because she married, she had the opportunity to rely more on her husband's career to afford her opportunities for personal exploration. Her husband, Carter, first noted that getting married had created an important impact on their educational trajectories. He stated, "I had an opportunity to go teach, but my current job right now has a better earning potential. For us, me making more money right now is important to me, so we can have a kid." He then turned to his wife to emphasize why this was important, adding, "Hopefully you don't have to work and be miserable at school, that's kind of the goal." His wife's misery in both school and work was clear to him, and he would later describe her relationship with education and work as "tumultuous."

You could tell Aria felt bad having this perception of her looming over the marriage. She explained, "Sorry, I don't hate teaching. Don't think that I do. I just feel, like, burned out from everything." In the case of Aria and Carter, the hope was to prioritize one career so that the other could stop or limit a career they found little personal enjoyment in. Based on the context of this conversation, apparently this couple worked under the assumption that Aria would be the primary caregiver for their future children, a role they apparently thought she would enjoy more.

Even though the examples I have given so far have been exclusively based on couples who prioritized the husband's career, this prioritization did not appear to be an explicit issue of traditional gender roles in all cases. Some millennial couples we spoke to prioritized the wife's education or career. For example, Connor and Sarah decided on an arrangement where Connor only worked part-time and mostly raised their daughter. Again, this was based less on gender and more on personal interest. As Connor explained,

> Sarah is much more career-driven than I am. I have found over these 6 months that our daughter has been alive that I really enjoy fatherhood, I really enjoy the moment-to-moment, the day-to-day aspects of it. I think that just kind of fits with our personalities that, where she is at, she's really driven at work and I kind of wasn't. Well, now I have a good reason not to be, and she's [referencing their daughter] sleeping in the other room right now.

I noted similar gender-flipped arrangements among many couples, suggesting that this prioritization mentality, for many millennials, is not simply about replicating traditional gender roles. In fact, in the case of one same-sex couple interviewed, they too saw the benefits of prioritizing only one career, in this case to manage childcare. Whitney and Claire, a same-sex couple who had young children, saw this focus on one career as a needed aspect of keeping balance in their home between employment and childcare. As Whitney put it, this was something they had naturally fallen into early in their relationship. She stated, "I would be the one that would stay home with kids and Claire would be the one that worked, so I do a lot of the childcare and housekeeping." Claire noted, "We had that discussion when we got engaged because of where we were in our life. We kind of needed to decide which career to put more energy into."

Giving up on Your Dream

For some millennials, this prioritization went further than just favoring one career over another. For these millennials, the decision to focus on one partner was not just a matter of reprioritizing, but to give up on their personal career dreams completely. Whether this meant switching career fields or settling for low-paying and part-time work in an area unrelated to their education, some millennials felt that any attempt to have two thriving careers was simply too difficult. Leo and Alexis had been married for over a decade and had two children early in their marriage. Despite having a busy, young family, both Leo and Alexis had been able to mostly maintain their individual career trajectories through a series of compromises and sacrifices. However, when Alexis became pregnant with their third child, she felt she simply no longer had the energy to keep everything going. She shared,

> I quit my job two years ago because I couldn't do it anymore. I couldn't be pulled all the different directions. I mean, Leo was extremely supportive of that. In my personal experience for me, I can't, there's just a limit that I have.

You can sense the millennial angst with Alexis; this desire to have it all and an assumption that other millennials can do it. It's not impossible; it's just that she has "limits."

Her husband, Leo, resonated with this tension too. He added this to his wife's thoughts:

> I think that there are only so many hours in the day, so I don't know that both partners in a marriage can have the same goal [for careers] and have everything be successful. I think if both partners are focused on marriage and kids, they're not focused on their career, so you're not really progressing there. Flip side, if both are focused on their careers and put everything else on the backburner, I think that that then causes the marriage piece to suffer.

Leo then turned to the tried-and-true mentality of millennials in me-marriage of long-term flexibility, sharing this as a possible solution to this dilemma:

> I think you can strike a balance if, for the next few years I'm focused on my career while Alexis focuses on our family, and we work together on our marriage. I think that's a balance that can be constructive.

The implication seemed to be that in a few years this arrangement might be reassessed and that he would be willing to sacrifice his career if Alexis wished to jump back into the job market.

92 *Balancing Education and Career*

Jess and Kevin were another example of this sacrifice of one partner's career. They were both in college when they met, Kevin planning on attending dental school and Jess studying to become a teacher. Eventually, they decided to focus on Kevin's more lucrative dental career. While Jess still planned to become a teacher someday, when asked about how marriage had changed or influenced their career and educational plans, Jess immediately noted that marriage had altered how she had approached the profession. She was teaching, but not in any meaningful way and certainly not in a setting where she felt there were long-term prospects of advancement. Jess noted that her husband's career, being the priority, had driven the decisions she had made. She explained,

> [My marriage has] completely defined where I've gone with my career. I taught high school English for a couple of years, and I potentially would have gotten further schooling rather than going straight into teaching for those couple of years if it hadn't been for marriage. And I definitely at this point would be doing something to further a career if it weren't for marriage.

Some millennials saw and vocally opposed this trend of couples placing emphasis on one partner's career while the other partner gave up their dreams. Ella, from previous chapters, noted this trend among her friends but appeared to connect it more with religiosity than a rational and thought-out decision-making process, stating,

> I also went to a Christian college, which ended up shaping a lot of my views. Unfortunately, a lot of what I saw was not good. Women would get married while they were in school, and then they'd drop out to focus on their husband's job, their husband's education. You never heard "I'm gonna focus on my wife." From the outside I saw a lot of focus on only one person in the marriage, and I decided that is something that I didn't want because marriage is about both people.

Ella, herself, was working full-time and finishing her degree, apparently hoping to avoid this trap that she viewed many of her female peers as falling into.

Do We Both Give Up?

Of course, one final option remains to be discussed. At least a handful of couples my team spoke to had concluded that trying to prioritize either partner's career might simply be too challenging given the complexities of the modern workplace. Whether they decided to give up one partner's career dreams or simply put one on the backburner, the sense of educational and career sacrifice regardless of the choice was a reality for several of the couples we spoke to. As employment opportunities for millennials increasingly involve travel and relocation, having two independent careers often pulls spouses in different directions (figuratively and literally in terms of location) in ways that seem impossible for many. Ava and Liam met while both were working on a local political campaign. As their relationship and

Balancing Education and Career   93

eventual marriage progressed, they explained that their marriage has prevented both of them from taking on career opportunities in locations that didn't make sense in their marriage. Liam noted,

> We have forsaken career stuff [because of marriage]. We live in rural South Dakota because we wanted to have a better place for us rather than someone's career. I'm from Detroit originally, I've had job offers in Seattle, but we've forsaken that because we want to be here. And it's better for our marriage that way.

Ava piped in with this: "And we both haven't taken jobs. I mean there were jobs in D.C., Atlanta, all over Montana that we could have taken. We thought this is the best place for us."

If you're getting a sense from these examples that career trajectories seem to be taking second priority to a lot of married millennials, you are not alone. I had the same thought. While generally hoping to have a happy and fruitful career, many millennials find that married life comes with an intentional decision to deemphasize career objectives in general. In our national study of millennials, we asked all our older millennials to rate how relatively important different roles were in their life. One of the options was their career. When completing this part of the survey, participants distributed a total of 100 points between the four priority areas, meaning that as they put more emphasis on one area, they had to take away from another. Here there were clear differences in priorities among married millennials compared to the never married. Married men placed an average of 20.29 points toward their career role. Never-married men put much more emphasis on their careers, averaging 33.68 points. Women likewise showed a difference, with married women placing, on average, 13.50 points toward career compared to an average 26.94 points for never-married women. While selection bias may again be a contributing factor here, it seems as though married millennials simply care less about their careers than millennials who opted out of married life. And remember, despite this lower priority among married men and women, they still, on average, earn more than the unmarried.

Levi and his wife, Violet, had been together for 11 years when they were interviewed and they provide an example of a more balanced attitude to this sacrificial approach to careers. They had faced many choices in their marriage that forced them to make hard decisions about each of their careers. Both Levi and Violet were teachers, putting an additional economic strain on their young family, which now included one young son. Levi noted that he did feel the need to sacrifice career opportunities for his marriage during the last 11 years. He stated,

> There have been advancement opportunities; there have been different places that I have been offered, but when talking between the two of us and how that would probably affect all three of us together, we've decided that each move would not be good for all of us combined. So, there have been places that we could have gone but would not have done just because of that.

94 *Balancing Education and Career*

Levi's wife, Violet, felt that marriage (or at least the thought of marriage) also influenced her education and work trajectory. In her case, she reported originally being fearful as a young adult of having to make the kind of sacrifices they had both made since getting married. She felt this fear of sacrifice altered the entire trajectory of their early relationship. She explained that she had a lot of big plans when she was in school, saying,

> One of my goals was to finish college. I wanted to get a job, work outside of home, etc. I told myself I'm not going to get married until after I graduated college because the likelihood of a girl finishing college and being married is very low.

This perception was based on experiences she had noted among her family and friends. "If you get married in college, usually the guy stays in college and finishes out, but the girl, a lot of the times, drops out," Violet explained. She did not want this to happen to her. Yet this perspective and quote come with interesting context in terms of her relationship with her husband. They began dating in high school and continued to date throughout college, a period of 7 years. Clearly this long courtship was partially based on Violet's desire to continue her education and because, as they both reported, they "weren't ready." As Violet said later in the interview, this delay was primarily motivated by a fear of lost opportunities. She explained that they often thought about marriage in this way as they dated:

> [We thought], maybe we should wait a few years; it will take some of the financial stress off us. It will take some of the emotional stress off us if we just wait a couple of years, mature a little more, get through college and get steady jobs before we get married.

Regardless of the specific decisions that millennials make in relation to their personal careers, it seems clear that millennial married couples are facing challenges brought about by their unique approach to me-marriage, their personal desire for individual fulfillment, and the realities of the modern employment landscape. Needing to sacrifice something, whether it be from one or both partners, seems to be an assumed byproduct of the decision to merge one's life with another.

Longing for Lost Opportunities

But if so many millennial married couples are sacrificing personal career ambition for their marriages, are they doing so happily? Recall the concept of reformatting that Justin used to discuss the natural shift he felt happened once he was married and had to consider another person in his career decisions. While Justin and his wife Monique's example of reformatting was described with a sense of pride and contentment about their decisions, other millennials, while acknowledging the reality of reformatting, expressed a sense of regret and resentment regarding this need to sacrifice and shift priorities. Some of the millennials we spoke to clearly felt that lost opportunities accompanied their decision to marry. While happy in

Balancing Education and Career 95

her current circumstances as a schoolteacher, Lucy expressed some frustration with the sense of career restriction that marriage had brought into her life. Like many millennial couples, Lucy and her husband had limited some of their career advancement opportunities for the sake of their family situation. But Lucy noted that these decisions did not mean she stopped thinking about these lost opportunities. She shared that she had moments that "make me rethink about the possibilities to take job opportunities at different places because I have to pick what's available right there in this location."

Juan, the young husband who kicked off Chapter 2, made a similar observation. At the time of the interview, he worked as a high school teacher. He reflected that he had lost opportunities for career advancement when he married, explicitly stating that marriage sometimes got in the way of a good job. For example, he explained that his wife and her career were a factor in them settling in their current location. He felt he had missed out on "some opportunities" because of this. For example, he noted,

> If you have a 3-month internship, that separates us for a while, that's harder to do when you're married. . . . If I decided that I'm going to do this but it's 3 months away, it's something that marriage gets in the way of. It's not really available for us at this point.

I think the phrasing here is important. Notice that Juan believes that marriage "gets in the way." There were moments in the interview when it seemed as if Juan could envision the more successful and lucrative career that he could have had if he had free rein of his personal time and location. Yet he acknowledged, perhaps begrudgingly, that marriage had taken some of that freedom away.

Interestingly, Juan's wife, Judy, had a similar sentiment. She had married early in her life and, while happy, couldn't help but wonder what life might have been if she had remained single. Remember, I already shared that she disclosed during her interview that she sometimes wished she had not met her husband until later in life, when the disruption to her career might have been minimized. Here's the quote I shared back in that earlier chapter, as it also serves as a clear example of the regret some millennials expressed:

> This is going to be contradictory because I got married so young, but I think [you should get married at] 30 to 35. I always joke and wish I could have hit pause. I always tell Juan I wish I could have pushed pause and met him later on because there are a few things that I have reprioritized, being married, that I think I would have prioritized differently had I not been married.

Chloe and Dylan shared a similar story of regret and the perception of lost opportunities. With three kids and a relatively early age of marriage, they had decided early in their marriage to have Chloe end her college career to stay home with the children. This derailment of Chloe's career and educational ambitions was not lost on either of them. Chloe explained, "I think if we hadn't married that young and didn't have kids I could have worked." This was said with just the

96 *Balancing Education and Career*

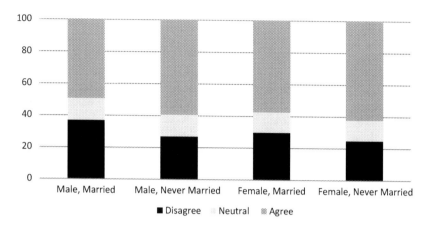

Figure 5.6 Percentage of Early 30-Year-Old Millennials Who Agreed With the Statement, "I Regret My Educational Decisions," by Marital Status and Gender.

slightest sense of remorse in her voice. Dylan picked up on this, trying to validate his wife's feelings. The early years of their marriage had been tough for Chloe, who struggled with a lack of identity and loneliness. He directly addressed his wife in his response, saying,

> Our getting married messed up your education and job and carried over to your other things. So, it kind of compounded. I think had you waited another six months to a year, you wouldn't have started out on such a rough foot.

While this regret came across through several of our interviews, our survey data provided a counterpoint to this observation. When comparing married millennials and their never-married counterparts in our U.S. sample of 5,000 millennials, I found that married millennials were slightly, yet significantly, less likely to regret their educational decisions, even after a series of demographic controls. I thought perhaps that there may be a gendered component to this, so I explored whether these results differed by gender. Interestingly, the findings did not differ by gender significantly ($p = .196$). Figure 5.6 shows the percentage of millennial males and females in their early 30s (split by marital status) that agreed that they regretted decisions they made about their education in their 20s. For both males and females, never-married millennials were about 10% more likely to agree that they regretted their educational decisions. It's fair to point out that over half of all the millennials in this sample, regardless of gender or marital status, agreed on some level that they regretted their educational decisions, so perhaps the take-home message here is that all millennials are struggling with their educational and career trajectories.

So how do we make sense of the fact that many married millennials may be frustrated by how marriage has hijacked or limited their careers, but also appear to regret their decisions around education less than their never-married peers? Perhaps the answer lies in the data I shared at the beginning of the chapter.

Married millennials, despite their frustrations, appear to be much better off economically than their single peers. Perhaps, on some level, millennials understand the economic benefits that marriage has afforded them. Regardless of any personal frustration with stunted ambition, they are able to note some level of personal benefit from the sacrifice they or their partners have made in their careers for the sake of the marriage. Clearly, however, while marriage appears to still benefit millennials economically, the path to economic and career success has only gotten more winding and challenging to navigate.

References

Addo, F. R. (2014). Debt, cohabitation, and marriage in young adulthood. *Demography*, *51*, 1677–1701.

Akers, K. E., & Kohm, L. M. (2018). Solving millennial marriage evolution. *University of Baltimore Law Review*, *48*, 1–38.

Amato, P. R. (2010). Research on divorce: Continuing trends and new developments. *Journal of Marriage and Family*, *72*, 650–666.

de Linde Leonard, M., & Stanley, T. D. (2015). Married with children: What remains when observable biases are removed from the reported male marriage wage premium. *Labour Economics*, *33*, 72–80.

De Vaus, D., Gray, M., Qu, L., & Stanton, D. (2017). The economic consequences of divorce in six OECD countries. *Australian Journal of Social Issues*, *52*, 180–199.

Edin, K., & Kefalas, M. (2011). *Promises I can keep: Why poor women put motherhood before marriage*. University of California Press.

Edin, K., & Reed, J. M. (2005). Why don't they just get married? Barriers to marriage among the disadvantaged. *The Future of Children*, *15*, 117–137.

Fry, R. (2010, October 7). *The reversal of the college marriage gap*. Pew Research Center. www.pewsocialtrends.org/2010/10/07/the-reversal-of-the-college-marriage-gap/

Gicheva, D. (2016). Student loans or marriage? A look at the highly educated. *Economics of Education Review*, *53*, 207–216.

Gorman, E. H. (1999). Bringing home the bacon: Marital allocation of income-earning responsibility, job shifts, and men's wages. *Journal of Marriage and the Family*, 110–122.

Harknett, K., & Kuperberg, A. (2011). Education, labor markets and the retreat from marriage. *Social Forces*, *90*, 41–63.

Hu, F. (2013). Homeownership and subjective wellbeing in urban China: Does owning a house make you happier? *Social Indicators Research*, *110*, 951–971.

Hymowitz, K. S., Carroll, J. S., Wilcox, W. B., & Kaye, K. (2013). *Knot yet: The benefits and costs of delayed marriage in America*. National Marriage Project at the University of Virginia.

Jordan, A. H., & Zitek, E. M. (2012). Marital status bias in perceptions of employees. *Basic and Applied Social Psychology*, *34*, 474–481.

Kalmijn, M. (2013). The educational gradient in marriage: A comparison of 25 European countries. *Demography*, *50*, 1499–1520.

Killewald, A., & Gough, M. (2013). Does specialization explain marriage penalties and premiums? *American Sociological Review*, *78*, 477–502.

Killewald, A., & Lundberg, I. (2017). New evidence against a causal marriage wage premium. *Demography*, *54*, 1007–1028.

Kuo, J. C. L., & Raley, R. K. (2016). Diverging patterns of union transition among cohabitors by race/ethnicity and education: Trends and marital intentions in the United States. *Demography*, *53*, 921–935.

Lee, G. R., & Payne, K. K. (2010). Changing marriage patterns since 1970: What's going on, and why? *Journal of Comparative Family Studies*, *41*, 537–555.

Lerman, R. I., Price, J., Shumway, A., & Wilcox, W. B. (2018). Marriage and state-level economic outcomes. *Journal of Family and Economic Issues*, *39*, 66–72.

Ludwig, V., & Brüderl, J. (2018). Is there a male marital wage premium? New evidence from the United States. *American Sociological Review*, *83*, 744–770.

McClendon, D., Kuo, J. C. L., & Raley, R. K. (2014). Opportunities to meet: Occupational education and marriage formation in young adulthood. *Demography*, *51*, 1319–1344.

Siassi, N. (2019). Inequality and the marriage gap. *Review of Economic Dynamics*, *31*, 160–181.

Zissimopoulos, J. M., Karney, B. R., & Rauer, A. J. (2015). Marriage and economic well being at older ages. *Review of Economics of the Household*, *13*, 1–35.

Zumbro, T. (2014). The relationship between homeownership and life satisfaction in Germany. *Housing Studies*, *29*, 319–338.

6 Mental Health and Physical Well-Being in Me-Marriage

Thomas and Madelyn met at a bar; this is something that may seem commonplace, if a little outdated, given how many millennial couples meet online rather than at a physical location. But there was more to this meet-up story than simply hanging out with friends and having a few drinks together that night. As Thomas put it, "To be quite honest, we met at a bar because we were kind of both full-on alcoholics . . . so 8 a.m. until 2 a.m., we were both at the bar. The same bar." Rather than meeting at a social event, Thomas and Madelyn met through their use of alcohol to escape life's difficulties and individual mental health challenges. These nightly, sometimes all-day, binges led to long conversations between the two. One night, Madelyn mentioned that she had nowhere to stay, having recently been kicked out of her apartment. Thomas recalled, "She needed a place to stay one night and I was like, 'You can come crash at my place, it's no big deal.' We really haven't been apart since." Madelyn piped in and agreed, saying, "He offered me a place to rest and I never left."

After they began dating, Madelyn and Thomas decided together to start living a healthier lifestyle. Madelyn explained, "We started making better decisions, started enjoying life and each other, and really turned our lives around individually and together." Thomas acknowledged that their joint recovery and reliance on each other had created not only a strong sense of commitment to their relationship but also a somewhat unhealthy level of reliance. He added, "we are really codependent on each other." Madelyn agreed, adding, "Now we are really codependent. I don't know if that's necessarily a good thing, but we are happy with each other, so I feel like that's what matters the most."

They began to live together and eventually had two children. It was the arrival of these children that made them start to talk about marriage and the legal benefits it would grant them. As Thomas put it, "The kids were kind of like the final signature on the contract." Despite their unstable beginning, they reported that things had been going well since they got married. Madelyn reported that conflicts were rare, noting, "We don't fight, we don't argue, we hold hands and peacefully enjoy every second that we can have together without the kids around. When the kids are up, it's family time." They felt like they simply "got" each other, largely based on their shared experience with substance use and mental illness. Madelyn went on to explain,

Our values are very similar. So the way we go through our day-to-day life, we are still absolutely compatible. I think we are definitely an oddity in that fact. I don't think I've seen that in my relationships in my entire life where people are that way. I'm grateful for that. I'm truly, truly grateful for that.

Thomas and Madelyn had gone through a major stressor related to their mental and physical health. They were young when they met but were clearly on a downward trajectory with alcohol. For both, their relationship had been key to finding the motivation and encouragement to push past their addictions. This story introduces the focus of this chapter: how marriage is influencing the physical and mental well-being of millennials. It is important to immediately acknowledge that millennials are still a relatively young generation. While some are approaching middle age, they are mostly not old enough to encounter significant health complications. For that reason, we do not have enough data to know how marriage will impact the long-term physical health of millennials. I will examine some data in this chapter, but keep in mind that it is likely a bit early to be drawing any major conclusions about the associations between physical health and marriage for millennials. Outside of some preexisting and chronic conditions, it's difficult to really examine much in the way of health differences between millennials and members of older generations.

Mental health and health-compromising behaviors are another matter, one that is worth spending some time discussing. While most of the millennials we interviewed refrained from overtly discussing any illegal activity, such as drug use, many discussed obstacles they have had in their marriages due to mental health challenges, which are a growing concern for many people in that age group (Twenge et al., 2019). When those rare instances of chronic health stressors did occur, such physical health issues could drastically alter life trajectories and decisions for married millennials. For example, Charles and Ruby met in high school and dated while Ruby finished college a few hours from their hometown. During this time, Charles worked, and they maintained a long-distance relationship for several years. After college, they moved in together and eventually married. They had been married for about three years by the time of their interview. Ruby had a chronic health condition. While much of their marriage followed the typical me-marriage routine, they did identify one area in which Ruby's health issues were especially relevant. Ruby shared,

> I have an autoimmune disease and so we weren't sure how pregnancy at an older age would be. So for the amount of kids that we want to have, and the kind of spacing we want to put between them, getting married young was the answer. We were not open to having children before marriage, so to be able to have the future and the family that we wanted, getting married at that time felt right.

Ruby's disease had altered the entire course of her marriage (and even her decision to be married). These uncommon but large effects show the need to examine how both mental and physical health issues are influencing the marriages of millennials.

In this chapter I examine the connections between health and marriage as much as possible at this point with this fairly young generation. I explore what previous research on this association has suggested and review data examining differences in health outcomes based on both age and marital status. For my interview data, I mostly focus on mental health, using the themes from those interviews to highlight some of the unique challenges and opportunities that marriage affords millennials in relationships where one or both partners struggle with mental health challenges.

The Historical Evidence

A large body of social science research has connected health behaviors, health outcomes, and marital status. When considering research in this area, it is important to remember that correlation and causation are separate phenomena. Given that there is almost always some uncertainty regarding when mental or physical health symptoms actually began, it is often challenging to know if any differences between married and unmarried individuals' health outcomes are due to the effects of marriage itself, or if the results are simply a selection effect caused by healthier people being more likely to date and eventually marry. There is probably some truth to both, but scholars have long argued that there is at least some causal relationship between marriage and health outcomes. For example, almost 30 years ago, Wyke and Ford (1992) suggested that increased resources and less stress due to perceived support were key causal factors linking marriage to better health outcomes.

One of the best-researched of these health outcomes is the area of risk taking. Married individuals, especially men, report significantly less risk-taking behavior than their unmarried counterparts (Bachman et al., 2013; Liang & Chikritzhs, 2012; Robards et al., 2012; West et al., 1996). The difference is noticeable across many behaviors, ranging from drug use (Bachman et al., 2013; Liang & Chikritzhs, 2012) to reckless driving (Whitlock et al., 2004). Some of these findings are hardly surprising. For example, married men engage in significantly less sexual risk-taking than single men (Astone et al., 2013), which is to be expected given the expectations of monogamy within a marriage. Risk-taking may also be the factor most susceptible to the selection effects I just mentioned. In fact, in their study exploring causal factors linking marriage to health outcomes, Wyke and Ford (1992) suggested that elevated risk taking among singles may entirely be accounted for as a selection effect.

More generally, a long series of studies has suggested that married individuals are healthier that those who never marry, in terms of general health outcomes (Aizer et al., 2013; Wang et al., 2011; Zheng & Thomas, 2013). Again, this research considered a wide range of outcomes and such differences seem to not be limited to the general self-reported health of married individuals. For example, Wang et al. (2011) found in a sample of over 100,000 colon cancer patients that married patients were more likely to seek treatment sooner and had a significantly higher survival rate. Scholars have noted higher survival rates of chronic and potentially terminal illnesses among married people across several diseases (see Aizer et al.,

2013; Sammon et al., 2012). Many of these studies suggest a gendered component to this increased survival rate, pointing out that such associations seem to be particularly true for men, although some unique health benefits have been found for women (Dlugonski & Motl, 2013). Aizer et al.'s (2013) large study of cancer survivors found that being married benefited both men and women, but the positive effect was stronger for men. Scholars have also noted that married people appear to have lower mortality rates than their single counterparts (Cheung, 2000; Lillard & Panis, 1996). This body of research has led to the assumption that married people tend to live longer and be healthier than single people. While this point is now rarely debated, whether it occurs due to selection or causation is still fiercely disputed.

Like the research on physical health, marriage and mental health are the subjects of much social science research (see Spiker, 2014). Links between being married and having better mental health have persisted for decades (Ennis & Bunting, 2013; Spiker, 2014; Williams et al., 2010). As recently as a few years ago, Simon (2014) argued that marital status continues to be one of the main drivers behind mental health differences across the population. Some scholars from earlier decades assumed that this link was due to increased loneliness and life stresses among singles and the socioeconomic benefits afforded to married couples, arguments that still are common today (Kessler & Essex, 1982; Pearlin & Johnson, 1977).

This association between marriage and better mental health outcomes continues with numerous studies suggesting that married individuals are less prone to depression, have lower lifetime occurrences of depressive episodes, and report fewer depressive symptoms than singles (Inaba et al., 2005; Meyer & Paul, 2011; Prince et al., 1999). Being married also predicts a lower likelihood of the onset of mental health problems (Scott et al., 2010) and a lower likelihood of suicide (Corcoran & Nagar, 2010). Following a common trend in this research, the findings on suicide suggest that this "marriage effect" is stronger for men than for women. Like research on physical health, scholars exploring links between mental health and marriage have often cited the increased social resources of having a spouse for emotional support and crisis management as one of the benefits of marriage (Williams et al., 2010). In many ways, links between marriage and mental health may be especially salient for millennials. Twenge et al. (2019) noted that mood disorders were on the rise during the early 2000s, suggesting that millennials as a generation may be reporting elevated rates of both depression and anxiety than older age groups.

Despite the robustness of these findings, research does suggest some caveats. Like any area of social science research, findings are not uniform, and some scholars have noted that married individuals may have unique health risks compared to singles (see Caputo & Simon, 2013). Scott et al. (2010) found that being married reduced the odds of mental illness but also that a marital separation or divorce increased the odds of the onset of mental health problems, suggesting that it may be only those who remain married who benefit from any boost to mental health. Some evidence suggests that differences in health based on marital status may diminish with age, with married individuals eventually "catching up" with their single counterparts as health naturally declines over time (Bulloch et al., 2017; Jang et al., 2009). It is also important to consider the fact that it may not be marital status that affects health at all but the actual processes and quality within that marriage. For example, in a large meta-analysis, Robles et al. (2014) suggested that higher marital quality was linked to a variety of positive health outcomes. In other words, positive relationship processes that create a relationship of support, warmth, and satisfaction may be the real reason we see health benefits associated with marriage. Given the strong belief that most of these health benefits can be traced to the additional resources a supportive spouse can bring, such findings are hardly surprising.

Another important aspect of this research lies in perception. Some scholars have argued that part of the health benefits of marriage may lie in the fact that married individuals tend to take more positive views of their own health, perhaps even overestimating their own health status (Zheng & Thomas, 2013). In a related finding, Ta et al. (2017) found that increased perception of stress, which mediated the relationship between marital status and anxiety, was the main reason singles reported elevated anxiety levels compared to those who were married. This and similar research may suggest a degree of self-fulfilling prophecy when it comes to health and marriage. Married people, as I have reported, may simply be more optimistic about their present and future—more satisfied with where their lives are. This may make them not only feel (and self-report) better health but also be more likely to engage in proactive health behaviors such as seeking out preventative care.

The pattern in the data here is similar to what I have presented in previous chapters. Generally, social science evidence suggests that being married is linked to a variety of positive physical and mental health outcomes. Exceptions exist, but this research is both robust and consistent. While I have already mentioned that fully exploring these questions among millennials is difficult given their age, it is worth at least attempting to analyze whether marriage is still linked to similar health benefits for millennials.

The Millennial Data

In my own research, I explored both mental and physical health among millennials and examined how marital status was associated with these personal health outcomes. I looked at physical health first. In my national sample of U.S. millennials, I explored trajectories of health by asking millennials to retroactively report on their health behaviors through their 20s. This provided a peek into not only how marital status may impact health but also how health may impact eventual transitions into marriage. As can be seen in Figure 6.1, marital status did appear to impact both respondents' exercise rates and serious health issues throughout their 20s. Those who were married in their 30s reported a small but consistently higher rate of exercise (this was self-reported and at least three times per week) than those who never married. On the other end of the spectrum, millennials who ended up marrying were significantly less likely to report a major health issue at any point in their 20s, with the never-married group reporting almost double the risk of a health issue at any specific age. To be clear, I am measuring marital status in the 30s in this analysis, meaning that these trends do not reflect the actual effect

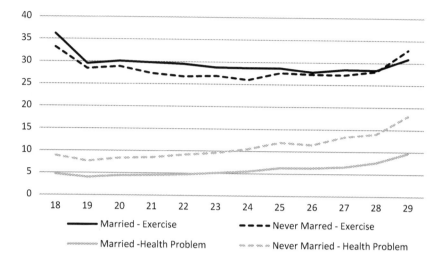

Figure 6.1 Percentage of Reported Exercise and Presence of Serious Health Problems From 18–29 by Marital Status for Millennials in Their Early 30s.

of marriage in all cases. Instead, they likely show that physical health has a selection effect on marriage, something I have already mentioned that scholars have suggested in the past. I start with this information because I think it is important context for the rest of the data I will share with you. As you will see, married millennials continue to show some health advantages compared to non-married millennials. However, data like those in Figure 6.1 indicate that much of this difference may have predated the marriages being studied. For millennials, like generations past, healthier people are more likely to get married.

Next, I turn to more contemporary assessments of health. I used this same dataset of 30-something millennials to compare the married individuals to the non-married on several indicators of their current physical health. First, I used height and weight variables to calculate all participants' rough body mass index (BMI) scores, a fairly robust overall measure of health and fitness. Once again, using the same set of controls as in previous chapters, I found that married millennials did not differ in their BMI scores compared to non-married millennials. I turned next to drug use and other health-compromising behaviors, such as binge drinking. After controls, I did not find any difference between married and never-married millennials when comparing their binge drinking or general drug use patterns, with one exception. Married millennials were significantly less likely to smoke marijuana and tobacco ($p < .001$) compared to never-married millennials. Figure 6.2 shows the raw percentages of millennials from each status who reported engaging in these behaviors in the last 12 months. Here, you can see a roughly 8% jump in tobacco use and a 10% jump in marijuana use among the never-married millennials.

Despite only slight differences in health indicators and behaviors, marital status did have a significant impact on millennials' satisfaction with their health. I found

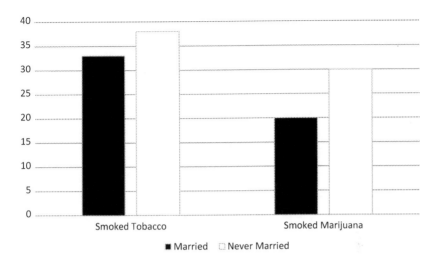

Figure 6.2 Estimated Means for Smoking Behavior by Marital Status for Millennials in Their Early 30s.

that married millennials were significantly more satisfied with their overall health than non-married millennials. The estimated averages after controls were relatively similar (married = 3.48, non-married = 3.23) but a clear and significant difference did emerge. Figure 6.3 breaks down each group's raw numbers based on three categories: dissatisfied, neutral, or satisfied with one's health. Here, you can see that while over 50% of married millennials were satisfied with their overall health, only 44% of never-married millennials felt the same way, a small but significant dip.

I examined mental health indicators next. In the same dataset I found significant differences in rates of depression when comparing based on marital status. Using a standardized clinical measure of depression and including divorced millennials in the model to explore whether ending a marriage impacted mental health, Figure 6.4 summarizes the estimated mean for each group after accounting for demographic controls. As you can see, married millennials reported significantly fewer depressive symptoms than both never-married and divorced millennials, who did not differ from each other. Like previous data I have shared with you, such findings suggest that divorce does not lower individual outcomes to a level lower than singles. Instead, divorce appears to merely erase any benefit to mental health afforded to married millennials.

Overall, the outcomes from these data continue to show a marriage-related health benefit, especially when it comes to mental health. But selection effects do need to be kept in mind, and I should note that there were no differences between married and never-married millennials across several indicators of overall health. My own interpretation of these numbers is that marriage may provide a small physical health benefit to some millennials and a larger mental health boost. Perhaps the most interesting finding rests in the differences observed in individuals'

106 *Mental Health and Physical Well-Being*

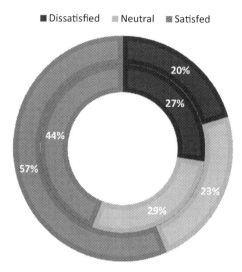

Figure 6.3 Percentage Satisfied With Overall Health for Millennials in Their Early 30s, by Marital Status.

Note: The outer circle represents married millennials, while the inner circle represents never-married millennials.

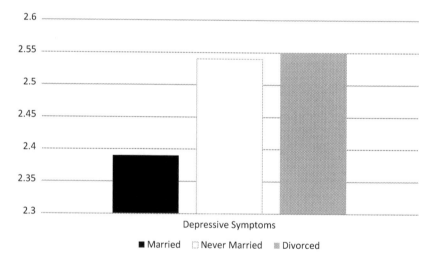

Figure 6.4 Estimated Means for Depressive Symptoms for Millennials in Their Early 30s, by Marital Status.

satisfaction with their own health. While this has been found in previous research as well, it is unclear why married millennials may have a more positive perception of their health. It may be related to similar trends I have noted in past chapters highlighting the unique stressors and frustrations of millennial singles, but this is

Mental Health and Physical Well-Being 107

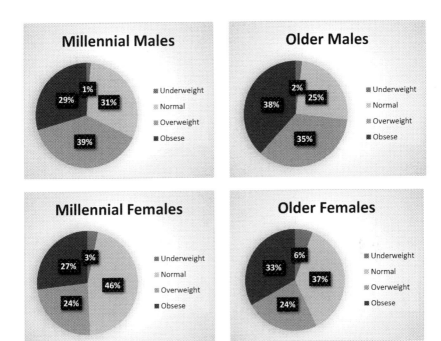

Figure 6.5 BMI Category by Gender and Cohort Among Newlyweds.

only speculation. These findings continue a trend of single millennials being less positive and less optimistic as they assess their lives during middle age.

You will notice I have not yet mentioned my other dataset from past chapters, where I have compared millennial married couples to older married couples to explore cohort differences. I will be completely honest: I almost did not even bother to run these analyses. After all, what would such data really show? When it comes to health outcomes, older married couples of the previous generations are obviously at a great disadvantage due to age, not their marriages. Showing that millennial couples are healthier than their older counterparts seemed at best pointless, and at worst potentially misleading. But, in an attempt to be thorough, I ran the models anyway. I was somewhat shocked by the results. I was able to explore two general markers of health in these data for newlywed couples of different ages. We collected enough information from these couples to calculate BMI and sort them into the following BMI categories: underweight, normal weight, overweight, obese. Figure 6.5 shows the percentage of the millennials and the older generations in each BMI category, broken down by gender. You can see that the distribution seems very similar across cohorts, although it does certainly slightly favor millennials. In fact, I found no differences for either males ($p = .26$) or females ($p = .15$) based on age cohort, meaning that older married couples were no more likely to be in a different BMI category (healthy or otherwise).

108 *Mental Health and Physical Well-Being*

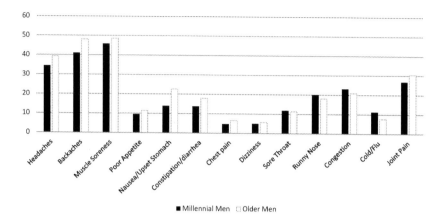

Figure 6.6 Percentage of Self-Reported Health Symptoms for Newlywed Men, by Cohort.

Next I analyzed a general measure of health to explore whether health problems were interfering with daily function. I did find the expected difference between generations for women ($p < .001$), with millennial women reporting significantly less health-related interference to their lives than older women. This was after controlling for a range of background factors, as I discussed in previous chapters. However, surprisingly, I found no differences between the men of various ages ($p = .61$). Turning to self-reported quality of sleep, a traditionally strong indicator of overall health (Ohayon et al., 2017), I once again found no difference between the millennials and older adults in their overall report of good sleep for either females ($p = .11$) or males ($p = .21$). The final thing I looked at was a count variable based on a series of questions asking the participants if they had experienced specific health problems in the last 4 weeks. Looking for cohort differences after controls, I again found what I expected for women ($p = .001$): millennial women reported significantly better health than their older counterparts. But, once again, I found no differences for men. Figure 6.6 shows the raw percentages of millennial and older men who reported each health problem. You can see that although the older men tended to report more symptoms compared to the millennial men in most categories, these differences were often small and overall were not significant. What about mental health differences across cohorts? Such differences may be slightly less prone to age-related confounding factors, at least in terms of depression. Again, I found no age-based differences for either men or women, after controls.

What is the explanation for this unexpected lack of differences, especially for men? After all, we would certainly expect to see some differences in health based on cohort simply based on age. The average age of the millennials in this dataset was under 30, while the older couples averaged close to 40 years old. At this point I do not have a good answer. The most obvious explanation would be that millennials may simply be less healthy as a group than older generations. While counterintuitive, this argument has some support. In 2008, the Centers for Disease

Control and Prevention released a report through the Department of Health and Human Services noting alarming rates of obesity and lack of physical exercise among millennial teens. A decade later, the insurance provider Blue Cross Blue Shield (2019) published a report suggesting that millennials may be significantly less healthy than previous generations as adults, noting high rates of hypertension, high cholesterol, and depression. If this is true, it may mean that marriage still provides health benefits to men, but millennial men have a lower base level of health than previous generations. Another possible explanation is that many health benefits may not appear until much later in life, at ages that very few of even the older couples in the dataset had achieved. Regardless, it is a non-statistically significant finding that is certainly worth continued exploration as both groups continue to age.

Me-Marriage and Mental Health

As I mentioned earlier in the chapter, most of the millennial couples my research team spoke to did not have pressing, chronic, or major physical health conditions and rarely spoke of illegal or other health-compromising behaviors. Remember, most were in their late 20s or early 30s and in the prime of their physical health. But mental health is another matter. Yes, most of the couples we spoke to were also doing just fine in that department. But a significant minority of the couples divulged how one or both partners had struggled at some point with mental health challenges. Given that research also suggests that mental health problems may be more prevalent among millennials (see Twenge et al., 2019), this is somewhat unsurprising. But how did these challenges influence marital dynamics, and what, if any, connection did they have to the themes of me-marriage I have outlined in previous chapters?

While the specific mental health challenges of the couples that spoke of these issues were varied, there were two common themes present in their discussions. One was the unique challenges that mental health conditions brought to modern marriage. The second was the unique companionship that marriage created that most couples highlighted as a critical resource, one that brought them to a positive, or at least manageable, place when it came to their mental health struggles.

Mental Health Struggles as a "Boulder" Roadblock in Me-Marriage

Let me first focus on the negative side of this topic: the unique struggles that mental health challenges caused for some of these millennial couples we spoke to. While the specific influence on their marriage varied based on the individual circumstances of each couple, one thing they all had in common was that mental health concerns made things harder and often stopped what they perceived as forward momentum in their marriage. This often came down to two things: a drain on personal and relational resources and an inability to negotiate and openly communicate about the complexities of life due to the symptoms of one or both partners. Oliver and Evie provide a compelling example of these issues. They met,

110 *Mental Health and Physical Well-Being*

like many other couples we spoke to, through an online dating site. They eventually had a daughter, and she was one of the main reasons why they married.

When they began to discuss during the interview how they divided household chores, they both began to talk about how this discussion had caused a fair amount of contention in their marriage, more than what many similar couples had discussed. These tasks were normal for any married couple, but Evie and Oliver reported that it almost broke their marriage apart. When pressed a little more, Oliver admitted that early in the relationship, when they tried to talk about simple things like who would cook or do the dishes, these conversations triggered deeper mental health issues for him that made such conversations difficult. He explained,

> There were a lot of conversations I wish we would've had before marriage. [My mental health] didn't really come up until we were further into being married. I would say we really didn't start addressing that until, like, three years into the marriage where we finally came to a place where we realized that we had to communicate or it wasn't going to work.

Oliver struggled with depression, and these contentious yet common discussions for newlyweds were difficult for him to handle during the first few years of marriage. As he put it, he had a "breakdown" at the end of their first year of marriage, unable to handle the stress it was creating in his life. As I have discussed, millennials have felt an increased desire and need to compromise with spouses on a variety of issues as both gender roles and life in general have grown more complex. Without being able to rely on social norms, Evie and Oliver were forced to create their own personalized me-marriage. For Oliver, this pressure was too much. Making household assignments requires both partners to be flexible and compromising, something Oliver was struggling with.

Evie also struggled during this time, reporting that, "the first year we got married was probably the worst year of being married." Evie was largely unaware of her husband's mental health issues, a surprisingly common story among the millennials my team spoke to. This made the first few years rough. As she put it, "the first and second year of our marriage, my husband had a lot of mental illness problems that he had to work through that I wasn't completely aware of." Oliver had mentioned that these issues had put his marriage on the brink of collapse, but Evie disclosed that another reason for this instability in their marriage was that Oliver had eventually turned to another woman for emotional comfort during this difficult time. She said,

> There were issues of emotional infidelity that we had to work through. It was kind of a make-or-break point that we were like, "either we're not going to work and you've got to leave or we're going to change how we do everything and we're going to rebuild our relationship." That's what we decided to do. We just decided that it was worth the effort to put in the work of changing things for us.

Mental Health and Physical Well-Being 111

Oliver realized that he needed more resources, especially individually, than he currently had. During this time of reflection he identified that his mental health struggles predated his relationship with his wife and could likely be traced to his childhood. Later in the interview he shared,

> I would say that a lot of the emotional stuff in the beginning [of our marriage] was more on my end. I had sort of repressed so many things from my childhood. I finally hit this breaking point where I was, at some points, hearing voices and waking up in cold sweats. I felt like I wanted to cry all the time. I needed to be on medication and therapy; we needed therapy. That allowed us to eventually just be more open with each other in general about frustrations and things like that.

He felt that, through utilizing clinical resources, they did eventually get to a place where he was able to be more open and honest in his communication. He added, "We started to feel more comfortable about saying whatever it was that we needed to say."

Oliver and Evie's experience highlights a few common patterns in the interviews my team conducted. As I noted, millennials with mental health issues often lack the needed resources to accomplish the unique tasks of me-marriage. In this case, the task of negotiating chores, a task that now more than ever requires compromise and coordination, was a major stumbling block. Oliver lacked the ability and skill set to navigate this part of his marriage. It was not until he accessed additional resources through individual and couples therapy that he was able to develop these skills. It was a lot of work, but one that Evie felt had benefited their relationship. She said this about how their relationship had improved since counseling:

> We started to really examine how we felt about how things were happening in the home, and it's just gone from there. It's a continuing conversation. It's not one that you have once and then you're done. You have it and then it might work that way for a bit and then you find a problem with it or you want to adjust something, but it's definitely something you keep at. We started talking about emotional issues between each other.

Evie and Oliver needed these conversations to get past the mental health obstacle in the way of their relationship. This metaphor of a physical object, a boulder in the path of marriage, resonated with many couples in which either or both spouses struggled with depression, anxiety, or other mental health issues. Simple things felt hard, or even insurmountable. Once Oliver and Evie were able to move the boulder in their way, they could return to the mundane and normal aspects of married life. In this case, that was assigning chores. Evie noted that the larger issues had to come first, saying, "I don't think we really started addressing house roles until later on." Oliver agreed, adding, "we had to address all that emotional stuff before we could really start to divvy up house chores." While mental health

112 *Mental Health and Physical Well-Being*

challenges can create a variety of struggles for married millennials, in the larger picture of me-marriage one of the clear problems it creates is stopping the forward momentum that millennials are yearning for in their relationships. Remember, they want marriages that are happy and fulfilling. They want relationships that are personalized to their own unique tastes and desires. They know that takes work, but they hope that the work is minimal and does not distract from their personal goals. Mental health issues often put the brakes on this progress. Like Oliver and Evie, many couples we interviewed noted that mental health struggles seemed to halt forward progress in the marriage.

Jace and Samantha were another couple my team interviewed who reported struggling with mental health problems during their marriage. They had been married for almost ten years and had two children. They had married young, mostly due to religious pressure they felt from their families and their larger religious culture. While they were both very religious when they first married, both had fallen away from organized religion over the course of the last decade, another common millennial pattern. Marrying early had put a strain on their relationship. As Jace explained,

> We got married and had children before going through school, and I think if those things had been switched, in terms of timeline, it would have been less difficult, less of a struggle. Because there were times where we were both in school full-time, I'm at work full-time, we had two kids, I'm pulling 17-hour days between class and work, and we honestly barely saw each other. I just think that's not the absolute best situation.

These early struggles were compounded by mental health challenges. Jace reported that both he and Samantha had a history of depression and anxiety. He noted, "We both also suffer from anxiety and depressive disorders and so some weeks, we just don't hold our weight, and we help each other out during those times."

Like Oliver and Evie, Samantha and Jace were going through a now-typical stressor for many millennials during this first decade of their marriage. They were trying to balance two educational and career paths, all while being newlyweds and eventually having young children. It is an increasingly complex arrangement, as I highlighted in Chapter 5. Again, mental health struggles halted much progress and caused a boulder in the path of their relationship. Jace felt a lot of this had to do with his being emotionally absent from his wife. His symptoms often included a retreat from personal interaction, making it hard for him to be a resource for Samantha when she was struggling with life stresses. Jace explained some of the unique challenges he felt their marriage had encountered during this time, saying,

> The one thing I don't think we have done the best in is emotional labor. From what I can tell, I'm not as bad as I could be but I'm definitely not actually pulling a full 50% of the emotional labor in our relationship. That's something that we discussed and that we're working toward.

Samantha saw a similar pattern in her husband's conflict behavior. She added,

Mental Health and Physical Well-Being   113

We have very different examples of parents. My husband's parents divorced when he was around 18. It had been a long time coming. His father was very abusive. My parents are still happily married so that was a very different environment. We had very different views on what a healthy marriage was. I had a pretty good foundation of how to deal with fights and how to deal with that kind of stuff. There were times when he would get nervous about having any fights early in the relationship, because his parents didn't fight in front of him. He didn't want his kids to see him being an awful person. He hadn't seen that people could fight and it could be healthy.

For Samantha, not having her husband as an emotional resource during school triggered many of her own symptoms. This also increased irritation, which led to even more conflict. As can happen in relationships with both partners dealing with mental health challenges, this led to a negative cycle of behavior, as Jace's own symptoms would often worsen because of these types of reactions from his wife. As Jace put it,

I grew up in a household with a lot of yelling, and it's just something that I don't deal well with. I have diagnosed PTSD from different things throughout my childhood, and one of my primary triggering activities is yelling. So, the fact that that was Samantha's main go-to [was hard]. There was a little bit when we first got together that I told her that is something that really puts me in a really negative space and makes it hard for me to come to a resolution. She very quickly said that was something she would work on. I think it was a combination of the fact that we both have a foundational belief of working together toward what's best, as opposed to doing what we think is best, or what is easier for us individually.

You can see that both Samantha and Jace felt they had largely overcome these issues from early in their marriage, but the road was certainly rocky, and they both reported that most of the relief did not come until after they had both finally finished school and established solid careers.

In just these two examples, you can see not only some of the specific challenges mental health problems created for these millennials but also two instances of couples who were able to overcome the roadblock in their way and at least get past the worst of their mental health problems. When millennials were able to toss this boulder aside, this often led to a resilient mindset when it came to marriage and a newfound view of what their marriage meant to them. Leo married his wife when he was 20 years old, and he had been with her for 13 years when he was interviewed. He was another millennial who had struggled with mental health problems, and he noted that he thought marriage was simply a piece of paper until he went through a serious bout of depression a few years into marriage. Going through this trial gave him a new perspective on his marriage. He explained,

I had really bad depression where essentially I lost all of my emotions, and I didn't feel anything. When you don't have emotions, you look at the world

114　*Mental Health and Physical Well-Being*

differently. You stop looking with your emotions at various things and you start to look at everything totally differently. Very straightforward.

Leo is likely describing a reaction to emotional flooding or feeling a strong rush of emotions (often negative). He reacted to this by distancing himself from his emotions. This was not the healthiest of reactions, but it gave him some perspective. He continued,

> It caused me to think more on things. After getting the help I needed, things changed. I couldn't have said I loved her [his wife] because I didn't have any emotions, but when I got everything back it was a stronger love than I had for her before, but it just made me realize that that piece of paper didn't matter.... With or without it, I'm still going to love her with everything I have.

This new perspective provides an illustration of the other major, and more positive, theme that emerged in my interview data.

Companionship Through Trial

While mental health struggles put a metaphorical boulder in the path of some millennial couples, the vast majority of those I spoke to that reported some level of distress related to mental health had often gotten to a place where they felt such concerns were no longer causing major issues within their marriage. Again, while circumstances were different, they all spoke about one resource that helped them move the boulder in their way: the companionship and strength of their spouse. Having a partner who was emotionally and physically present seemed to be the one common source of strength for many of these couples. While many with mental health difficulties often struggle to find strong interpersonal resources outside of family members (who can often be the source of such difficulties), marriage provided many millennials with a partner who was invested in their well-being. I just reviewed the struggles that Samantha and Jace had gone through, but Jace also reported that they felt things had started to turn the corner once they had completed school. Here's his explanation for why:

> We're heading into a much better situation right now than we were just a year or two ago because we were just going through school. Samantha just finished getting her master's and was starting work. During that time, we were sacrificing to get through school. During that time period, we kind of had to tighten the valves with whatever the needs of our kids were. We lived for several years below the poverty line while raising kids, and knowing that, for the both of us, there were difficulties of knowing that you want to do X, but we know we really need to do Y for the kids, and knowing that we were in that struggle together, I feel that was strengthening.

While there were some instrumental obstacles in their way, Jace felt like it was the strength of his marriage itself that had also been a key factor in their success in overcoming the boulder of mental health.

Mental Health and Physical Well-Being 115

I introduced you to Elise, a mid-20s woman with self-proclaimed "psychiatric issues," back in Chapter 3 where I reviewed some of her mental health struggles. Elise was another millennial who spoke highly of the resource her marital relationship brought her when it came to her mental health. Interestingly, interpersonal resources first came in the form of help from extended family rather than her husband. She noted that, at one point during her marriage, she had to end her employment due to the stress it was causing her. She decided to stay at home and take over the caretaking duties of her young child. Both during and after her employment, she relied heavily on her mother to help her in some caretaking duties, explaining,

> I couldn't do it [her previous job]. I'm a stay-at-home mom now and I'm able to handle it, but at the same time, I still need my mother on the weekends to take her for a couple hours so that I can have some sanity.

Elise had a long history of being very dependent on her mother. Yet over time, she started to rely more on her husband for this type of support. As she explained this shift, she noted, "That's the reason why I got married. That's why we got married." It was a little unclear at this point about what exactly this reason was. Upon further prompting, she explained that it was the increased shift in dependence from her mother to her husband that was appealing to her. Simply having someone around all the time to help out was essential to her well-being, and a spouse provided that for her. While her husband may not have helped much in the practical parts of her life due to his own employment, she did appear to rely heavily on him for what she labeled as "stability." She noted,

> I knew I needed somebody that was stable. I needed somebody that at least had an income. Not that we make tons of money, but we make enough to survive. I wanted somebody to complement me in terms of being able to be there. I could not deal with immaturity, even though I'm still immature.

It became clear during the interview that Elise was mostly referencing emotional stability here. She recognized her own shortcomings when it came to relationships and her inability to stay focused for long periods of time. She felt that finding someone as a resource to help her was one of the main benefits of marriage itself. Companionship and the high amount of social capital it provided was essential for her own well-being.

This unique support that marriage provided was an important resource for those struggling with mental health problems. Certainly, marriage was not the only romantic union that could provide it, but in the minds of these millennials, stability was best found within marriage. Remember, me-marriage is centered on personal benefits. For some millennials with a history of mental health problems, this personalized benefit came in the form of a supportive partner who was willing to dedicate themselves to be a personalized resource. Addy and Sawyer provide a great example of this belief. Addy had a rough childhood growing up, reporting emotional abuse from her father who eventually abandoned her family. Addy was raised by a single mother who tried to make ends meet. She loved her mom but

116 *Mental Health and Physical Well-Being*

noted that she was rarely there for her when she was growing up. This led to depression and anxiety, things Addy was desperately struggling with as a young 20-something still living at home and working a low-paying job.

When she met Sawyer at a party one night, she felt she may have finally found someone who could give her what she needed. After a late first night together, their relationship progressed quickly. Wanting to escape her mother's house, Addy moved in with Sawyer just 2 weeks later. Their relationship eventually became a source of emotional and mental healing for Addy. Here's how she put it:

> I'm not patient. But Sawyer taught me how to be happy with just being okay. Knowing that not everything is going to be perfect. As long as you're happy, it's okay. Now that I'm older I can see that I wanted to be happy as a child. I just wasn't happy; I wasn't happy. I couldn't express myself, and I had a lot of trauma from my dad's abuse and my mom's neglect. I didn't have the proper outlet at the time to work through that, and I think now that I'm nearing 30, I've had time to heal and I've had time to reflect and I've had time to get the proper care and treatment to see that the only thing that I wanted was to be happy, and being with Sawyer makes me happy. Are all of my dreams and fantasies in my head going to come true? Absolutely not, but that's okay because I always expect more in my own fantasies than what's obtainable. I think everybody does that. I think we always expect more from our fantasies than what reality always is. I think that's okay as long as you're realistic about it. I think being with Sawyer in our marriage has taught me that I've got to learn to be a little more realistic and still be okay with that.

How did Sawyer deal with his wife's struggle with mental health? As he put it,

> I don't really set my expectations that high .... I don't need a lot. Everybody has needs and stuff, but my needs are being met, so I'm okay. I'm not super needy. There are people out there who kind of see marriage like, "What if I don't get my needs met, what am I going to do?" Okay, it's not like a prison. You can do other stuff.

Luckily for Addy, her husband did not seem to require a lot of reciprocal emotional support, at least based on his own report. But for Addy, the resource of a spouse was essential to her current well-being.

However, this marital support didn't mean that Addy's mental health struggles were gone. They continued to flare up, making stable employment difficult for her. But even as she jumped from job to job, she felt that Sawyer and her marriage had been her rock. She explained,

> I couldn't take [work] anymore; the stress was messing with me physically and mentally. Sawyer and I had a clear conversation about me quitting and finding a new job .... So, in 2015, I quit that job. I took a risk and I quit with no support. Then I was working on a call center, which I've also recently quit. When I found out I was pregnant, I couldn't handle it emotionally anymore.

I always really wanted to be a teacher so Sawyer and I discussed it, and Sawyer is the solo income earner right now. I'm taking this summer off, which is a good thing because I needed it, and then I'll go back to school next month. I think in our marriage we've always supported and encouraged each other to do the things we want to do. Without Sawyer, I don't think I ever would have gone back to college to get my teaching degree. I think that we make each other stronger when it comes to making those decisions because it's scary to think that he might try something new and fail. But I think, for me, I can't fail as long as I have Sawyer there telling me that I can do it.

Here you can clearly see the unique millennial take on marriage as a mental health resource. As noted, these problems may have compounded the modern stresses of marriage, which in Addy's case centered on navigating a complex educational and career landscape. Addy's mental health symptoms made holding any job for longer than a few months difficult, but Sawyer was willing to support his wife and work with her challenges. Perhaps this is why millennials are somewhat uniquely suited to deal with the instability that often comes with mental health problems. Their lives are already fairly unstable due to trying to balance and navigate both partners' hobbies, ambitions, and needs. Modern me-marriages simply require a large amount of flexibility, and perhaps this is one area in which that flexibly can benefit millennials.

As one final example of the resource marriage was to millennials with mental health problems, let's return to Oliver and Evie. Oliver's mental health struggles had put a strain on their early marriage. But, in hindsight, they both recognized the unique resource their marriage had been during that time period. Evie explained,

> During our first kiss, I had this explosion kind of thing in my head. There was a moment where I realized that this person was going to impact my life in a really big way, and I didn't know what it meant at the time. It kind of freaked me out a little bit. I think we have this connection to each other. It made working out all the other stuff feasible because we were so close. That helped us navigate all of the things that we did wrong because we had that underlying connection with each other.

Oliver felt this connection too, adding, "I can't quite explain it, but yeah. There was always an underlying comfort and desire to be together that has powered us through the bad moments and the unforeseen moments." It was this comfort that gave these struggling millennials a special perspective on marriage.

So, what are the takeaways when it comes to health and me-marriage? My data suggest that this may be another area in which the traditional benefits of marriage appear to be continuing. While data on physical health is currently limited, both my quantitative and qualitative data show a mental health benefit for millennials who are married. Interviews suggested that much of this benefit may be traced to increased social resources and spousal support, a factor traditionally mentioned in this area of scholarship. Apparently, the mental health benefits of having a

118　*Mental Health and Physical Well-Being*

loving spouse transcend many of the other recent cultural shifts when it comes to marriage.

Of course, there are some exceptions to this general trend. While mental health seems to be better among millennial married couples than singles, and marriage continues to provide many of the same resources as seen in previous generations, millennials are also reporting some unique difficulties when it comes to mental health problems. Specifically, in an increasingly complex world where marriage needs to be more adaptable, mental health problems often seem to halt any progress or movement forward in a relationship, a problem that seemed to cause a great deal of distress among millennials who wanted marriage to reduce, not create, stress in their lives. I should also remind you that the physical health data were decidedly mixed. Again, this may be due to the fact that clear health benefits will only appear later in life or may suggest that such physical health benefits may be slipping as marriage becomes a less normative arrangement. While the general trend in this area is similar to past cohorts, it is important for scholars to continue to monitor whether married individuals report better health outcomes moving forward as the millennial generation ages.

References

Aizer, A. A., Chen, M. H., McCarthy, E. P., Mendu, M. L., Koo, S., Wilhite, T. J., Graham, P. L., Choueiri, T. K., Hoffman, K. E., Martin, N. E., Hu, J. C. & Nguyen, P. L. (2013). Marital status and survival in patients with cancer. *Journal of Clinical Oncology, 31,* 3869–3876.

Astone, N. M., Pleck, J. H., Dariotis, J. M., Marcell, A. V., Emerson, M., Shapiro, S., & Sonenstein, F. L. (2013). Union status and sexual risk behavior among men in their 30s. *Perspectives on Sexual and Reproductive Health, 45,* 204–209.

Bachman, J. G., Wadsworth, K. N., O'Malley, P. M., Johnston, L. D., & Schulenberg, J. E. (2013). *Smoking, drinking, and drug use in young adulthood: The impacts of new freedoms and new responsibilities.* Psychology Press.

Blue Cross Blue Shield (2019, November 6). *The health of America: The economic consequences of millennial health.* Blue Cross Blue Shield. www.bcbs.com/sites/default/files/file-attachments/health-of-america-report/HOA-Moodys-Millennial-11–7.pdf

Bulloch, A. G., Williams, J. V., Lavorato, D. H., & Patten, S. B. (2017). The depression and marital status relationship is modified by both age and gender. *Journal of Affective Disorders, 223,* 65–68.

Caputo, J., & Simon, R. W. (2013). Physical limitation and emotional well-being: Gender and marital status variations. *Journal of Health and Social Behavior, 54,* 241–257.

Centers for Disease Control and Prevention. (2008). *2007 National youth risk behavior survey overview.* CDC. www.cdc.gov/HealthyYouth/yrbs/pdf/yrbs07_us_overview.

Cheung, Y. B. (2000). Marital status and mortality in British women: A longitudinal study. *International Journal of Epidemiology, 29,* 93–99.

Corcoran, P., & Nagar, A. (2010). Suicide and marital status in Northern Ireland. *Social Psychiatry and Psychiatric Epidemiology, 45,* 795–800.

Dlugonski, D., & Motl, R. W. (2013). Marital status and motherhood: Implications for physical activity. *Women & Health, 53,* 203–215.

Ennis, E., & Bunting, B. P. (2013). Family burden, family health and personal mental health. *BMC Public Health, 13,* 255.

Inaba, A., Thoits, P. A., Ueno, K., Gove, W. R., Evenson, R. J., & Sloan, M. (2005). Depression in the United States and Japan: Gender, marital status, and SES patterns. *Social Science & Medicine, 61,* 2280–2292.

Jang, S. N., Kawachi, I., Chang, J., Boo, K., Shin, H. G., Lee, H., & Cho, S. I. (2009). Marital status, gender, and depression: Analysis of the baseline survey of the Korean Longitudinal Study of Ageing (KLoSA). *Social Science & Medicine, 69,* 1608–1615.

Kessler, R. C., & Essex, M. (1982). Marital status and depression: The importance of coping resources. *Social Forces, 61,* 484–507.

Liang, W., & Chikritzhs, T. (2012). Brief report: marital status and alcohol consumption behaviours. *Journal of Substance Use, 17,* 84–90.

Lillard, L. A., & Panis, C. W. (1996). Marital status and mortality: The role of health. *Demography, 33,* 313–327.

Meyer, D., & Paul, R. (2011). A cross-national examination of marriage and early life stressors as correlates of depression, anxiety, and stress. *The Family Journal, 19,* 274–280.

Ohayon, M., Wickwire, E. M., Hirshkowitz, M., Albert, S. M., Avidan, A., Daly, F. J., . . . Vitiello, M. V. (2017). National Sleep Foundation's sleep quality recommendations: First report. *Sleep Health, 3*(1), 6–19.

Pearlin, L. I., & Johnson, J. S. (1977). Marital status, life-strains and depression. *American Sociological Review,* 704–715.

Prince, M. J., Beekman, A. T., Deeg, D. J., Fuhrer, R., Kivela, S. L., Lawlor, B. A., . . . Copeland, R. M. (1999). Depression symptoms in late life assessed using the EURO–D scale: Effect of age, gender and marital status in 14 European centres. *The British Journal of Psychiatry, 174,* 339–345.

Robards, J., Evandrou, M., Falkingham, J., & Vlachantoni, A. (2012). Marital status, health and mortality. *Maturitas, 73,* 295–299.

Robles, T. F., Slatcher, R. B., Trombello, J. M., & McGinn, M. M. (2014). Marital quality and health: A meta-analytic review. *Psychological Bulletin, 140,* 140–187.

Sammon, J. D., Morgan, M., Djahangirian, O., Trinh, Q. D., Sun, M., Ghani, K. R., . . . Karakiewicz, P. I. (2012). Marital status: A gender-independent risk factor for poorer survival after radical cystectomy. *BJU international, 110,* 1301–1309.

Scott, K. M., Wells, J. E., Angermeyer, M., Brugha, T. S., Bromet, E., Demyttenaere, K., . . . Kessler, R. C. (2010). Gender and the relationship between marital status and first onset of mood, anxiety and substance use disorders. *Psychological Medicine, 40,* 1495–1505.

Simon, R. W. (2014). Twenty years of the sociology of mental health: The continued significance of gender and marital status for emotional well-being. In R. J. Johnson, R. J. Turner, & B. G. Link (Eds.), *Sociology of mental health* (pp. 21–51). Springer.

Spiker, R. L. (2014). Mental health and marital status. In *The Wiley Blackwell Encyclopedia of Health, Illness, Behavior, and Society* (pp. 1485–1489). John Wiley & Sons.

Ta, V. P., Gesselman, A. N., Perry, B. L., Fisher, H. E., & Garcia, J. R. (2017). Stress of singlehood: Marital status, domain-specific stress, and anxiety in a national US sample. *Journal of Social and Clinical Psychology, 36,* 461–485.

Twenge, J. M., Cooper, A. B., Joiner, T. E., Duffy, M. E., & Binau, S. G. (2019). Age, period, and cohort trends in mood disorder indicators and suicide-related outcomes in a nationally representative dataset, 2005–2017. *Journal of Abnormal Psychology, 128,* 185–199.

Wang, L., Wilson, S. E., Stewart, D. B., & Hollenbeak, C. S. (2011). Marital status and colon cancer outcomes in US Surveillance, Epidemiology and End Results registries: Does marriage affect cancer survival by gender and stage? *Cancer Epidemiology, 35,* 417–422.

West, G. B., Moskal, P. D., Dziuban, C. D., & Rumbough, L. P. (1996). Gender and marital differences for risk taking among undergraduates. *Psychological Reports, 78,* 315–320.

Whitlock, G., Norton, R., Clark, T., Jackson, R., & MacMahon, S. (2004). Motor vehicle driver injury and marital status: A cohort study with prospective and retrospective driver injuries. *Injury Prevention, 10,* 33–36.

Williams, K., Frech, A., & Carlson, D. L. (2010). Marital status and mental health. *A handbook for the study of mental health: Social contexts, theories, and systems* (pp. 306–320). Cambridge University Press.

Wyke, S., & Ford, G. (1992). Competing explanations for associations between marital status and health. *Social Science & Medicine, 34,* 523–532.

Zheng, H., & Thomas, P. A. (2013). Marital status, self-rated health, and mortality: Overestimation of health or diminishing protection of marriage? *Journal of Health and Social Behavior, 54,* 128–143.

7 Parenting Within a Me-Marriage

I mentioned Aiden and Ella in the last chapter. They were recently wed, celebrating 2 years of marriage when they were interviewed, and they had a young daughter living at home with them. They met through an online dating site where Aiden had made first contact with Ella. As Ella described it,

> I messaged with a lot of guys. He messaged me and we started talking. I remember he called me to ask me out the first time we met, which I thought was really nice cause a lot of times when you are meeting people online, they don't call you. The first time we met, we met at the bookstore here in town and went out to dinner and then just kind of hit it off.

They started dating, eventually became exclusive, and, after a while, they started to talk about their future together. Interestingly, Aiden noted that he had never really planned on marrying. As he put it, "I kind of hadn't really put that [marriage] in my goals." He had other goals, more personal goals, that he wanted to accomplish. He was a millennial after all, and his personal goals seemed more important than tying himself down to another person for the rest of his life. These individual ambitions did not appear extravagant, however. As he put it, "When I met her, I was going to work and getting KFC and hanging at Starbucks all night viewing the internet. So, I wasn't really doing much." So, perhaps it was the general thought that marriage might hamper his personal freedom that made Aiden hesitate.

Ella had her own concerns. She shared,

> When I was 19, I found out that I have an autoimmune disease that is going to make having kids fairly difficult. Playing with young kids, you know, running and chasing and moving is going to be hard for me.

Ella's disease was progressive, and she knew she had a limited window if she wanted to have any children and still be an active mother. This concern weighed on her when she started to get serious with Aiden. She explained,

> When I met Aiden, we had all the same values. We moved really fast because I knew, I won't say it's my biological clock, but I think that was part of it.

122 *Parenting Within a Me-Marriage*

I wanted to have as much time with my kids as I could. My parents, they worked a lot growing up. My dad was on-call a lot and I didn't see him a lot. I felt that being younger would afford me more opportunities to really spend more time with my kids.

Ella shared these concerns with Aiden, a conversation that put them on an accelerated track for both marriage and parenthood, despite Aiden's reservations about marriage.

They married and immediately began trying to have children. Their little girl eventually came about a year into their marriage. For both Aiden and Ella, mixing parenthood with a young marriage brought with it some unique challenges. Aiden noted that it was challenging to explore their new marriage while also balancing the demands of a baby. It was easy to let the marriage slip. As he put it,

I think a lot of people, they have babies and try to have hobbies . . . . Some people get so far apart they are just roommates with a baby. They just turn into glorified roommates sometimes, so I guess you have to put the work into [the marriage].

Putting in the "work" was something Aiden was committed to. You could tell he was nervous about the long-term toll becoming parents so early might have on his young relationship with his wife. Ella expressed similar concerns, noting that they both recognized the extra effort they needed to put into their marriage to keep it a top priority in their lives. She added,

I think we do check in with each other, we do make sure that we're happy. I think [we talk] when we start to feel like it isn't a priority. I mean our kids and our belongings wouldn't be there without our marriage. I don't think any of that would be there without our marriage.

While Aiden and Ella took a quick and non-normative route to parenthood compared to their peers (at least in terms of timing), their concerns and challenges of trying to balance parenthood and marriage are age-old quandaries. This challenge of balancing the unique complexities of a me-marriage with the stresses of parenthood also highlight some of the uniquely millennial approaches to this transition. The transition to parenting is one of the most stressful and life-altering moments in a person's life. But in the increasingly complex and individualistic world of millennials, a world that has created the me-marriage relationships I have outlined in previous chapters, what unique challenges and opportunities does millennial parenthood within such marriages afford? Is this transition into parenthood the same as it has been in the past, or are there new and unique challenges for modern millennials? This chapter is dedicated to exploring this question by examining married millennials who have become parents and looking at some of the ways parenthood has put a different spin on me-marriages.

The Historical Evidence

What has past research had to say about the transition to parenthood? The answer is; quite a lot. Here I provide some broad historical context on trends and themes in the research in this area, but I do not attempt to provide a complete review of this varied area of study. Much of this research has focused on broad fertility patterns across the world, a topic less relevant to the present conversation. One trend to note is that marriage and parenthood have become increasingly separate phenomena in recent decades. Non-marital fertility is on the rise in most parts of the world (OECD, 2020; Smith, 2019). Increasing numbers of couples are opting to begin families while cohabiting instead of waiting until marriage, and these unions are largely unstable environments for children (Lichter et al., 2016). While non-marital fertility may be on the rise, other scholars have noted that marriage remains the most common relationship in which children are conceived across countries (Perelli-Harris et al., 2012).

A large volume of research suggests that the connection between parenthood and marriage is complex and varied. As I mentioned already, the transition to parenthood has long been viewed as a major stressor in one's life and, as such, has been a major focal point of social science research on relationship quality for many decades. Many scholars have examined the correlates, processes, and outcomes associated with becoming parents in general (see Boivin et al., 2018; deMontigny & deMontigny, 2013; Nomaguchi & Milkie, 2003). Scholars have also examined in a fair amount of detail the impact that becoming a parent has on relationship quality and process for married couples. Generally speaking, becoming a parent puts stress on any couple's relationship, and this stress can impact multiple relational processes (Tavares et al., 2019). This stress, and the draining of resources that accompanies it, is often associated with negative outcomes (Bouchard, 2016; Mitnick et al., 2009; Twenge et al., 2003). It would be fair to point out, however, that some scholars have noted that the declines in marital quality seen among new parents may simply be documenting a similar decline seen among all married partners, regardless of whether or not they become parents (see Mitnick et al., 2009). In other words, perhaps we see a decline in quality when couples become parents simply because we expect to see one. It is also important to keep in mind that many of these outcomes are moderated by unique birthing and child situations. Birthing complications (Howe et al., 2014), postpartum depression (Choi, 2016), and developmental delays (Baker et al., 2002), all put unique stressors on marital relationships that alter the specific effects the transition has on any particular couple.

Given the breadth of research done in this area, several high-quality meta-analytic studies have examined relational quality over the transition to parenthood. A meta-analysis by Twenge and colleagues (2003) found that marital satisfaction tended to be significantly lower for parents compared to non-parents and that marital satisfaction also declined with the number of children. A later meta-analysis found very similar findings across over 30 studies, noting a small but negative association between parenthood and relationship satisfaction (Mitnick et al., 2009).

124 *Parenting Within a Me-Marriage*

Exploring trends across research, they noted that most studies pointed to conflicts about roles within the family as the main reason such dips in satisfaction were found. Dew and Wilcox (2011) argued a similar process, noting that decline in a mother's marital satisfaction could be traced to feelings of unfairness in how roles were assigned after having children. They also noted decreased time spent together as a couple after a child was born as another primary mechanism for explaining declines in marital satisfaction. Traditionally, many scholars have found what is referred to as the "u-shaped" pattern of marital satisfaction during the transition to parenthood. This pattern involves a dip in satisfaction during the transition to parenthood and while children are young. Satisfaction is then found to rebound as children age and leave the home, creating a "U" pattern over time. While this pattern is far from uniform, continued evidence of its existence as a broad and normative trend persists (Keizer & Schenk, 2012).

Parenthood also appears to influence individual well-being. Large studies have documented declines in life satisfaction, mental health, and personal health across the transition to parenthood (Bernardi et al., 2017; Keizer et al., 2010), although some research has suggested that millennials may get a life satisfaction boost from parenthood (Switek & Easterlin, 2018). Like research on relationship quality, the bulk of this individual-focused research suggests that becoming a parent takes away personal resources and adds personal stress, a recipe for the commonly seen overall declines in well-being. Of course, for some couples, becoming a parent may be perceived as a wanted and exciting transition. Such perceptions may account for other research suggesting that mental health may improve for some individuals during the transition to becoming a parent (McKenzie & Carter, 2013).

Like many things that could impact the quality of a marriage and personal well-being, couple characteristics and processes are important considerations that can shift the effect of children on a marriage. Whether a couple originally intended to get pregnant appears to be an important factor that changes the effect of becoming a parent (Bouchard et al., 2006). Rosen et al. (2017) found that empathy between partners was key during the transition to parenthood. Among couples with more expressed empathy, relational quality improved, including increased sexual satisfaction and desire among females. Given the previously noted importance of conflict about roles within the marriage, gender role beliefs and attitudes have also been found to be key contextual factors that impact the transition to parenthood (Katz-Wise et al., 2010).

Perhaps one of the most important factors in determining how parenting will impact marital process and quality is the quality of the relationship *prior* to the pregnancy. Becoming a parent does not drastically change the very nature of the relationship in most marriages. Instead, parenthood can exaggerate both the positive and negative qualities of any relationship that existed prior to the pregnancy occurring. Le and colleagues (2016) examined cohabiting couples during the transition to parenthood and documented that couple dynamics that existed prenatally were one of the most powerful and important factors in well-being during this transition.

The timing of pregnancy and children is also an important contextual factor and is likely relevant to married millennial parents, many of whom have transitioned

Parenting Within a Me-Marriage 125

to parenthood sooner than many of their peers. Helms-Erikson (2001) argued that married couples who transition to parenthood early in their marriage may be more at risk for negative marital quality down the road. This timing effect has been noted by other scholars as well (Mitnick et al., 2009).

Together, this research suggests a common theme of parenthood as a normative stressor that generally has a negative impact on relational quality by both lowering couple resources and introducing additional points of conflict into the relationship. However, numerous contextual factors moderate and alter this association, creating a complex web of factors that makes it difficult to predict just what effect a child will have on any given marriage. But this research does provide a foundation and some expectations as we now examine the marriages of millennials and see if parenthood status alters or changes what their relationships look like.

The Millennial Data

Before venturing any further into this topic, I should remind you that this book is focused on marital relationships and not child development. The question of whether children fare better in marriages versus other types of relational unions is a very important one, but it is also a very different question than the one I am attempting to answer (for examples of this type of work, see Björklund et al., 2007; Fomby & Cherlin, 2007). Rather, the main questions here are (a) how is becoming a parent and the presence of children impacting the marriages of millennials, and (b) is that impact similar to what we have seen in the past?

So, how is relationship quality impacted by the presence of children? Since I know at least one reader is curious, let's get one thing out of the way. Yes, having children did have an impact on the sex lives of millennials. In my data, having children was significantly related to having less sex and being less satisfied with sex, but only for women. With that out of the way, Figure 7.1 outlines the data from our national sample of 30-year-old millennials who answered questions about relationship stability and satisfaction. I broke the sample down across four categories, separating the parents with children at home from those without children living in the home and then separating the sample again based on whether the subject was married or not. Figure 7.1 shows that, while there is an ever so slight dip in both satisfaction and stability for married millennial parents compared to married millennials without children, this difference was not significant. (These models once again included all the normal controls I have referenced in previous chapters.) What you can see clearly from both graphs is that the one group that appears to be suffering is the group of unmarried parents. These millennials reported significantly lower relationship satisfaction and less stability compared to millennials who were married, regardless of whether or not they had children. Generally, those who were unmarried but did not have children reported similar outcomes on stability and satisfaction as other groups, although there was a significant difference in relationship satisfaction between this group of unmarried millennials and the married millennials without children.

Overall, this may suggest that many of the relationship differences I noted in Chapter 4 between married and unmarried millennials in terms of relationship

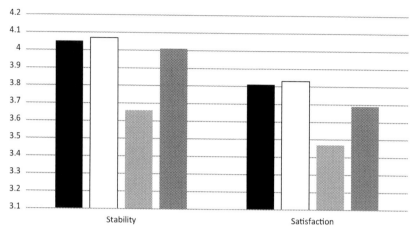

Figure 7.1 Estimated Means for Relationship Stability and Satisfaction by Marital and Parenthood Status for Millennials.

quality may largely be attributed to unmarried parents, who appear to suffer the most when it comes to relationship quality. It also suggests that marriage provides an important buffer for millennials when it comes to becoming parents. While unmarried parents were reporting significantly lower relationship quality compared to their peers who were not parents, parenthood did not appear to have any significant effect on relationship quality among those who were married, something that did not fall exactly in line with research on previous generations.

Naturally, becoming a parent does impact relationship quality for millennials. Figure 7.2 plots both relationship satisfaction and stability, based not only on the presence of children but also on the number of children. While not monumental, there is a clear linear trend toward lower relationship quality as the number of children increases. Parenthood also appeared to impact individual well-being when I focused on those outcomes. After controls, I found differences in depression rates among millennials based on parenthood and marital status. In this case, the news appeared positive. Married parents reported the lowest rates of depression on a standardized depression scale of any group (estimated average = 2.38), which was significantly lower than the average reported by both unmarried parents (estimated average = 2.54) and unmarried non-parents (estimated average = 2.57). While lower, their average was not significantly different than married non-parents (estimated average 2.47). For life satisfaction, parenthood status appeared to have little impact on average reported life satisfaction for millennials after controls. As noted in a previous chapter, life satisfaction was significantly higher for married millennials, a trend we see repeated here, regardless of whether they were parents or not. There were no significant differences between married millennials in terms of life satisfaction depending on whether or not they were parents.

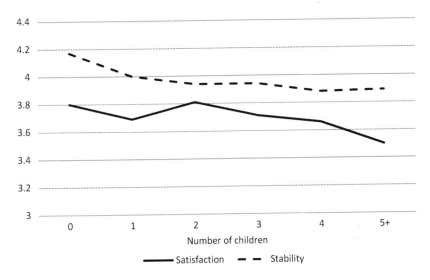

Figure 7.2 Average Relationship Satisfaction and Stability by Number of Children for Married Millennials.

So far, the results seem pretty positive. Millennial parents, at least in the U.S. data I had access to, appear to be faring well. But as noted previously, some of these trends may simply have been related to marriage itself, not parenthood. What if we examined more closely just the millennial married couples themselves? Do the results for people who have elected to become parents look different than the results for those who have not? I used the national U.S. sample of newlyweds to dig deeper into that question. When I examined a regression model predicting parenthood status based on a range of demographics in our sample of millennial newlyweds, I found that being a parent was predicted by several demographic variables. Having more education reduced the likelihood of becoming parents, something that other scholars have noted as well. On the other hand, being previously married, racial differences between partners, longer relationship length, having cohabited prior to marriage, and being more religious all independently increased the likelihood that millennials in the sample were parents. These findings mostly line up with traditional demographic markers that make parenthood more likely. But what about their relationships? If we control for demographic factors and dig deeper into just the married couples, does parenthood influence the marriages of millennials?

The answer would appear to be yes, but in some gendered ways. Figure 7.3 outlines the estimated means, after controls, on both stability and relationship satisfaction for millennial parents and non-parents, split by gender in the large sample of newlyweds. Unlike the other data I explore, here I found significant differences ($p < .01$) for both outcomes based on parental status. There was a significant dip in satisfaction levels for both male and female millennial parents, perhaps confirming some fears millennials have when it comes to the effect of

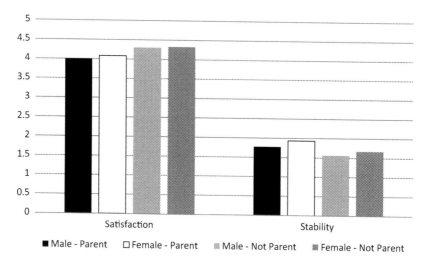

Figure 7.3 Estimated Means for Relationship Satisfaction and Stability by Parent Status and Gender for Newlywed Millennials.

becoming a parent on relationship quality. However, stability goes the opposite direction. I found that both male and female millennial parents reported better stability in their relationship than non-parents. In both cases it's important to point out that these are results from cross-sectional data—meaning, it is impossible to know if individuals in less satisfying but more stable millennial relationships are more likely to transition to parenthood, or if becoming a parent is actually changing the nature of the relationship. Regardless (and the answer is likely both), while the effects are small, clearly millennials are experiencing differences in marital quality based on parental status, something seen in social science for many decades and that suggests that me-marriages remain highly susceptible to the stresses and impacts of parenting.

Let's turn to more process-oriented variables, things like conflict and relational aggression. These variables are where results get a bit more gendered. Figure 7.4 plots the differences between parent and non-parent husbands and wives on overall conflict and relational aggression. These are estimated means after control variables have been taken into account. While the means may look very similar, the differences between millennial men with and without children are significant in both cases (although the analysis examining general conflict was barely significant, $p = .035$). Interestingly, the trend goes in the opposite direction for each variable. While millennial men who are parents reported less overall conflict in their relationship, they also reported significantly more relational aggression. Remember, relational aggression is focused on passive aggressive behaviors, so perhaps male parents are shifting the type of aggression they engage in after becoming parents. It's an interesting gendered finding that bears some additional future attention.

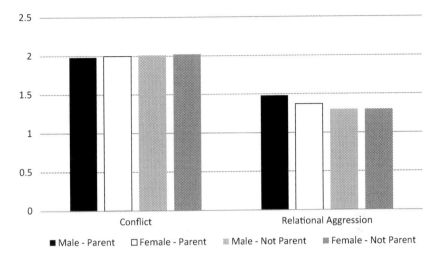

Figure 7.4 Estimated Means on Overall Conflict and Relational Aggression by Parent Status and Gender for Newlywed Millennials.

The Salience of Marriage and Children

As with previous chapters, this quantitative approach to the impact of children only tells us part of the story. The interviews my team conducted with married millennials, many of whom were parents, shed some additional light on how millennials are balancing parenthood with marriage. Some of these themes echo previous scholarship on past generations, while others appear uniquely millennial and may provide insights into some new directions for parenthood scholarship in the future. One thing remains clear when it comes to most millennials: marriage and parenthood remain intertwined. Despite higher non-marital child-bearing rates across almost all countries, parenting is still largely done within the confines of marriage, particularly for those with at least a college education. In our study of older millennials, 79% of married millennials reported at least one child. That was compared to only 36% of never-married millennials who reported at least one child. National data show similar trends. Married couples report significantly higher fertility rates than non-married couples (Monte, 2017; Stone, 2018). In a recent report for the Institute for Family Studies, Stone (2018) argued that many of the dips in fertility in recent years are actually explained by declining marriage rates.

But perhaps more important than these raw numbers are the words of millennials themselves, which appear to indicate that they still connect marriage and parenting. This is not to say that they necessitate being married to having children ("to each their own" is the common millennial mantra), but there remained among them a strong sentiment that marriage, especially the implied commitment and stability marriage brought, was still the ideal setting for raising children. This

130 *Parenting Within a Me-Marriage*

certainly seemed to be the case for Aiden and Ella, from the beginning of the chapter. Like Aiden, Denzel, from a previous chapter, noted that this connection between marriage and children was one of the main reasons he married his wife of 3 years, stating that the main driver to his marriage was that, "Lanelle told me she wasn't having no more kids with me unless we get married." His wife would later provide more context for perhaps why she put this pressure on him, stating,

> I think, for me, my upbringing kind of plays a big part in that. I was brought up in a two-parent household, my parents have been married my entire life. So, my thought process of how things operate in the household, for me, it takes two to make a kid. And not everybody has children, but I've always wanted children, and I think [marriage] is a solid foundation for the family.

You will remember Elise from a previous chapter as well. Her husband had given her an ultimatum about getting her own mental health issues figured out or he threatened to leave. Despite all of the individual and relational stresses on her marriage, her views on the connection between marriage and having children were similar. She went into marriage for the sole purpose of providing a stable family for her children. She said,

> I got married because I wanted children. I didn't want my children to grow up without a father because I knew what it was like growing up without a father. He was there, but he wasn't "there." I knew that I didn't want that for my children. I wanted my children to have somebody they could go to on a daily basis and do things with, do family trips, things I didn't get really as a kid. That's basically the reason why I got married was because I didn't want my kids to deal with the things that I dealt with. I didn't want to do that to my kids.

While it may seem slightly old fashioned, this concept of needing to get married prior to having children came up in many of the interviews we had with millennials. While the norms surrounding the need for marriage may have largely eroded, the need to sequence marriage before childbearing was still salient for many millennials. Like others, one couple, Doug and Celeste, suggested that the decision to marry should be centered around children. When asked about their views on the timing of marriage, Doug explained you should get married when you are "mature enough to have kids." Stability seemed to be another common theme for many millennials who expressed these views. Grace, currently in her second marriage, linked marriage with her desire for stability in her children's lives. She explained, "I wouldn't have continued to have kids had I not had somebody that I knew I was going to be with and committed to and all that."

Educational status and socioeconomic resources were key players in how millennials saw the connection between marriage and parenthood. As noted before, research has suggested that much of the upward momentum in the rate of non-marital childbearing is happening among the least educated and lowest socioeconomic segments of the population. For the educated and well-off, marriage

Parenting Within a Me-Marriage   131

and childbearing still appear to go together. I had introduced Ben in some of the early chapters of the book but have yet to mention his wife, Sophia. Sophia was a schoolteacher of low-income children and had a unique perspective on this issue when we interviewed her. She said,

> With teaching elementary school, and I teach at a really, really low-income school, a lot of those kids come from either single-parent homes or have siblings from different dads or different moms. Seeing the lack of stability that comes from that is really shocking for a lot of those kids. I think marriage is really important because I think people function better with other people, and so when you have that long-term commitment that is a legally binding thing, I think a lot of times couples that stay married longer tend to be more involved in other things with their communities. Personally, from my experience, their kids for the most part turn out to have a little more stable home lives.

Sophia isn't wrong in her assessment: stability is a key part of healthy child outcomes (Craigie et al., 2012; Gross et al., 2001) and has long been connected to research suggesting that having married parents does benefit children's well-being (Brown, 2010).

Syed and Marcy had an interesting view of the connection between marriage and children. They had no biological children of their own but had served as foster parents for several children. Marcy felt that their marriage brought a unique benefit to these children, stating,

> One thing that we see with the children that come into our home is that most of them that have been placed in our home were from homes where there were not two-parent families. They haven't been in homes where the two people that may have been in the home were married. So, they get to see that particular dynamic and hopefully they leave with a better perspective of what marriage is or what marriage looks like.

She then shared a specific experience they recently had that, in her mind, confirmed this belief. She added,

> There was this very young child, a toddler, and she really was kind of curious about what marriage was about. The dynamics with a two-parent household— that was something she had never seen before. I think it's those small things that we don't realize make a big difference in the lives of some kids.

But perhaps the best example of this continued strong millennial connection between marriage and parenthood came from Sam and Avery, a couple who expounded on the benefits of open communication in Chapter 4. Theirs was a whirlwind romance. They met on Tinder and connected after messaging for a few days, like Aiden and Ella. While Aiden and Ella had a quicker courtship than most millennials, Sam and Avery were another thing altogether. To say their

132 *Parenting Within a Me-Marriage*

relationship continued at an accelerated rate would be an understatement. Two weeks after meeting, they moved in together. Two weeks after that, they found out they were pregnant and decided to get married. This pregnancy and upcoming wedding created an interesting decision point for them regarding the logistics of the wedding. The wedding was set for when Avery was 8 months pregnant, and she did not want to spend the money on a lavish wedding day and a dress she did not feel comfortable in. So, they went in the opposite direction. As Sam explained,

> We got married in our pajamas in our living room. We got up, got married at 8, went back to bed and spent the day just snuggling, watching TV . . . . We weren't really up for anything other than just kind of relaxing, and you know, rubbing her feet.

A year later they had a larger, more traditional wedding ceremony. So why rush into marriage given their constraints and plans to marry in a "real" ceremony later? For Sam and Avery, there was a push to make their relationship seem more legitimate and create the stability for their new child that other millennials also reference. With Sam, there was a pragmatic element as well. As he added, "It was important we were legally married, should anything have happened at the hospital. I mean, to make decisions. If we weren't legally married." But it was also clear that the first reason, the desire for legitimacy, was also at the top of his mind. He went on to add, "I wanted it to be very clear that, you know, she was born and we were married. So there wasn't any confusion or anything like that." The implication was that the confusion he referenced was in relation to his commitment to Avery. He did not want anyone to think he was not committed to the relationship, and marriage provided a symbolic way to express that commitment.

For Sam and Avery, this link between marriage and parenting was one of the main benefits of marriage and something they continued to reference at other points in their interview. Later, when asked about the importance of marriage, Avery shared, "Like in our case, it was definitely easier to be married when I gave birth to my daughter, just legally speaking, to give him parental rights and have him on the birth certificate. All that was way easier." These examples suggest that, at least for many millennials, the tight connection between marriage and parenthood has not disappeared. The decision to marry and the decision to become a parent were interconnected rather than separate decisions for many.

It was clear in many interviews that this thinking extended not only to decisions about transitioning into marriage but also to decisions about transitioning out of marriage. There was a sense among the couples we interviewed that children still do better within marriage. The stability that marriage affords children was seen as a key factor in the developmental success of children. The importance of a good marriage for parenting appeared to remain strong for most millennials. Lucy, without any children of her own, noted that marriage was needed for children, "because children need two adults for households. They need a good steady relationship to see what relationships should be like for them." This sentiment was echoed by other couples. Omar and Kennedy agreed that marriage is the best relationship arrangement for children, with Omar noting, "Marriage

Parenting Within a Me-Marriage   133

improves the lives of those that are married, but also marriage provides the structure needed to raise the next generation." His wife agreed, adding, "Yes, that would be my thought too. Children need that solid ground to stand on, they need that stability."

As illustrated, many millennials altered their own marital timing simply to keep what they viewed as a critical normative sequence in place. While fertility patterns in much of the world have continued to shift toward less marital childbearing, many millennials appear to be holding firm to this social norm. Many also continue to hold a strong belief in the importance of a strong marital relationship on the health and well-being of children. While millennials have shifted both their marital behaviors and approach to marriage in many ways, these views and attitudes toward the interconnection between marriage and parenthood appear to be one area where millennials look very similar to past generations.

The Timing of Children

Of course, this discussion has largely glossed over an important aspect of this parental transition: the timing and the actual decision to have children. Married millennials in their late 20s and early 30s who have already had children of their own are mostly in the "early" timing category. In most developed countries, first childbirth often happens right around the age of 30 (Livingston, 2018), meaning that many millennials who have opted to become parents already have opted to do so slightly earlier than normal. For our millennial parents and non-parents alike, the decision to have children was discussed with the weight and the significance it held for many of these couples. They understood the resources, time, and sacrifice parenthood required. In me-marriages, marriage is focused on personal goals and ideals, and the concept of sacrifice as tied to parenthood was a challenging one for many to consider. Like with the decision to marry, many millennials expressed concern about becoming parents and the implications such a choice would have on their lives.

Jose, a young and happily married millennial with no children of his own, expressed an almost bewildered attitude when he tried to make sense of trying to balance parenting and marriage. He had a hard time even conceptualizing how being a parent and being married would even be possible. He said,

> I don't know; it's hard because we don't have kids. And when I look at people who do have kids, I'm always like, "How the heck could you handle a marriage and having children at the same time? Like, that's too much." But I don't know, I mean my parents did it. They have a beautiful marriage, they had kids, and they have careers.

He knew through example that this was normal behavior; having children was something a lot of married people did. But being young and married and already struggling trying to balance all the personal goals and hobbies he wanted to continue to do made parenthood seem daunting, a common sentiment among the millennials we spoke to. The mere thought of adding a child to that mix seemed

134 *Parenting Within a Me-Marriage*

too much. Jose went on to rationalize that maybe if your marriage was strong enough, you could make it work, adding, "I don't know why you couldn't have success in parenting. Obviously, I feel the more your marriage is flourishing the more everything else does. Like when our marriage is better, I'm better at work." In the interview there was almost a sense of Jose trying to convince himself that he would be okay if he decided to become a father down the line. The fear of making the parenting plunge too soon was a tangible one for Jose and for many others. As noted in the data presented earlier in the chapter, these millennials have some cause for concern as parenthood does appear to put some strain on marriages.

But despite the concerns of Jose and others, some millennials transitioned into parenthood fairly smoothly. Remember, trends and averages are just that: they represent what average people experience, not everyone. In our interviews, success in the timing and transition to parenthood seemed to be most likely when both spouses had clear, direct, and complementary beliefs about childcare roles, often with one spouse staying at home to manage that part of the couple's life. I already noted that conflict about roles was one of the most common contextual factors that led to decreases in marital quality during the transition to parenthood. Justin and Monique, from previous chapters, were one such successful couple that reported a rather smooth transition and a clear sense of role identity when it came to childcare and parenting. They had a 6-month-old son who was born early in their marriage. They had dated for about a year before getting married, and they found out they were pregnant 6 months after their wedding. Justin explained that they had transitioned into parenthood without much of a hassle, with Monique settling into the role of being the main caregiver. This, in Justin's mind, made the transition a lot easier. He explained,

> I'm glad that Monique's okay being a stay-at-home mom because I know that's something I couldn't do. It's important to me that she has what's important to her and just having her with our son is super important. I think we just are complementary in the way that we just do what we enjoy, you know? I don't cook out of obligation, I do it because I enjoy it. She takes care of the baby really well and does it [because she enjoys it], not because she feels like she has to or because she's in trouble if she doesn't.

Like what scholars have argued for decades, there were many contextual factors that millennials appeared to think were important to help make the decision to become a parent and eventually create the right balance between one's marriage and parenthood. Perhaps the most common factor expressed by the millennials I interviewed was the desire for a period of time between the wedding and having a first child. This time to be alone as a couple was viewed as critical to most millennials, so critical that if you didn't have it, many millennials worried that the transition to parenthood would do irreparable damage to the relationship. Allison, whom I have referenced several times, was one such millennial. Like others, she brought up parenthood in the context of discussing the ideal time to get married. As she put it,

Parenting Within a Me-Marriage 135

I think if you want to have kids, then yes, I think there's an ideal age for marriage. I think it's about 25, because it gives you some time. Your brain is more developed. My mom thought that I was too young because I wasn't yet 25 and my brain was still developing. I don't think it's like a switch that you turn 25 and, all of a sudden, you're ready. But I do think it's important that you, like, have time to grow and understand yourself as an adult, as an individual, so that you understand what you want in a partner. Then, if you are planning to have kids, it's optimal to have kids before you're 30, just, like, for the physical health benefits to both the mom and baby. You then have some time to be together as a married couple before you introduce kids.

For Allison, it was important to give yourself enough time to grow as a couple before attempting to introduce children. She went on to explain that this generalized belief had a very specific effect on her own life plans. She noted,

> Our plan is when I'm almost done with my Ph.D., we're planning to have kids, definitely before I'm 30. So, in the next, like, 2 to 3 years. We will have been married for, like, 4 or 5 years. You need a certain amount of time married before you have kids.

Age and sequencing were important for another reason when it came to parenthood. Many millennials reference 30 as a magic number when it came to fertility, sensing a closing biological window that caused some anxiety for millennials, despite advances in fertility treatments in the last 20 years. Cyrus and Heather were a bit, as they described it, "older" when they met through an online dating site. In their early 30s when they married, they expressed a strong desire to jump right into parenthood, something they both obviously felt was not an option without marriage. When Heather explained what she was looking for when she was dating, she shared this:

> I know that we were both looking for someone that attended church regularly, someone that wanted a relationship with Christ as the center, and then obviously I think that we both had that thought that we wanted to get married and have a family. The thought was, we're going to get married; we're going to have kids. We didn't really have much option on that one . . . I was 31. We had to speed up our life. We got there very quickly as far as everything—we got pregnant within 3 months and then lost that one and then got pregnant again with my son. Now I'm pregnant again!

Later, Cyrus noted that getting married earlier would bring benefits as it would speed up the timetable to parenting. He said,

> One of the advantages of getting married younger is that we can start our kids younger and then you're a younger parent. Because the concern I have is I'm going to be older when he's [their son] only 20-something, so it kind

136 *Parenting Within a Me-Marriage*

of cuts down that time where guys are the healthiest to be able to do certain things with his kids.

Stella, a young mother with a 2-year-old son, expressed a similar sequencing of life and how it had impacted her marital decisions. She explained,

> I intended to have children before I was 30, and I wanted to be married before I had a child. I wanted to be married and have a child before I was 30. Just because the older you get, with women, the more chance of genetic issues with babies, so that's why I had that goal.

These first two themes show the sequencing and timing pressure that many millennials feel. Many still believe in the connection between marriage and parenthood. But they also know that their biological parenting window may be shortened if they delay becoming parents too long into their life. With their desire to delay marriage for personal pursuits and their belief that marriages need several years to develop prior to children being introduced, the window for parenthood often feels tight for many we spoke to. There was a general sense of timing anxiety among many millennials, of wanting to have it all when it came to family life, marriage, and parenting, yet wanting to space out transitions as to not overwhelm their personal life trajectories.

Parenting is Number One and Putting Marriage by the Wayside

The concerns of some millennials that parenthood would change and make marriage more difficult are, as already noted, not unfounded. Turning to the transition to parenthood itself, one thing that was common among married millennials with children was the sense that parenthood had replaced their spousal role as the most important (and stressful) aspect of their lives. Madison, a young mother, laughed when my team asked her to rank her life priorities. She explained, "I think right now parenting is the number one thing that we focus on in our life. Being good parents." Her husband, Caleb, added, "It's stressful." Referencing the balance between marriage and parenting. Nathan and Bella, another couple with young children, had a similar thought. During the interview, Bella said, "For me, our daughter usually comes first, and then our marriage, and then everything else just after that." Her husband? He simply said, "Yeah, I agree with that."

This wasn't a concern for only the parents we spoke to. Many non-parents expressed a very specific fear that children would distract from the happy and successful marriages they were enjoying. For Vivian, who didn't have children yet, the prospect of becoming a mother came with a fear of a changing marital relationship, something she appeared to have thought quite a bit about. She shared,

> That child is going to become your priority. And not that I think the marriage has to suffer because of that, but I think there has to be an understanding that we may not be able to have a date night every week. We'll just be tired at the

Parenting Within a Me-Marriage 137

end of the week or because we're up all night or we have a fussy child or whatever that case may be.

Vivian appeared to have a plan in place to try to fit in this added complexity to her life. She went on to explain how she thought her marriage might survive the arrival of a baby, explaining that part of this was simply mindset, adding,

> I think as long as everybody's in agreement of what's the priority and can understand. I think that's just a part of it, and I think that when you think of family, I don't think you need to separate the family from the marriage. I think the marriage is a part of the family that you're building and creating it. It just may be that there may not be as much alone time for a couple of years, until that child's a little more independent.

This view of the interconnection between marriage and parenthood would be a first step in her mind.

But this "good attitude" did not address the more pressing question on the minds of many non-parent millennials. How would you balance everything? Vivian had an answer for that too. It was all about resource allocation and taking on a mindset of continually shifting priorities. She shared,

> I think there will be times where the focus does shift. You say, "we want to have kids and this is what we want to do," and as long as you're on the same page, I think that marriage is always going to be a focus and important, but it just may not be number one. It may be that we take our date nights, they're just going to kind of die out for a little bit until we can do them again. You find time in other ways.

But what is the reality? The millennials who actually were parents likely had similar plans in mind but often felt like something was slipping away as they focused more and more of their energy into their children. In the interviews we conducted, this change was sometimes met with some resentment among millennial parents, often the male partners who were not doing the majority of the child rearing in the home. For example, Jason and Emery had four young children at home, and Emery noted that Jason was not always thrilled with how much attention and energy the kids took out of her. She noted,

> It's really easy to focus on the kids; I'm totally guilty of it, focusing on the kids too much. Or putting the kids' needs above Jason's. And he's told me before, or reminded me, that you just can't do that. It's really easy to do because the kids are so demanding and they consume so much of my day, but our relationship for sure has to be number one.

I referenced Stella earlier in the chapter as another millennial who believed that children came before marriage and that she had planned to have children prior to 30 to avoid any potential health risks to her children. Stella had been married

138 *Parenting Within a Me-Marriage*

to her husband for 7 years and had a very energetic 2-year-old when we spoke to her. Their son had so much energy that they needed to take turns completing the interview because he simply would not sit still long enough for them to speak to the research team at the same time. Stella was very clear that she felt her role as a parent had overtaken her role as a spouse. She said, "I would say marriage is not first, which sounds awful. My son is first, and work is second, and he's [her husband] last. Which is sad, but that's how it's been lately." Stella seemed frustrated by this admission. She did feel like this priority could shift a little day-to-day, adding,

> I think it all depends on what's going on. Some days work necessarily doesn't need to take priority, so a kid could be one, but sometimes your husband has needs and the kid is fine so you can shift them.

But as she thought about it more, she admitted that her husband's needs rarely did come to the forefront, something she attributed to the unique needs of a child. She added, "I feel like a child is number one because they're helpless. I feel like until the child can do things on their own, they're number one."

Aaron and Hailey provided another excellent example of this line of thinking. They also had some interesting insight into balancing parenting and me-marriage as they had already entered into a parenting stage most millennials my team spoke to had not yet explored: parenting teenagers. They married very young, right out of high school, and started having children immediately. By the time we interviewed them, their three children were entering their teenage years. Like other millennial parents, they agreed that parenting had taken over as the top priority in their lives, but they also perhaps provided a bleaker look at just how far their marriage had fallen down the ladder of priorities over the years. Hailey shared this when asked about her priorities:

> I think that, for me, marriage is, like, third. I put my children first. I put my housework second and then my marriage third. I think it's only because I've been with my partner for so long that I'm comfortable and I know that I don't have to constantly be worrying about it. I can worry about other things and not [the marriage] because it's in a groove, so to speak.

Hailey seemed rather upbeat about her de-prioritization of her marriage. She attributed this to the growth she had witnessed in their marriage over time, quickly explaining that she didn't always have this perspective. She elaborated:

> When we were first married, marriage was the first priority. I won't lie because I was constantly worried about it. I was like, "Is something going wrong? Are we going to last? Is there going to be a divorce?" But, the longer I'm married, the less I worry about it.

I said their perspective was bleak, but perhaps you take Hailey's words as simply a stance that expresses a lot of confidence in her marriage. Perhaps, but I have the benefit of knowing how her husband, Aaron, responded to the same question.

Parenting Within a Me-Marriage 139

When asked where marriage ranked for him, he said this: "I think it's in the top ten. The kids go first." This took both the interviewer and Aaron's wife a bit by surprise. Hailey quickly responded to this answer, "Top ten? Thank you. I'm so glad I'm in your top ten." Her husband was reassuring, "You're in my top ten, don't worry." He then went on to explain what things were higher than marriage in his mind: "You know, the kids and then having money to pay for the things and the job, work." Hailey had a sarcastic addition, "Then his games." Perhaps this is an extreme example, but Hailey and Aaron showed a clear illustration of marriage taking a strong backseat to other priorities over time once children entered the mix.

Unlike Hailey and Aaron, Kayden and Sadie were a younger couple already struggling with some of the same prioritization issues that Hailey and Aaron referenced, but these issues appeared much earlier in their child's life. As a young couple chasing around an energetic young girl, much of this change was simply about time and energy. Kayden shared,

> I think we're a lot more exhausted physically and mentally than we were a couple years ago, just with putting all of the energy on our daughter. I think that's a challenge for us, how to really support [each other] if one person's fallen behind in the housework. I told Sadie a couple days ago that I need to hire someone. I need to sit down and make a list of what we need to get done and I just need to get some help because I'm not going to be able to get all of this done. I think those are kind of the two biggest things I can think of right now. Just not having as much time as we used to, as we are adjusting to that, is a challenge. And then when we feel like we are really falling behind on stuff, coming to the other person and letting them know.

The use of the word challenge by Kayden is a good one that summarizes both the empirical research on parenthood transitions during marriage and how many millennial parents spoke about the transition in their interviews.

As one final example, Nolan and Autumn had two small children and noted that having kids had changed their marriage. They had met in high school but did not have children until 10 years after they started dating. Autumn noted, "I think it's definitely a harder stage of marriage right now with little ones." Nolan agreed, saying, "It's a lot harder." But Autumn was optimistic, sharing, "I think we're pretty good at teamwork. He comes home and I'm like, 'here are the kids.' I need to go away for a minute. We're good at both working together on that, I think." Nolan and Autumn acknowledged the toll that parenting had taken on their marriage, admitting that their relationship was probably no longer the top priority in their life. Autumn shared,

> I mean, I think at this point it's hard. Little kids need so much of you . . . . Marriage kind of takes, I don't want to say a backseat, but it's harder to find a time to connect when you're trying to even just parent . . . . It's more challenging. But I think it's always something that we want to. It's hard to find time for ourselves, but we try to.

140 *Parenting Within a Me-Marriage*

You will notice a theme of time being a precious resource among these millennial parents as they talk about the challenges of parenting and the common theme of parenting overtaking marriage as a top priority in life. Time was perhaps the single most valuable resource for these married couples. Children took a lot of their time, making couple time between spouses almost sacred in nature. As Autumn later said with some frustration, "we don't get a lot of personal time together." In fact, she went into even more detail, expressing specific frustration with the frequency of their physical intimacy, referencing her questionnaire for the study and adding, "I was answering the intimacy questions and I was like, yeah, one time in a month . . . . It's hard with little ones; it's difficult at the moment."

It was clear that the millennial parents we spoke to felt like their role as a parent had shuffled the priorities in their marriage and brought the role of "spouse" down the priority ladder, often regulating it to the number-two spot. But this does not mean that millennials all felt that their healthy relationship was simply a casualty of parenthood. Axel and Mia, whom I mentioned in Chapter 4 as balancing two demanding careers, agreed that becoming parents had put their marriage firmly in the number-two position, but they offered a more optimistic twist on this theme. When asked about priorities, Axel shared,

> I would say I probably rate marriage number two. We are kind of focused on being parents. We almost have a 2-year-old, so we work together on that to make that work the most. I feel very strongly that parenting is a very loving but also a very self-sacrificing thing, so we work together to kind of hold each other up to make sure we are the best parents we can be.

Notice that while Axel believes that his marriage has taken a backseat to the pressures of parenting, he clearly feels the benefits of a solid and stable co-parenting relationship with his wife. Having said that, Axel also expressed a common anxiety of many millennial married parents: What if marriage kept slipping further down the priority list? He wanted to make sure that did not happen, adding,

> It's [marriage] one of those things that you almost expect, you almost expect it to work out, but it requires a lot of maintenance, and if you aren't careful, then it can fall by the wayside. We are trying to make sure it doesn't fall by the wayside.

For her part, Axel's wife, Mia, agreed with most of what he said. She added,

> We still try to check in with each other and make sure that our marriage is doing good. We have a date night when we can get it. I think that is important to being a good parent. Being happy wherever you're at, and if you're in a marriage and you're unhappy, I think your kids will know that. I want to make sure that our marriage is in good working order because I know that that will bleed into how I parent. Like Axel said, I would probably put them neck and neck, with parenting slightly above marriage right now.

Parenting Within a Me-Marriage 141

Mia offers an important insight here, another theme echoed by many millennials we spoke to. I have mentioned in past chapters that many millennials view me-marriage as a relationship that offers personal benefit. You keep your marriage strong and your spouse happy because that offers, in many of their minds, the best opportunity for personal happiness and satisfaction. But Mia's comment offers some perspective on how this view had shifted for many millennial parents. Their desire to maintain and keep their marriage happy has shifted away from being primarily motivated by personal happiness. Instead, this was replaced with a concern that problems in a marriage could make parenting harder or adversely affect children. For millennials, the connection between one's marriage and one's ability to parent was woven into almost everything they said about parenting. Ruby, a new mother of one young daughter, went so far with this thinking that she insisted that her spouse was still her top priority. In her mind, this was critical to her parenting. She explained,

> It's kinda hard being new parents because we're still trying to figure out the murkiness of that. I think I personally place a pretty high priority on our marriage because, at the end of the day, the reason we are family is because we're married. And the reason we have a family is because we're married. So, I'm gonna put my husband's needs and the needs of our marriage above my personal time, which is not always the best thing, let's be honest. Sometimes you need that personal time, and you need to have time for yourself too, so you don't get lost. I think I do place a very high priority on him and my marriage and a very close second would be our daughter. I think that's where I stand.

In Ruby's example, you can sense the unique millennial tug-of-war happening for many parents between a continued desire for personal time and space, a desire for a happy marriage that is personally fulfilling, and a desire to be and stay a good parent. This tension leads many millennial married parents to start to put (or at least desire to put) extra resources and energy into their marriage, energy they perhaps never felt was needed prior to becoming parents.

In Chapter 4 I noted that Jordan and Aubrey had recently sat down to talk about their marriage and making it a priority. For some extra context, much of this was due to the stresses of parenthood. They recently had a new baby and recognized that their marital relationship had taken a backseat. They wanted to reprioritize things. As Aubrey explained,

> I think when we talked about it, we both agreed that even though our child takes up the majority of our time, our relationship should still be our first priority. I explained that it was our relationship that created the child, so our relationship should be priority number one, even though he takes up a lot of our actual physical time. We can still try to make our relationship our first priority.

Jordan was on board with this new direction in their relationship, although he acknowledged, "In practice, it's pretty difficult . . . between him [their son] and

142 *Parenting Within a Me-Marriage*

work, especially with my work stressors. Trying to find a new job and just life in general." But Aubrey was determined, saying, "I think it is hard to make marriage a first priority, but we're trying to work on that more."

This concept of rededicating oneself to one's marriage to reconcile the new focus on children was a common one in our interviews. However, this shift in focus was often a challenge. Thomas and Madelyn, from the last chapter, agreed that they would like to try to reinvest in their marriage but had struggled putting anything into action. Thomas stated, "Honestly, our relationship, as far as marriage goes, kind of had to take a back burner to primaries, like our kids and all that. But if I ever got the opportunity, I'd like to move that up the list." Madelyn also yearned for more time in the day to put resources back into her marriage, sharing,

> I think it's hard because, I make sure my job is taken care of because I'm the manager, so I have the most responsibilities there. I make sure that the kids are taken care of because I have to make sure they have a nice warm place to sleep at night. But in my heart, [my husband] comes before everything else. Our marriage, as far as spending time together and stuff, is on the back burner because there's other things that have to come first. But in the grand scheme of things, he's pretty much it. We just don't get to necessarily focus on our marriage as much as we'd like to. I don't know the last time we had alone time together except for naptime or bedtime, and then we are usually both so tired so we don't do anything anyways.

While a common desire, attempting to keep marriage in the forefront of their minds was difficult for many parents.

Collectively, the story when it comes to married millennials and parenthood appears to be one that is similar in most ways to previous generations. Transitioning to becoming parents is a major stressor and challenge for many millennials, one that can take a toll on both the quality of and the satisfaction with one's marital relationship. However, the data on millennials suggest that many millennial married parents are actually doing quite well, often with relationship quality that is very similar to the quality of non-parents. Many millennials also seem to continue to adhere to long-held normative ideals about the interconnection of marriage and childbearing benefiting children through the stability it offers. There is a lot that is decidedly non-stereotypically millennial and perhaps simply human about how these married couples are approaching parenting.

However, there do appear to be some millennial wrinkles to this formula. The desire of millennials to balance personal happiness across multiple domains in their lives makes parenthood perhaps more challenging and scarier than in generations past, something that may account for the dropping fertility rates seen in many parts of the world. Millennials actively fear the toll parenthood will take on their relationships and feel more personal agency when it comes to deciding on the timing of becoming a parent. Millennials who elect to marry are already a unique group, a collection of individuals who largely believe that marriage will enhance, not distract, from their personal goals. The sacrifice assumed to accompany

Parenting Within a Me-Marriage 143

parenthood puts additional stress into the minds of millennial parents and non-parents alike. Combined with the unique timing pressures millennials find themselves in due to delayed adult transitioning and ticking biological clocks, this stress creates a recipe for another area of life where elevated anxiety may continue to be the norm.

References

Baker, B. L., Blacher, J., Crnic, K. A., & Edelbrock, C. (2002). Behavior problems and parenting stress in families of three-year-old children with and without developmental delays. *American Journal on Mental Retardation, 107,* 433–444.

Bernardi, L., Bollmann, G., Potarca, G., & Rossier, J. (2017). Multidimensionality of well-being and spillover effects across life domains: How do parenthood and personality affect changes in domain-specific satisfaction? *Research in Human Development, 14*(1), 26–51.

Björklund, A., Ginther, D. K., & Sundström, M. (2007). Family structure and child outcomes in the USA and Sweden. *Journal of Population Economics, 20*(1), 183–201.

Boivin, J., Bunting, L., Tsibulsky, I., Kalebic, N., & Harrison, C. (2018). What makes people try to conceive? Findings from the international fertility decision-making study. *Human Reproduction, 6,* 90–101.

Bouchard, G. (2016). Transition to parenthood and relationship satisfaction. *Encyclopedia of Family Studies, 1*–5. https://doi.org/10.1002/9781119085621.wbefs007

Bouchard, G., Boudreau, J., & Hébert, R. (2006). Transition to parenthood and conjugal life: Comparisons between planned and unplanned pregnancies. *Journal of Family Issues, 27,* 1512–1531.

Brown, S. L. (2010). Marriage and child well-being: Research and policy perspectives. *Journal of Marriage and Family, 72,* 1059–1077.

Choi, E. (2016). Marital satisfaction and maternal depressive symptoms among Korean mothers transitioning to parenthood. *Journal of Family Psychology, 30,* 516–521.

Craigie, T. A. L., Brooks-Gunn, J., & Waldfogel, J. (2012). Family structure, family stability and outcomes of five-year-old children. *Families, Relationships and Societies, 1,* 43–61.

deMontigny Gauthier, P., & deMontigny, F. (2013). Conceiving a first child: Fathers' perceptions of contributing elements to their decision. *Journal of Reproductive and Infant Psychology, 31,* 274–284.

Dew, J., & Wilcox, W. B. (2011). If momma ain't happy: Explaining declines in marital satisfaction among new mothers. *Journal of Marriage and Family, 73,* 1–12.

Fomby, P., & Cherlin, A. J. (2007). Family instability and child well-being. *American Sociological Review, 72,* 181–204.

Gross, S. J., Mettelman, B. B., Dye, T. D., & Slagle, T. A. (2001). Impact of family structure and stability on academic outcome in preterm children at 10 years of age. *The Journal of Pediatrics, 138,* 169–175.

Helms-Erikson, H. (2001). Marital quality ten years after the transition to parenthood: Implications of the timing of parenthood and the division of housework. *Journal of Marriage and Family, 63,* 1099–1110.

Howe, T. H., Sheu, C. F., Wang, T. N., & Hsu, Y. W. (2014). Parenting stress in families with very low birth weight preterm infants in early infancy. *Research in Developmental Disabilities, 35,* 1748–1756.

Katz-Wise, S. L., Priess, H. A., & Hyde, J. S. (2010). Gender-role attitudes and behavior across the transition to parenthood. *Developmental Psychology, 46*(1), 18–28.

Keizer, R., Dykstra, P. A., & Poortman, A. R. (2010). The transition to parenthood and well-being: The impact of partner status and work hour transitions. *Journal of Family Psychology*, *24*, 429–438.

Keizer, R., & Schenk, N. (2012). Becoming a parent and relationship satisfaction: A longitudinal dyadic perspective. *Journal of Marriage and Family*, *74*, 759–773.

Le, Y., McDaniel, B. T., Leavitt, C. E., & Feinberg, M. E. (2016). Longitudinal associations between relationship quality and coparenting across the transition to parenthood: A dyadic perspective. *Journal of Family Psychology*, *30*, 918–926.

Lichter, D. T., Michelmore, K., Turner, R. N., & Sassler, S. (2016). Pathways to a stable union? Pregnancy and childbearing among cohabiting and married couples. *Population Research and Policy Review*, *35*, 377–399.

Livingston, G. (2018). *U.S. women are postponing motherhood but not as much as those in most other developed nations.* Pew Research. www.pewresearch.org/fact-tank/2018/06/28/u-s-women-are-postponing-motherhood-but-not-as-much-as-those-in-most-other-developed-nations/

McKenzie, S. K., & Carter, K. (2013). Does transition into parenthood lead to changes in mental health? Findings from three waves of a population based panel study. *Journal of Epidemiology and Community Health*, *67*, 339–345.

Mitnick, D. M., Heyman, R. E., & Smith Slep, A. M. (2009). Changes in relationship satisfaction across the transition to parenthood: A meta-analysis. *Journal of Family Psychology*, *23*, 848–852.

Monte, L. M. (2017, March). *Fertility research brief.* United States Census Bureau. www.census.gov/content/dam/Census/library/publications/2017/demo/p70br-147.pdf

Nomaguchi, K. M., & Milkie, M. A. (2003). Costs and rewards of children: The effects of becoming a parent on adults' lives. *Journal of Marriage and Family*, *65*, 356–374.

OECD (2020). *Share of births outside of marriage.* Organization for Economic Co-operation and Development. www.oecd.org/social/family/SF_2_4_Share_births_outside_marriage.pdf

Perelli-Harris, B., Kreyenfeld, M., Sigle-Rushton, W., Keizer, R., Lappegård, T., Jasilioniene, A., . . . & Di Giulio, P. (2012). Changes in union status during the transition to parenthood in eleven European countries, 1970s to early 2000s. *Population Studies*, *66*, 167–182.

Rosen, N. O., Mooney, K., & Muise, A. (2017). Dyadic empathy predicts sexual and relationship well-being in couples transitioning to parenthood. *Journal of Sex & Marital Therapy*, *43*, 543–559.

Smith, R. D. (2019). Marital fertility patterns and nonmarital birth ratios: An integrated approach. *Genus*, *75*, 1–15.

Stone, L. (March, 2018). No ring, no baby: How marriage trends impact fertility. Institute for Family Studies. https://ifstudies.org/blog/no-ring-no-baby

Switek, M., & Easterlin, R. A. (2018). Life transitions and life satisfaction during young adulthood. *Journal of Happiness Studies*, *19*, 297–314.

Tavares, I. M., Schlagintweit, H. E., Nobre, P. J., & Rosen, N. O. (2019). Sexual well-being and perceived stress in couples transitioning to parenthood: A dyadic analysis. *International Journal of Clinical and Health Psychology*, *19*, 198–208.

Twenge, J. M., Campbell, W. K., & Foster, C. A. (2003). Parenthood and marital satisfaction: A meta-analytic review. *Journal of Marriage and Family*, *65*, 574–583.

8 Religion and Spirituality in Me-Marriages

When Ashley began to seriously date as a young adult, her Christian faith was an important part of her life. Faith in Christ was one of the main criteria Ashley was using while trying to find an eventual marriage partner. At her university, she struggled to find dating partners who shared her faith. Ashley felt that without this commonality, her relationships could go nowhere in the long term. She wanted to marry a man with a similar faith and religious conviction. This created, as she put it, "my shallow dating pool." But she was determined to marry and often would at least give non-religious men a chance. However, as she neared the end of her degree, she was about ready to give up. At the time, she was dating a man who had no real religious beliefs or background and she was ready to be done—maybe with dating altogether. She explained, "I just knew that my faith couldn't be a part of that relationship. I was like, 'this isn't going to work.' So we ended up breaking up." After the breakup, Ashley remained frustrated.

Next, she met Preston, engaging in a brief sexual fling with him at a mutual friend's get-together. Preston was Catholic but was not attending church at the time they met. As he explained, "I was raised Catholic and kind of stopped going to church in college. At that point when we started dating, we weren't going to church regularly." But he was clearly religious and had rather conservative views of marriage. As he explained, "I think . . . marriage is supposed to be between a man and a woman. Other religions can have different perspectives and they're more than welcome to do that." His views on gender were likewise traditional. He noted, "The husband should be the spiritual leader as well as leader of the household." Such a background may have seemed to be exactly what Ashley was looking for, and at first, she was excited about finally finding someone who potentially matched at least some aspects of her religious zeal.

But after a few of their early dates, Ashley felt that Preston was not devoted enough for her to continue the relationship. She felt their relationship was based too much on the physical elements of their relationship. She explained how she came to him, ready to break up. She said, "I was like, 'So, we're going to break up because I need to love Jesus, and this isn't going to work. We need to quit what we're doing.'" But Preston wasn't ready to give up so easily, explaining to Ashley that he too "loved Jesus" and would do what it took to keep the relationship going. Ashley felt a bit stuck. She continued the story, saying, "I was like, dang it; well, we're going to have to go to church then. So, we went to church after that."

146   *Religion and Spirituality in Me-Marriages*

But going to church didn't seem to fix things. Preston was going to church with her but didn't seem to *want* to go. She explained,

> It seriously was all downhill from there. It was just like, well, he's not going anywhere. We're at church together, and it was really weird because he was raised Catholic, and I was just going to bible churches, kind of non-denominational, nothing exciting. And he shows up and he's like, this is crazy. I didn't think it was that exciting, but compared to a Catholic mass, this is free-flowing hippie stuff.

Despite Ashley and Preston having similar beliefs, the expression of their religion was still causing issues.

For Preston's part, he also felt a disconnect with Ashley when it came to religious engagement and practice, explaining, "I felt so out of place all the time in the churches she was dragging me to." To Ashley's credit, she eventually agreed to attend a Catholic mass to help her understand their different backgrounds. As she put it, "Once I went to Catholic mass, I really got it. It was very rigid. This is very routine." Their relationship was on rocky ground, or as Preston put it, "When we first started dating, we weren't in a good place, faith-wise." However, their issues ran deeper than just faith. Preston was unsure if he really wanted a relationship at the time. He noted,

> I can't say I was really looking for dating at the time. When I was in college I was focusing on college. I'd never really been in a serious relationship before her, and when we started seeing each other, I wasn't really looking for anything at that point. It just kind of happened.

Ashley noted the same thing, adding,

> I was really not looking for him; we had actually met about two years before that on my brother's dorm floor. And I remember seeing him from afar. . . . I was dating a friend of his so . . . we knew each other.

Somehow, Preston and Ashley managed to get past these early struggles and eventually became united in an active, non-denominational Christian faith. They married shortly after Preston graduated from college with a degree in engineering. Ashley had also graduated. Now a stay-at-home mom, Ashley said she was "really using that college degree to its fullest extent." When they were interviewed, religion was still at the center of their marriage. Preston noted the important role their religious community had in the trajectory of their engagement and marriage after they had settled on a more unified view of religion. He shared, "We did premarital counseling and everything from a biblical perspective. We've done quite a few Bible studies and everything on marriage. We're going through one together right now and it's really helped to build our marriage."

Preston and Ashley are just one example of the many ways millennials are attempting to make sense of their own spiritual and religious journeys while also

Religion and Spirituality in Me-Marriages   147

attempting to navigate the road toward marriage. In many ways, religion and marriage have been intertwined for generations (see Waite & Lehrer, 2003; Wilcox & Wolfinger, 2007). Millennials are certainly still finding this association to be true in their lives. In some ways, religion appears to hold some millennials back from the generational shift I have been discussing, making them (and their relationships) resemble times of old. As I have alluded to in previous chapters with some of my examples, it was often the religious millennial couples who appeared to engage in marital dynamics (and hold beliefs about marriage generally) that were similar to the baby boomers who preceded them. Religious millennials are also much more likely to get married than non-religious millennials (Lehrer, 2004; Wilcox & Wolfinger, 2007). In our own national study of older millennials, married millennials were more likely to report that religion was important, more likely to attend church regularly, and more likely to pray often compared to never married millennials. This was true even after controlling for several background factors.

Is Religion Still Relevant to Millennials?

Of course, such religious millennials appear to be a dwindling group. There has been much discussion surrounding millennials' retreat from religion (Shimrom, 2018; Riess, 2018). Several sources have noted decreasing religious attendance (Wallace, 2018; Wisniewski, 2015) and less affiliation with religious organizations (Smith et al., 2011) as evidence of a global retreat from religion among the younger generations. While such a dramatic storyline certainly has important nuances and is far from universal (see Willoughby et al., In press), clearly there have been important shifts in the religiosity and spiritualty of millennials that are worth noting.

As I explained, much of the discussion centered on the religious lives of millennials has focused on their behavior. Millennials appear to be retreating from ongoing religious behaviors, such as attending church regularly or praying, and clearly seem to be less inclined to affiliate with a particular religious organization. Religion and religiosity also appear to be an area in which moral relativism, a concept I noted early in this book, has really taken hold. Millennials bristle at how many religious faiths hold beliefs that label certain behavior or people as bad or "sinful." But to call millennials anti-religious would be inaccurate. Most millennials still report a belief in God (Pew Research Center, 2020), and many consider themselves spiritual (Arnett & Jensen, 2002; Singleton, 2012). Religion and spirituality may be changing, but they are far from lost concepts to this generation. For example, Mia, who grew up in a Christian home, had left her church but still considered herself religious. She explained, "We don't go to a Christian church anymore but we lead a spirituality meditation gathering at our house. So I would say that we are definitely spiritual."

Of course, religious scholars would be quick to point out that it is hardly uncommon to see a younger generation appear to leave the religious faith of their families of origin or to desert religion altogether. This pattern of leaving religion only to return again during major family transitions such as marriage and having children is a common phenomenon of generations past (see Marks & Dollahite,

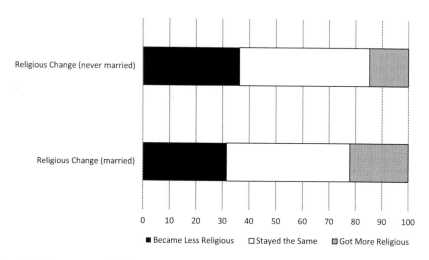

Figure 8.1 Percentage of Self-Reported Religious Change From 18 to 29 for Millennials in Their Early 30s, by Marital Status.

2017; Palkovitz & Palm, 1998). What is less clear is if and how such patterns may be repeating. The simplest explanation about millennial marriages and religion may be that the phenomenon is simply a replication of this long-noted occurrence of marriage being a catalyst to return to religious faith.

Our national study of adults in their early 30s provides some evidence to support this theory. We asked these millennials to report their average church attendance from when they were 18 until their current age. For those who had gotten married during this time span, 31.5% reported a decrease in religious attendance during that time. Never-married millennials reported a slightly larger decrease in religious attendance, with 36.3% reporting a decrease. Perhaps more telling and in line with previous research, among married millennials, 22.2% reported an increase in their religious attendance. This was compared to only 14.7% of never-married millennials who reported a similar increase (see Figure 8.1).

Perhaps millennials' religious retreat can even be partially attributed to their lower marriage rate. If fewer and fewer millennials are marrying, fewer of them are experiencing the common catalyst that was bringing their parents and previous generations back to religious faith. But the data show that, despite the fact that marriage appeared to bring some back to religious faith, the most common trajectory for millennials, both the married and the never married, was away from religion.

In many ways, this discussion of religion and millennial marriage can be broken down into two areas. On the one hand, we have the majority of millennials attempting to navigate their own unique take on religion and spirituality that no longer involves organized religion. Such millennials are attempting to blend this new approach to religion with their new and modern approach to marriage. This

Religion and Spirituality in Me-Marriages   149

approach creates a unique aspect of me-marriage that I will tackle in the next section. On the other hand, we have a smaller group of more traditionally religious millennials that warrants discussion—those who either remained religious or who have returned to faith and are approaching marriage in unique and differing ways than many of their peers. This will be my second focal point of discussion in this chapter as I attempt to help you understand the unique connections between religion and marriage among this unique subgroup of millennials.

Individualized Religion and the Spiritual Disconnect From Marriage

Like with many previous topics we have covered thus far, me-marriages have created a unique spin on the connection between religion and marriage. This has a lot to do with how millennials have transformed the role religion now plays in most of their lives. As mentioned earlier in this chapter, scholarship on the trajectory of religious faith has found that young adults often report a decrease in religious behavior and religiosity before returning to a life of faith upon forming a family. Some millennials (perhaps at an accelerating level) may be following an alternative life path when it comes to religion, one where they gradually fall away from any connection to a religious community and remain disconnected from faith for the rest of their lives. These millennials may label themselves as atheist or agnostic, and religion likely does not play any significant role in their marriages. While many millennials may follow this pattern, religious scholars have noted a new, third option, one not seen in previous generations. This unprecedented path blazes a new trail between embracing organized religion and leaving it behind. This third path is connected to the increasingly individualized nature of the lives of millennials. Millennials appear to desire an ability to adapt their religious faith in a way that maximizes personal benefit and fits their own unique take on the world. Adapting religious faith often means creating a uniquely individualized religious perspective that may combine ideas from multiple faith perspectives or be a combination of traditional faith beliefs and personal interpretations. Some scholars have called this concept "congregations of one" (Arnett & Jensen, 2002) to capture the idea that many millennials have crafted personalized religious faiths that fall outside the traditional concept of faith communities.

Such individualized religion has an interesting impact on the marriages of such millennials. Before jumping into the unique intersections between marriage and religion for religious millennials, I want to take a short detour that focuses on this topic of individualized religion, as it was a common topic in my interviews. Sam and Avery provided a typical example of this individualized approach to spirituality. Avery had a law degree but was staying home to care for their two young children. Sam did not come from a particularly religious home, but Avery had been raised Catholic. However, she was clear that she no longer considered herself Catholic, explaining, "I elected not to continue that particular indoctrination into my adult life." When the topic of religion came up in their interview, both Sam and Avery were adamant that organized religion felt too constraining for them. Sam noted

150 *Religion and Spirituality in Me-Marriages*

that when someone has to put their faith inside of the box of organized religion, "there seems to be a lot of giving up of your own power, your own ability to think, your own personal agency." Sam did feel that spirituality was an important part of this life; he simply felt that organized religion would hamper what he called "his journey." He continued to explain, saying, "You're giving up your control of your own spiritual and emotional journey to somebody that may not care or have your interest at heart." There was a clear sense of distrust in the minds of both Sam and Avery when it came to organized religion. They mentioned God and noted that being spiritual was important to them but felt that spiritualty was best cultivated on the individual level, within their marriage.

As religion has become individualized, the ties between marriage and religion for most millennials have become somewhat vague. Take Hunter and Zoey, a couple I briefly mentioned in Chapter 2. As is typical for millennials, they had been raised in religious homes but considered themselves loosely Christian and more spiritual. Zoey explained it this way: "We're both very liberal Christians, kind of have fallen off going to church but we were married in a church." When asked how marriage was related to their faith, Hunter thought the connection was probably there, but in a rather vague and ambiguous way. He struggled articulating any connection, finally settling on his desire to teach generic moral values to his children. He stated, "I think the values are there [in his religious beliefs]. We want to teach our son and any other future children our religious beliefs as well." But even here, both Hunter and Zoey seemed hesitant to suggest that they would decide the religious beliefs of their children. Zoey immediately chimed in with, "Let them [their children] have the choice." Hunter agreed, adding, "Yeah. I'm not as critical on going to church every Sunday. My beliefs are my own kind of thing." This "own kind of thing" belief system is typical of millennials and their new, individualized approach to religion.

If religion was influencing their marriage, Zoey at first felt any connection was more tied to cultural expectations than any specific beliefs or doctrines. She noted,

> I think that part of that [connection between religion and marriage] is yes, marriage is an institution and a part of religion. So I think that [religion] definitely did influence where we got married and why we wanted to get married.

When pressed a bit more, Zoey felt that perhaps her religious beliefs were tied to marriage when it came to commitment, adding that she felt her religious beliefs dictated that if "you are married to someone, you commit yourself to them for your life." When asked the same question, Hunter said, "I think supporting each other is a big one I got out of it. And honesty with each other." Zoey threw in one more potential connection, "Yeah, love unconditionally." Commitment, honesty, and unconditional love: These hardly feel like attributes that are deeply interconnected with specific religious doctrine. As many millennials have opted for a more individualized set of religious values and beliefs, it may be becoming harder and harder to find specific applications in their lives, marriages or otherwise, that are dictated by such beliefs. On the whole, religion, or even the unique millennial

Religion and Spirituality in Me-Marriages   151

spirituality many embrace, may be having less and less practical connection to their marriages.

The Unique Marriages of Religious Millennials

With that short overview of the majority completed, let me turn the remainder of this chapter over to a more in-depth exploration of the more traditionally religious millennials who have gotten married. While most millennials have veered toward individualized religion, a significant minority still holds religious beliefs and engages in religious practices in ways similar to previous generations. In both my quantitative and qualitative data, many of these couples and individuals appeared distinct compared their non-religious or even spiritual peers. Their outlook and behaviors in marriage suggested a very different marital culture that has some interesting implications for this unique minority group moving forward. While the majority of these trends come from a Christian perspective, we also spoke to some millennial couples from a variety of traditional faith groups. A focused analysis of these interviews revealed four key themes related to how such millennials were either approaching or acting in marriages in ways that appeared in contrast to many of their peers and some of the themes presented earlier in this book.

Dating With a Purpose

The first theme I found regarding how religion influenced the marriages of the religiously devout was regarding how they sought to find their eventual spouse. It was clear as many told their courtship stories that their religious faith shifted their dating and courtship trajectory prior to marriage. This shift often involved the couples taking a greatly accelerated path from dating to marriage and gave them a clearer focus during the dating phase of life. Religious millennials spoke of being almost singularly focused on marriage while dating, and they appeared to be eager to tie the knot once they felt they had found the right partner. Let's return to Justin and Monique, a religious couple I have discussed in previous chapters. Their experience is a good example of this accelerated timetable. Justin met Monique at a local church function and they began dating shortly after. They dated for 4 months before becoming engaged. Their wedding followed 6 months later. As Justin put it, "we didn't really have any setbacks in dating; it was just kind of a really great steady thing." Interestingly, their age of marriage (mid-20s) was similar to that of their non-religious married peers; it was only their courtship timetable that was vastly different.

Victoria was another religious millennial who likewise felt her religious faith made dating more about marriage than anything else. She explained,

> I had superficial relationships in high school, but then once I went through my first serious college breakup, I was like, "Okay, if I'm not ready to get married, then I don't wanna date." So for a while I just focused on my studies, and then, when I was ready, I just decided I wasn't gonna date anyone if they

152   *Religion and Spirituality in Me-Marriages*

didn't want to get married. I made that very evident in whoever started to pursue me. If I was interested in someone, I was like, "The purpose of dating is for marriage."

While Victoria was in no specific hurry to marry in college, she wanted to be clear with any potential suitor that if he wanted to date, he needed be prepared to start talking about marriage quickly.

Some religious millennials felt that they could get "left behind" if they did not focus enough on trying to get married. Mia married at what she considered "old" for marriage, 25. She noted that her highly religious peer circle put a lot of pressure on her to hurry up and find a partner. She explained,

> I think I had a lot of marriage envy the summer I turned 23, or maybe that fall. Because all of my friends, or it felt like all of my friends, were either married or engaged and were graduating, and I had kind of done an alternative path. I had taken a year off of school, so I was graduating behind everyone, and I wasn't dating super seriously. I didn't see myself getting married to the person I was dating in the near future at that time. So yeah, I was disappointed and that added to my stress, like, what's wrong with me? Did I make the wrong choices? Am I a bad Christian? Stuff like that.

Mia identified this time in her life as a turning point, one that would lead to her eventual husband a year later.

There are several potential explanations for this accelerated pace into marriage among religious millennials. One often-cited reason is fairly pragmatic and is tied to one specific aspect of romantic relationships, physical intimacy. Religious young adults are much more likely to abstain from various forms of sexual intimacy (Burris et al., 2009; Hardy & Willoughby, 2017). A desire to accelerate toward marriage and the freedom of sexual intimacy such a union creates for many religious couples may provide some extra motivation to get down the aisle (and into the honeymoon suite!). This was one of the reasons Victoria gave for her marital-focused dating. She said, "because once you start to become close with someone, intimacy follows. Why are you becoming intimate with someone that you wouldn't want to marry?" Another potential explanation lies in the concept of the soul mate, which, while not a new idea, has certainly been embraced by millennials, especially religious ones. One of the hallmarks of the millennial generation has been their emphasis on and desire for a soul mate. Scholars have noted a rising trend among younger cohorts to hold strong beliefs in soul mates and general romanticism (Leslie & Morgan, 2011; Wilcox & Dew, 2010). In some cases, searching for faith and searching for soul mates is intertwined. For religious millennials, soul mate belief often comes in the form of a belief in Godly or divine assistance in finding the partner "God intends." For example, in a 2006 study, researchers found that it was common for religious married couples to believe that there was divine involvement and intervention in their marital lives (Goodman & Dollahite, 2006).

Religion and Spirituality in Me-Marriages 153

Preston and Ashley, from the beginning of the chapter, were a good example of this thinking. Remember, they had a rather turbulent and troubled early relationship as they attempted to navigate their slightly different faith backgrounds. When reflecting on this time, Ashley added this to why she felt like she ended up with Preston. She shared,

> It definitely makes me realize how lucky I am to have somebody that I do truly believe that God put in my life, because there is no reason I should have ended up with him. It makes me think, "Yep, God knew exactly what I needed." And He's like, "There you go. You get him." And I'm forever grateful for that.

Ashley, like several other millennials we spoke to, felt God had put her partner in her path, a sort of divine matchmaking game that Ashley felt helped her overcome some of her early reservations.

Religion's impact on premarital trajectories goes beyond just being tied to the general desire for marriage and a soul mate; it also appears to be a clear priority for religious millennials in selecting an eventual spouse. For some religious millennials, there was a clear sense that religion helped them thin the herd when it came to dating, and they believed this thinning process eventually made marriage easier by creating an environment of shared values. Jackson and MacKenzie, two devout Catholics, explained it this way: MacKenzie noted that her strong religious beliefs were a key factor in whom she would consider dating. She explained that the main attributes she focused on while dating were "core values . . . like, social issues." Why was this important to her? This wasn't just about an underlying set of values she felt were important. She felt this shared value set would make her marriage easier. She explained, "I feel like it's just easier if you already have the same value system, because there's a whole lot that you don't have to talk about, because you already know. . . . There's no argument." This thinning of the dating herd mentality rang true to Jackson too, who noted, "if you go as far as, like, filling out a dating profile by putting 'Catholic,' that eliminates a lot of people." Jackson carried that logic over into the dating pool he was faced with while in college, explaining,

> At the time, our university had, like, 20,000 or 18,000 people. Most of those people were guys, so I'm trying to weed out between 8,000 women. If I say "Catholic," the group was only maybe 40 people. Immediately my dating pool went down very, very quickly.

Jackson alluded to a double-edged sword here, being able to focus on shared values, which he assumed would help create a strong marriage. But also, such a religious-minded focus could drastically limit the dating pool to the point where finding a viable partner seemed difficult.

While these trends are mostly focused on the premarital phase of life (and are less relevant to our main discussion), they are important to note, as they suggest

154 *Religion and Spirituality in Me-Marriages*

that many religious millennials started their marriages from a slightly more marriage-focused and religious-centric view of dating than many of their peers. It is also important because such thinking carried over into the second theme I noted: unlike many of their peers, religious millennials appeared willing to place marriage at the top of their life priority list.

Marriage is Number One

The second theme we found in this group of religious millennials was the strong emphasis they put on marriage itself. This is not to say that all married millennials don't value their marriage, but we have already noted several times how many married millennials are struggling as they attempt to prioritize marriage, career, and other aspirations in their life. I have noted that me-marriages are now largely based on the delicate balance of individual pursuits and interests and are built on a foundation of individual happiness and satisfaction. Many religious millennials, while often ascribing or articulating similar values and thoughts, appeared to place more importance on the marital relationship itself than other millennials did. There was a strong sense of joint purpose among the religious millennials my team interviewed. Justin, one of the most religious men we spoke to, argued that marriage was not just *a* top priority, it was *the* top priority. He stated,

> For me, marriage is *super* important. I would say it tops the priority list. As far as, like, work, school, even being a parent. I think two, like, really big pieces of advice that are super important to us is to not prioritize your kids or anything above your marriage. At first that sounds, like, counterintuitive but it's worked really well for us.

His wife, Monique, seemed to agree. Later in the interview she stated,

> But marriage in general, it literally is, like, the best thing ever, and like Justin said, we put our marriage above everything else except God. We think a lot of people should do that, whether it's over kids and other family members, career, education, stuff like that—our marriage succeeding is literally the most important thing to us.

This "marriage matters at all costs" mentality is a bit in contrast to the more laissez-faire attitude from previous chapters that dominates the minds of most millennials. I noted how both Justin and his wife put their marriage over their children, something almost none of the less religious millennials in my sample did. Religious millennials seemed aware of these new and emerging themes and seemed displeased that marriage was often taking a backseat. Some religious couples seemed to take issue with "others" in their generation whom they often viewed as disrespecting the central importance of marriage. Ava, who grew up Roman Catholic, noted in her interview that, "I think marriage isn't just a con- tract, and I think that in our culture, it is just a contract with people our age. For us [her and her husband], it was a bigger personal commitment too."

Religion and Spirituality in Me-Marriages 155

Returning once more to Ashley, she too had similar struggles with her cohorts. Throughout her interview she referenced "traditional marriage," which, to her, seemed to be centered on what she considered a traditional focus on the importance of one's marital role. She stated,

> I think the traditional form of marriage is still something that's needed. We use marriage as this disposable thing. Like, "It's okay if it didn't work out, we're just going to divorce and just move on with our lives." That just makes me sad, because that's not what it's for. You might as well just date somebody at that point; don't get married.

There was some passion in Ashley's voice, and she seemed genuinely offended by the views of other millennials. She seemed frustrated that anyone would approach marriage with anything less than 100% energy and effort. She continued, "[Marriage] is important, but the traditional version of marriage, where you get married and you're forever."

Jackson and MacKenzie felt similarly, believing that their religious view of marriage set them apart from their peers. They had met at a college ministry program and, as I mentioned earlier, both were devoted Catholics. MacKenzie felt that their religious beliefs put their marriage on a different level than the marriages of most of their peers. She noted in her interview, "For us, marriage is definitely for a different purpose than for someone who doesn't believe in what we believe in. For us, yes, of course it's necessary; it's critical to who we are." Notice how MacKenzie felt like their marriage was qualitatively different than others; it had a different "purpose." It seemed like this purpose may have been tied to what they perceived as the motivations of others to marry. Jackson continued, "for other people, it's for tax purposes; we can just break up and be done. You're not fully committed." He felt his mindset was different, more focused and driven. He added, "I'm not backing out, I'm here, we're going to figure it out! To have that marriage as a decision which is making you fully commit to a person, it's to me tough to have that kind of commitment." Jackson, like other religious millennials, felt that this view elevated not only the purpose of marriage but also his own marriage. He explained that this view influenced "the way that we act in our marriage and our roles that we take in our marriage." There was clearly a sense from Jackson that he felt this type of marriage was preferred compared to the secular marriages of others.

Such a view, that religion elevates marriage in not just importance but also in stature and priority, ties to the scholarly concept of sanctification (Mahoney et al., 2003). Sanctification means to give something divine or spiritual significance and is a common occurrence in the lives of religious millennials. For example, consider sacramental bread or communion. Across Christian faiths, the act of eating bread holds special and spiritual significance because of the religious symbolism tied to it. Marriage can likewise be sanctified in the minds of religious couples. In fact, research has suggested that such sanctification can elevate marital quality and is linked to positive marriage outcomes (Hernandez et al., 2011; Hernandez-Kane & Mahoney, 2018).

156 *Religion and Spirituality in Me-Marriages*

Although our interviews were predominantly with Christians, the connection between spirituality and marriage was not limited to Christian millennials. Allison, a practicing member of the Bahai faith, also noted a connection. She explained,

> I became Bahai as an adult. I think I was 18. The Bahai faith has reinforced the value of marriage for me. It has shifted my understanding of the purpose and the value of marriage in terms of raising kids who know God and using the family as a unit to spread love and unity throughout the community and throughout the world. I guess it's given me some new ideas about marriage but largely reinforced what I already felt about it.

Cyrus, a deeply devoted Christian, was passionate about how his faith connected to the importance of marriage. He believed everyone felt an innate desire for marriage, whether or not they chose to acknowledge it. He said,

> I think, basically, it's [a desire for marriage] ingrained. As humans, I think most people want that relationship. Nowadays, secular humanism and just the wisdom of the world says don't get married; you're best single; and just sleeping around, you don't have to commit to anybody. That's not God's design. When you're a Christian, you have that yearning desire to fulfill God's designs. So, there it is naturally, just by creation. We believe that we would love to be married and share life with one person, committed, have that family, stay close-knit. There's no need to keep seeing all kinds of other people. I think people innately know that if you try to do that—stay single pretty much all your life, or just have a boyfriend or a girlfriend that you're never really married to—life ends up becoming lonely because you never really, truly have that loving commitment. We are just people of commitment, I believe.

This sense of higher commitment was another sub-theme tied to this general principle. Another religious couple, Jeremy and Katie (one Catholic and one Lutheran), felt this deep commitment to each other that they associated with religion. Their slightly differing faith backgrounds made this connection difficult to articulate, but it was clear they both felt faith was a central aspect of what made their marriage work. During the interview, Jeremy said, "I'm pretty sure our marriage is mostly held together with prayers, duct tape, and a strange sense of commitment to each other." That strange sense of commitment was similar to what other religious couples had noted about this "elevated view" of marriage. Later on, Jeremy articulated this commitment in clearer terms when asked why he felt it was important to work out differences in a marriage:

> Because you committed to something! That's why. I mean, if you commit to something, you put your word and your honor and your trustworthiness behind it. And by divorcing, I would say, you failed at your word and your honor and your commitment to love and honor your spouse and to care for and provide for them!

Religion and Spirituality in Me-Marriages 157

This commitment helped save Jeremy and Katie's marriage during the rough voluntary separation of 4 months that I referenced in Chapter 4. As Katie noted,

> A lot of it for me was faith because I was like, "Yeah, I'm really unhappy right now and things are really bad, but I made a promise that I would stay with him." I knew no one would fault me if I said, "Nope! I am up and out of here! I'm done." But I wanted more for myself and for my word to mean more. My word means everything, and a failure to keep that commitment was really important. I mean, had we not been married, we probably wouldn't be together anymore.

Marriage and Sacrifice

A third theme that emerged from our interviews with religious millennial couples was what appeared to be a decidedly different approach to the individual focus at the heart of me-marriages. While many religious millennials still had hints of, or even strong beliefs in, the individualistic nature of modern marriage, for a handful of highly religious millennials, marriage appeared to be a clear marker of service and sacrifice. Their approach and mindset were often actively focused against their own self-interest. In fact, many of these couples appeared to believe that marriage based on self-interest was problematic. This thinking was often tied to religious doctrines associated with suffering and personal sacrifice.

Jose and Joselyn were strong in their Christian faith and drew parallels between their belief in Christ and their marriage. Jose noted a common connection that many of the other Christians reported. He explained, "We're both Christians and we believe in the Bible. The Bible obviously talks a lot about marriage and it gives us this model of Christ loving the church like the groom loved the bride." He admitted that he didn't fully understand all the implications of this New Testament parable, continuing, "I don't think I'll ever fully get that; it's kind of hard to understand the analogy." However, it was clear that he felt this mentality influenced his marital behavior. As he put it,

> What you do see is Christ laying down his life for the church, and in a marriage you make sacrifices for each other. It is a love that is completely unconditional and completely forgiving and completely sacrificial. . . . I don't think you can have a healthy marriage without Christ at the center of it.

Jose clearly resonated with this idea of sacrifice, the idea of giving up oneself for another.

Jose's wife, Joselyn, noted what marriage meant to her, saying,

> Companionship. I think both of us know that there's always at least one other person out there that has our back no matter what, and is putting us first no matter what. We do have friends that will usually have your back and usually be nice to you, but are they willing to sacrifice their own happiness and well-being just for you? To sacrifice their comfort? I think that's one of the biggest

158 *Religion and Spirituality in Me-Marriages*

benefits of marriage, that sense of peace of mind knowing that you are never alone. Knowing that someone always has your back.

Joselyn didn't seem to understand that her belief that a marital partner would give up their comfort or happiness for their spouse was foreign to many other millennials. As I have detailed in previous chapters, the very notion of sacrificing personal happiness in a marriage goes against the very principle of me-marriage that so many millennials currently hold. Marriage is supposed to enrich and increase personal happiness, not detract from it (let alone any notion that this self-sacrifice of personal happiness is actually at the core of what marriage should be about). While most millennials likely understand that some degree of personal sacrifice is needed in marriage, the central and essential nature of sacrifice for religious millennials was very unique.

Victoria, whom I mentioned earlier and who had been married for 7 years, shared a similar thought. She believed that marriage was given by God to help reduce self-focus. She explained this about marriage,

> Well, it's really fun. I think it's just really cool how God uses it to show you how selfish you are. You think you're a pretty laid-back person, and then you get married and you're living alongside someone, and you're like, "Oh, that really annoys me, like, a lot."

Let me pause here and remind you that this concept of annoyance was the very reason most millennials felt you should (a) cohabit prior to marriage and (b) end a relationship if you do in fact find out these "annoying" things about your partner. But for Victoria, such annoyances were needed and important. As she put it, "It's just really refining. It challenges you to be more selfless and to care about the other person, put the other person's needs above your own." Similar to Joselyn, Victoria turned the basic principle of me-marriage upside down. Her marriage wasn't about her at all. It was about sacrificing one's personal happiness for one's partner. Victoria did not seem upset or frustrated by the idea of sacrifice, quite the opposite. She finished her thought saying, "It's great! It's awesome to walk through life with someone and to know that you essentially will never be alone and you have a partner to face life together with."

Violet and Levi, a religious couple with a 4-month-old, provide one final example of this sacrificial element in their marriage. When asked how they navigate decisions and responsibilities in their marriage, Levi explained it this way: "We compromise. Absolutely." He noted that there were various work demands in his life, adding, "There are definitely some things that I have been asked to do at work; there are some things that I have been wanting to help out with at work." But he noted that he had largely decided to ignore these tasks, even the ones he wanted to do. Notice how he elected to word his next explanation. He said, "I just have never been able to [get to those things] because I need to . . . [pause] . . . get to help out with the family." Notice that he quickly revised his wording from "need" to "get." Levi felt that sacrificing work for family and marital obligations was an

Religion and Spirituality in Me-Marriages 159

opportunity. What were these home-based tasks he was sacrificing for? Nothing beyond mundane chores and everyday responsibilities. He said, "I help out with our 4-month-old son because he's still a handful . . . . There [are] priorities at home that take precedence over anything that happens at work."

His wife Violet felt she made similar sacrifices, particularly in her social life. She added,

> For instance, going out with friends and stuff like that. One of the ways that I see us ranking our marriage highest is when it's last minute and someone asks, "let's go." We always ask each other, not necessarily for permission but just out of respect for each other and the fact that we put our marriage first. If something is more needed at home, then we'll just say, "no, sorry, next time," and put our spouse over our friends. Even if it sounds like a lot of fun. That's how we kind of show that it's [the marriage] number one.

For both Violet and Levi, the sacrifices they made—whether at work or with friends—were symbolic sacrifices. Their sacrifices were how they showed themselves and each other that their marriage was their top priority. While religious millennials certainly have not cornered the market on this mentality, religion appears to play some role in this unique marital perspective, especially given that the majority of the millennials we interviewed struggled even listing their marriage as their number one priority.

The Magic Ingredient? The Power of Religious Community

The final theme I noted in the interviews with the more religious millennials was related to the power of social resources within a religious community. While many social networks offer many forms of social support, these couples often noted the specific marital resources that were available to them through their religious communities. For many of them, this took the form of premarital counseling and marriage enrichment courses, something only the religious couples in the sample mentioned. Ashley and Preston were among this group, with Ashley sharing a quote I shared earlier, "You know we did premarital counseling from a biblical perspective; we've done quite a few Bible studies and everything on marriage. We're going through one together right now and it's helped to build our marriage."

Ben and Sophia also attended premarital counseling before getting married. In their case it was with a local pastor, and Sophia explained the important role the counseling played in helping them prepare for marriage. She explained,

> We had premarital counseling—with the pastor that married us—before we got married and it was really intensive and really eye-opening for us. I think he and his wife really helped us see that this is a huge deal, like, this is really big.

Ben likewise felt this counseling was pivotal in their relationship, reshaping how he looked at marriage. He jumped in and added,

160 *Religion and Spirituality in Me-Marriages*

> I would say a large portion of how we think about marriage was going through premarital counseling with the pastor that married us. . . . It helped guide us a lot because our faith does dictate a lot about how we value marriage and how we see marriage.

I call this religious-based relationship education the "magic ingredient" for religious couples. Why? Because decades of research have suggested that such relationship enhancement programs can have strong and important positive effects for couples (Halford & Bodenmann, 2013; Hawkins et al., 2008). Premarital educational programs have been shown to significantly improve the likelihood of success in marriage (Stanley et al., 2006), and relationship education programs have also been shown to improve relationship well-being (Hawkins et al., 2008). The problem with almost all of these forms of education is that couples rarely have access to them, or they at least seem unwilling to access them. Many religious couples, often supported by their faith communities, are encouraged or even required to engage in these types of enrichment activities prior to their church-based wedding or after marrying.

Ava and Liam had a unique experience with this "magic ingredient" of religious-based relationship education. While Ava grew up as a Roman Catholic, Liam did not (instead having a Protestant upbringing). When they were married, they wed in a traditional civil ceremony with friends and family. After their wedding, Liam eventually converted to the Catholic faith. In the process of receiving his religious education to become confirmed, Ava and Liam decided to, likewise, prepare for sacramental marriage. This secondary marital ceremony and the education that accompanied it was a turning point for Liam in his and Ava's marriage. He felt this education elevated their marriage to the next level. He explained,

> It was a different kind of commitment for me. We got married in front of our friends and family. It was my dream to get married where we did and that was important to me. But it [sacramental marriage] was something I didn't know I wanted, which was great and it was a very spiritual experience.

Liam went on to explain how he felt the preparation that went into his "second" marriage to his wife was instrumental in teaching him how to be a more caring and thoughtful spouse.

Marcy and Syed felt that their faith community and the elevated view of marriage that came with it was the only reason they held things together during the first few years of marriage. They had been married for 4 years when they were interviewed and attended a non-denominational Christian church. Syed explained,

> I tell people, if it wasn't for spiritual guidance and our faith and the leaders we have in our church, our colleagues that have been there for us, we probably would already be clearing our divorce papers. When you first come into marriage you just think, "this is too much." You're so intense in those moments and you think that it's always going to be like that when, really, you're going

Religion and Spirituality in Me-Marriages 161

through a valley time and you're going to start going back up from there. Some of the meetings that we've had at our church and stuff [have] kept us together. Because no matter what we go through, we go into our faith community and are able to kind of heal stuff from there.

While many of the religious millennials we spoke to seemed to treasure these general educational moments found in religious communities, there was one other element of this social community that appeared to be critical to many of these couples. This element was the role of informal mentoring in many religious communities. This social resource was less organized but seemingly just as important. Many of the young couples we spoke to mentioned informal mentors who took a keen and direct interest in the success of their marriages. Carter and Aria noted that their faith community group was a large source of strength in their marriage. This influence often came from simply being around older couples and seeing the success of their marriages. When speaking of their faith community and what it brought to their marriage, Carter noted that the personal impact he felt had less to do with any specific religious education and more about what he saw around him. He said,

The biggest thing is teaching. Students aren't gonna remember half the things you said, but they're gonna remember how you acted and how you made them feel. I think that's the same with marriage. We're in a community group that meets weekly. We're the youngest, and I think the oldest couple is in their 60s. To be able to be in a community with them and talk with them and see what they've gone through, it's kind of helped us. They're in a different season of life than we are in marriage, but I think that family's influenced us both.

Victoria shared a similar experience about a pastor and his wife. She shared, "Our pastor at the church I was going to and his wife, they were Jamaican, and they were super hospitable and would have us over all the time." These regular visits had a powerful impact on Victoria. Again, this did not appear to be based on anything that was said or any spiritual guidance that was given. Victoria and her spouse were influenced merely through a positive marital example. She continued,

Their sensitivity towards one another and how they communicated, how they made each other a priority, they just demonstrated what love looks like in good times and in times where they were struggling. When you have people in your home a lot, you can see that more readily than if you're just sitting across the academic desk or just passing each other on church on Sunday or on the street. When you begin to bring people into your home and break down those barriers of communication, then you can see more easily what marriage looks like.

This tangible example of a couple going through ups and downs but remaining committed to each other had stuck with Victoria and changed how she acted toward her husband.

162 *Religion and Spirituality in Me-Marriages*

While other millennials spoke of mentors in their life (often parents) when it came to marriage, the consistency with which religious millennial couples mentioned these experiences suggested that their religious communities were providing perhaps more opportunities to interact and engage with older couples who might provide guidance and socialization of healthy marital practices. Combined with the access to the educational resources I mentioned, this unique combination of resources provided by many religious communities may be at the heart of some of the unique perspectives that religious millennials had about their marriages and the increased priority they seemed to place on them.

An Explosive Glue?

While religion appears to be a strong glue holding many millennial couples together, this glue appeared to be largely contingent on the continued shared faith of partners. Looking back at the patterns I have outlined in this chapter, shared faith is clearly central to many religious millennials. It was often shared faith that brought such couples together while dating, and that same shared faith that gave many a unified and unique perspective on their marital roles. But what would happen if one partner decided to shift their religious perspective at some point during the marriage?

When this question was posed to many such couples, they often quickly came to the same conclusion: It would be disastrous. When asked how their marriage would be affected if one of them left their religious faith, Monique had this to say:

> Having that [shared faith] and then suddenly not having that would just be so heart-breaking to me. A very, like, practical side says that I would find it as a risk to have that with my son if Justin left the church.

Monique is fairly dramatic here, suggesting she wasn't sure she would feel comfortable even raising a child with her husband if he lost his faith. She brought this line of thinking to its inevitable conclusion, adding,

> I don't know if we'd be together because then my son would grow up in a household where I'm afraid he'd get mixed signals, and I want my son to be raised in the church and to have a strong testimony. Seeing divided parents, I'm just not a risk-taker like that. It would be just so heart-breaking, but I don't want to risk, one, becoming casual in my own faith because it's easier when my spouse isn't, and then, two, risking my son and his development.

Notice here that Monique is talking about risk. Apparently to her, the risk of being a single mother was lower than the risk of a marriage without shared faith.

This view on the loss of shared faith was something often articulated by the more religious couples I have shared stories about in this chapter. Victoria was clear that shared religious faith (in her case, Christianity) was a deal breaker in any relationship. When asked about what was important to her in any relationship, she quickly responded, "Obviously he has to be a Christian. That was at the top

Religion and Spirituality in Me-Marriages   163

of the list. And not just taking it lightly, taking it seriously and being committed to the Lord. That was my number one thing." For Victoria, having a husband leave the faith would be undermining the very foundation on which she created the relationship.

Jose and Joselyn expressed a similar idea. Jose said that, when considering Joselyn as his wife, he was looking for a few specific things. He started by saying, "I think it was important to see a servant heart in someone who wasn't just self-absorbed." When asked to follow up on what this meant to him, he acknowledged that these were attributes he ascribed to a specific religious faith, adding, "Well, a big thing was also being a fellow believer with me. Sharing the same faith with Christianity." Like others, Jose felt that not having this shared faith would create a large burden on his marriage. He explained that not having a shared religious faith would "automatically [create] a huge hurdle in your relationship if you're not believing the same things." His wife agreed, adding, "It's just nice."

Taken all together, religion is an interesting moderator and contextual factor for many millennial marriages. For some, perhaps a shrinking minority, religious faith has served as both a boundary that has held back many of the changing tides of me-marriage and a factor that has created some unique marital dynamics not shared by non-religious millennials. For others, religious faith is one more factor millennials are trying to both individualize and balance in a world of changing relational dynamics. Faith, though not the only factor, was one more component that helped some millennials make sense of the confusing relational world around them. Remember, we started this discussion with Preston and Ashley, a religious couple who had met during a one-night stand. Yet this hookup had ended in not only marriage, but in a marriage that has persisted for a decade. They noted their religious identity as a key ingredient to this unique trajectory, with Ashley saying,

> We do feel that God is in our marriage and, like, God ordained this marriage. Because there's no reason we should be together. There's no reason we should have lasted. It was a one-night stand. It should have gone away. It should've been a poor mistake and we should have learned from it and moved on, but nope. God's like, "Oh, I think you two are good." So, here we are.

Such unique perspectives on marriage taken by religious millennials suggest this is a group that may continue to diverge from the majority of their cohort as perhaps they continue to develop and expand on their own unique brand of me-marriage.

References

Arnett, J. J., & Jensen, L. A. (2002). A congregation of one: Individualized religious beliefs among emerging adults. *Journal of Adolescent Research, 17*(5), 451–467.

Burris, J. L., Smith, G. T., & Carlson, C. R. (2009). Relations among religiousness, spirituality, and sexual practices. *Journal of Sex Research, 46*(4), 282–289.

Goodman, M. A., & Dollahite, D. C. (2006). How religious couples perceive the influence of God in their marriage. *Review of Religious Research, 48,* 141–155.

Halford, W. K., & Bodenmann, G. (2013). Effects of relationship education on maintenance of couple relationship satisfaction. *Clinical Psychology Review, 33*(4), 512–525.

Hardy, S. A., & Willoughby, B. J. (2017). Religiosity and chastity among single young adults and married adults. *Psychology of Religion and Spirituality, 9*(3), 285–295.

Hawkins, A. J., Blanchard, V. L., Baldwin, S. A., & Fawcett, E. B. (2008). Does marriage and relationship education work? A meta-analytic study. *Journal of Consulting and Clinical Psychology, 76*(5), 723–734.

Hernandez, K. M., Mahoney, A., & Pargament, K. I. (2011). Sanctification of sexuality: Implications for newlyweds' marital and sexual quality. *Journal of Family Psychology, 25*(5), 775–780.

Hernandez-Kane, K. M., & Mahoney, A. (2018). Sex through a sacred lens: Longitudinal effects of sanctification of marital sexuality. *Journal of Family Psychology, 32*(4), 425–434.

Lehrer, E. L. (2004). Religion as a determinant of economic and demographic behavior in the United States. *Population and Development Review, 30*(4), 707–726.

Leslie, B., & Morgan, M. (2011). Soulmates, compatibility and intimacy: Allied discursive resources in the struggle for relationship satisfaction in the new millennium. *New Ideas in Psychology, 29*(1), 10–23.

Mahoney, A., Pargament, K. I., Murray-Swank, A., & Murray-Swank, N. (2003). Religion and the sanctification of family relationships. *Review of Religious Research, 44*, 220–236.

Marks, L. D., & Dollahite, D. C. (2017). *Religion and families: An introduction.* Routledge.

Palkovitz, R., & Palm, G. (1998). Fatherhood and faith in formation. *The Journal of Men's Studies, 7*, 33–52.

Pew Research Center. (2020). *Younger millennials.* Pew Research Center. www.pewforum.org/religious-landscape-study/generational-cohort/younger-millennial/

Riess, J. (2018, July 16). *Why millennials are really leaving religion (it's not just politics, folks).* PBS. www.pbs.org/wnet/religionandethics/2018/07/16/millennials-really-leaving-religion-not-just-politics-folks/34880/

Shimrom, Y. (2018, June 13). *Losing their religion: Younger adults are less religious, and not only in the U.S.* Religion News Service. https://religionnews.com/2018/06/13/losing-their-religion-younger-adults-are-less-religious-and-not-only-in-the-us/

Singleton, A. (2012). Beyond heaven? Young people and the afterlife. *Journal of Contemporary Religion, 27*(3), 453–468.

Smith, C., Christoffersen, K. Davison, H. & Herzog, P. S. (2011). *Lost in transition: The dark side of emerging adulthood.* Oxford University Press.

Stanley, S. M., Amato, P. R., Johnson, C. A., & Markman, H. J. (2006). Premarital education, marital quality, and marital stability: Findings from a large, random household survey. *Journal of Family Psychology, 20*(1), 117–126.

Waite, L. J., & Lehrer, E. L. (2003). The benefits from marriage and religion in the United States: A comparative analysis. *Population and Development Review, 29*(2), 255–275.

Wallace, J. W. (2018, September 9). *Young Christians are leaving the church – here's why.* Fox News. www.foxnews.com/opinion/young-christians-are-leaving-the-church-heres-why

Wilcox, W. B., & Dew, J. (2010). Is love a flimsy foundation? Soulmate versus institutional models of marriage. *Social Science Research, 39*(5), 687–699.

Wilcox, W. B., & Wolfinger, N. H. (2007). Then comes marriage? Religion, race, and marriage in urban America. *Social Science Research, 36*(2), 569–589.

Willoughby, B. J., Dollahite, D. & Marks, L. (In press). Diverse trajectories at the intersection of religion and sex during emerging adulthood. In M. Van Dulmen & E. Morgan (Eds.) *Sexuality in emerging adulthood.* New York, NY: Oxford University Press.

Wisniewski, M. (2015, November 2). *Americans becoming less religious, especially young adults.* Reuters. www.reuters.com/article/us-usa-religion/americans-becoming-less-religious-especially-young-adults-poll-idUSKCN0SS0AM20151103

9 Gender and a Role-Less Marriage

Simon and Greta both had strong and promising careers, one in education and one in engineering. Both had recently started new jobs within the last two years. Their relationship, however, was one that dated to the middle years of their childhood. They had known each other for a long time, since meeting in a church youth group when they were in the eighth grade. Simon's family moved frequently because of his father's job in the military, so they only lived near Greta for a few years before moving away again. Several years later, Simon moved back into Greta's town and developed a deeper friendship with her in high school. They eventually attended the same local university and started to go on what they jokingly called "friend dates."

As you might imagine, these "friend dates" eventually became real dates, and a romantic relationship bloomed in their later years of college. Once their formal dating relationship was established, and their feelings for each other were clear, things moved fairly rapidly. They were engaged and married within a year. They were a religious couple, with Simon noting that "it felt like God was telling us" to get married when the time came. When my team spoke with Simon and Greta, they had been married for almost two years. Their views on marriage seemed very centered on gender, early in the interview. When asked about the benefits of marriage, both Simon and Greta felt like men and women benefitted in different ways because, as Greta put it, "we think that men and women have different roles in marriage, so the benefits affect those roles." Greta felt that her role, as a woman, was "mostly to support Simon." Her husband's role, on the other hand, was to be in charge. As she put it, "Simon's job is to lead us . . . . Simon has the decision power, and my job is to give support to that." Simon agreed, noting that "it's the wife's job to submit, and it's the husband's job to not make submitting a bad thing." This statement reflects a pretty traditional view of gender, perhaps one that would have been more standard and generally accepted a hundred years ago.

Yet despite this seemingly extreme or even antiquated view of gender roles, the actual day-to-day life of Greta and Simon's marriage seemed at odds with their general perspective on gender. One might expect that Simon would want Greta to engage in traditional feminine roles around the house: cooking, cleaning, and likely preparing for motherhood. But this was not the case. Both were working, and they did not have (nor did they seem in a hurry to have) children. Greta's role as a wife did not seem to be centered on motherhood. In addition, they did

166 *Gender and a Role-Less Marriage*

not seem to have a distinct separation of labor in their home. As Greta explained, "When [we] first got married, I think we decided that [roles] would be shared." It seemed clear that Greta wasn't expected to be the only one cooking and cleaning, but rather that these would be shared tasks. Of course, like many married couples, they realized that some separation of tasks was needed. She continued, "as it started going, we decided that there needed to be more, not assignments, but just an understanding of who does what better than the other." Notice that even when assignments were given, they were based more on merit than on any cultural expectations. Greta seemed to shy away from the suggestion that anyone was "in charge" of anything, despite her earlier description of a male-led home.

Simon chimed in, again suggesting that what they actually did on a day-to-day basis was not determined by him (as the male leader), or even by any semblance of traditional gender roles. Instead, he explained that this task assignment would ebb and flow based on each person's needs. He explained,

> There's definitely times where one of us has a busier week at work or, back when we were at school, has a busier week at school and so one of us would have to take more of the chores that week ….We'd have to rebalance back out.

Both Greta and Simon noted that this arrangement sharply contrasted with their parents' marriages, where clearly defined roles (often based on gender) were the norm. This had caused some minor tension early in their marriage. Greta gave this example:

> When we first got married, I think the biggest issue was grocery shopping. My dad did a lot of the grocery shopping in my house and Simon hates it, so it was just very odd for me to have to do most of that.

Notice why Greta had taken on the grocery shopping—not because the man of the house told her to (at least not that she implied) and not because of skill. No, she did it because her partner "hated" the task. Again, this did not seem to be based on gender or on Simon's demands that she do it. Additionally, the assumption appeared to be that if Greta "hated" a task, it would be Simon's job to do it.

Greta and Simon represent an interesting yet common case when it comes to roles and gender in millennial marriage. On the one hand, they were perhaps the most traditional couple my team interviewed when it came to their stated beliefs about gender and gender roles. Yet their behavior was decidedly unique from that of their parents and oddly ungendered, a pattern of role assignment and implementation that is, as I will illustrate in this chapter, uniquely millennial. The focus of this chapter is this new balancing act of old ideas about gender and gender roles with new millennial cultural ideals of gender neutrality.

Why focus on gender and gender roles? The obvious answer is that no conversation about marriage would be complete without some discussion of gender. Gender studies and scholarship have greatly expanded in the last several decades. Like many topics in the social sciences, studying gender and gender dynamics in relationships has only grown more complex. Issues of gender identity (Matsuno &

Budge, 2017; Perry et al., 2019) and increasing variation and complexities in gender roles and gender expectations (Coltrane, 2000; Jackson & Bussey, 2020) have created a vast diversity of ways in which gender may impact the marital relationships of millennials.

How is gender relevant in the marriages of millennials? I should pause to make a quick but important caveat. While I will address sexual orientation, same-sex couples, and millennial couples in open relationships in the next chapter, you will find this chapter to be largely focused on heterosexual and monogamous relationships between one man and one woman. That decision is largely pragmatic, as most of the research on gender and gender roles among married couples is based on such a heteronormative framework, as is most of my own quantitative and qualitative data.

The changes from previous generations associated with gender roles within millennial marriages have created unique dynamics as millennials wrestle with the continued normative expectations of both men and women while also attempting to reach what they consider a more ideal state of gender neutrality. They are mostly fiercely egalitarian when it comes to how they talk about gender, but they also speak in gendered ways, clearly assuming that men and women have slightly different wants, needs, and expectations when it comes to marriage. Most millennials appear to still recognize the enduring power of gender and sex differences in their marriages. Scholars have long debated the nature vs. nurture elements of gender and sex (Bradshaw & Ellison, 2009; Eagly & Wood, 2013; Fausto-Sterling, 2005) but tend to agree that sex and gender differences do exist. Overall, I personally find compelling evidence that gendered differences arise from both biological and environmental factors. (For example, see Mendelsohn & Karas, 2005, for an interesting examination of cardiovascular gender differences, and see just about any study on the effects of parental socialization on gendered behavior, such as Chaplin et al., 2005, or Fredricks & Eccles, 2005). Regardless, the millennials I spoke with were not interested in a conceptual debate on the nature and origin of gender differences. Instead, they were grappling with how gender influenced their own me-marriages and trying to make sense of gender roles in a marital environment that focuses on individual choice and a growing lack of social norms.

A Role-Less Marriage

The roles (whether explicitly assigned or passively assumed) in marriage that are based on gender have undergone a lot of transition in the last few generations. Almost 30 years ago, Amato and Booth (1995) noted that shifts in gender role beliefs toward more non-traditional roles, then becoming common among women, were potentially impacting marital quality and processes. They found that when wives adopted more non-traditional roles, their perceived marital quality decreased. The opposite was found for husbands. This finding was replicated a few years later (Barber & Axinn, 1998). A few years after that, Thornton and Young-DeMarco (2001) noted a consistent shift across several datasets in attitudes toward more gender equality in marriage and family. Since then, numerous scholars have

168 *Gender and a Role-Less Marriage*

noted that gendered behavior in marriage has continued to change in the last several decades (Coltrane, 2000; Knight & Brinton, 2017), mostly in the direction of more gender equality and less traditionally defined gender roles in families.

While it may be clear that gender roles are less rigid than in generations past, it is less clear how millennials are approaching this new gender landscape in their own marriages. As my team spoke with married couples about issues of gender, it became increasingly obvious that many of them had created a uniquely millennial take on gender roles. Several millennial couples we interviewed spoke of gender roles that had transcended traditional task delegation. These were marriages where roles and tasks had little to do with gender; indeed, many of the couples we spoke to bristled at the thought that tasks should be assigned in any way based on gender. For example, Cole and Serenity, married for about three years, were clear to each other early in their marriage that their relationship was not dictated by gender roles. Serenity noted that she felt some of her married friends were still shackled by traditional gender roles. She said,

> If Cole only works 40 hours one week, he helps a lot with the housework. I think that's essential to any relationship. I have friends who are stay-at-home moms, and the husbands work 40 hours a week, and when they get home they sit down and do nothing and she's still working, and that's unfair.

She viewed the dynamics of her relationship differently, believing that she and her husband had been able to move beyond these rigid roles. She continued, "I think Cole is very good at sharing the load, and he doesn't think that the house and kids are mine because I'm the woman. We don't have gender roles, we split everything fairly equally." Cole agreed, adding, "Even after work at a 12-hour shift I come home and I do my chores real quick. I take the baby and feed her, let [Serenity] get some extra sleep before I go to sleep." As you can see, both Cole and Serenity felt very proud of the equality of their relationship.

Some couples that did have more traditional gender roles seemed frustrated by being stuck in what many, especially women, considered dated gender norms. Aaron and Hailey, a couple I introduced in Chapter 7, both worked but Hailey felt she was often stuck with the traditionally feminine roles in their marriage. When asked if men or women benefited more from marriage, she had a quick and strong answer:

> Men! One hundred percent men! Honestly, I do all the housework. He does help when I tell him specifically what to do, but he gets to play the husband role .... He likes coming home to the wife and children, so to speak.

Aaron thought about interjecting here, likely to try to defend himself. But before he could get a word out, Hailey quickly turned to him and added, "Am I wrong?" His meek response: "I don't know. I haven't thought about it." She apparently disagreed, adding only one word, "Bullcrap!"

Yet, oddly enough, this shift, at least in perception, away from segregated gender roles does not appear to be because millennials are actively attempting to avoid the gender roles of generations past. Instead, it seems tied to a desire to not have "roles" at all in a marriage. Their frustration with assigning roles has less to do with frustrations with gender and more to do with frustrations with assigning *anything* to just one person. Having a role, whether assigned based on gender or other means, implies a structure and inflexibility that is at odds with the personalized nature of me-marriages. Instead, millennials appear to long for *role-less* marriages where tasks inside and outside of the home are not really assigned to anyone.

These "role-less" marriages are ones in which there are no longer clearly defined roles within the marriage. Instead, tasks and roles are fluid and can shift from person to person on any given day. I am about to barrage you with a series of several examples of this concept from my interviews. Many are iterations of the same theme, but it is hard to describe how prevalent this theme was without showing, at least to some extent, how common the language was that millennials used to describe this role-less marriage across a variety of contexts and situations.

Ava and Liam provide a good starting example of this way of thinking. Ava had this to say when asked if assigning roles equally in her marriage was important to her. She said, "It's not important to me at all. I do not care who does the dishes as long as they get done." We followed up and asked how, then, she and her husband figured out who exactly was supposed to get things done. She explained,

> We kind of have an understanding in our relationship . . . . If the grass needs to be mowed, someone's gotta do it, and if I'm able, it doesn't matter, I just do it. That's just kind of my background; we had chores and stuff as a kid, but if you saw it needed to be done, you better do it.

While Ava appeared to attribute this mindset to her childhood, her example rang true for almost all the millennial couples we spoke to.

Couples we interviewed had various ways in which they would negotiate these shifting and transitioning roles. For example, Trevor and Lucy had created a system where one partner could take over a task from the other at any point. What would illicit this change? For them, it was stress. If one spouse was getting frustrated or stressed about their daily tasks, they would let the other spouse know. As Lucy explained,

> I feel like for [assigning roles] we just help if one is struggling and, like you said, if one of us is overbearing it becomes a conversation of, "Hey, this is how I feel about it and this is what I feel like you're doing." We just kind of talk about it if we have a problem.

This conversation was not simply about seeking emotional support. Instead, Lucy explained that these conversations were meant to transition one's roles to the other, a sort of code for letting your partner know it was time to switch up the roles.

Brock and Chelsea, married for about a year and both working when we spoke to them, had a similar arrangement. Brock first explained that he felt they had

170 *Gender and a Role-Less Marriage*

made at least some role assignments based on individual talents and strengths, explaining,

> I think we look at each other's strengths and what we've demonstrated that we're able to do well and what maybe we'll have an aptitude for or a stronger desire to do. And maybe looking at the amount of sweat equity that goes into certain duties or activities. That may equal five other duties in terms of one being super heavy intensive and then somebody else may do five other duties that may amount to that.

Regardless of what you might think of Brock's chore-related math, his wife Chelsea was less convinced that they had clear roles. Rather, like many others, she seemed to think jobs got done more based on convenience rather than aptitude. She followed-up her husband's statement with, "I would say that, depending on what's going on in life, one person might do more housework than the other person. So, for me, it just kind of ebbs and flows depending on what's going on."

Millennials noted repeatedly that marital partners needed to be nimble and observant of their spouse when it came to daily tasks so that they knew when to step in and take over a responsibility. Omar and Kennedy were another couple who spoke of this role-less marriage and the need for keen observation. Kennedy explained that they did not have assigned roles in their marriage. There was no need for them, in her mind. As she put it, "If you see something that needs done, you do it." Omar agreed quickly with this. To them, tasks around the house were not one person's job. As Kennedy further explained, "It's not the responsibility of just one person." It is on this very topic where millennials appear, ironically in some ways, the least me-centric. There was a clear sense from many couples that this role-less marriage arrangement, an arrangement that ignored or defied any traditional sense of gender, was about *joint* and *shared* responsibility. When asked how he and his wife found the right balance in these roles to make sure one person was not being overburdened, Omar said simply, "Just pay attention . . . . When stuff needs to be done and someone's overtaxed, you just step in."

This joint venture was not just about picking up subtle and non-verbal cues from one's spouse. It also involved being open and honest about when you needed help. Trent, married for 2 years, agreed, stating, "If I need help, I ask [my wife] for help. If she needs help, she asks me for help. Otherwise, we just do what needs to be done." Again, there was a clear theme of unity in this process. As I mentioned earlier, while very few of the millennials we spoke to argued that their role-less arrangements were an active rebellion from the gender roles of the past, they clearly seemed negative, in some cases overtly so, about clear divisions of labor for husbands and wives. Trent's wife, Becky, took this notion even further, arguing that dividing tasks or specializing in roles would have a detrimental effect on marriage for anyone, stating, "I feel like if you are dividing labor, you have bigger problems."

Chloe, who had been married for 11 years after a courtship of less than one year, was perhaps the most straightforward about this concept when she explained how roles were assigned in her marriage. She stated,

Gender and a Role-Less Marriage 171

It's more of, it needs to get done, one of us will do it. If dinner needs to be made and I haven't done it, my husband will make it. My husband does most of the yard work, but we've moved and I've started to do a lot of the yard work, mowing the lawn and things.

For many, including myself, this type of fluidity may sound exhausting. But millennials seemed to thrive in this role-less wonderland. Chloe found this type of marriage almost cathartic, noting that, "I think, for me, it's the emotional break. If you want to go do it, then you do it; if you don't want to go do it, then you don't do it."

Was this role-less nature simply based on the small and day-to-day tasks of marriage, like dishes and laundry? It did not appear so from our interviews. This flexibility and genderless role assignment extended for many millennials to larger work–family life decisions as well. For example, Sam and Avery took a stance on careers similar to the one many millennial couples took on dishes. Avery explained that their decisions around who would work and who would stay at home with their first daughter were largely based not on salary, not on individual strengths, and certainly not on gender. They were based on an almost daily reassessment of what each person in the relationship wanted individually. Avery noted that their current arrangement was certainly very fluid. When asked if roles centered on childcare had been static or changed often in her marriage, Avery noted,

It definitely has [changed]. When my daughter was born, after maternity leave, I went back to work, and then when I didn't wanna, he stayed home with her. Then when I didn't wanna be away from her anymore, and I wanted to stay home, then he went to work.

That would seem to create a rather chaotic work situation for both her and her husband, but Avery and Sam seemed fine with that. Avery continued, "And then, when we moved, we both applied to different jobs, and whoever got the job first got to go to work." At the time of the interview, Avery was staying at home and doing the majority of childcare-related tasks. But she was very clear with us that this could change at any time, saying, "If I wanted to go to work tomorrow, I could." Her husband, Sam, immediately chimed in after that, saying, "Yeah, and I would stay home." He paused for just a minute here before adding, after a bit more thought, "I would probably have to give two weeks."

Putting the Me Into Me-Marriage Roles

Of course, it is human nature to fall into pattern and routine. Despite efforts to not assign roles in any official capacity, millennials inevitably create some patterns in their lives, and falling into regular family roles appeared common. Perhaps it is in this more subtle application of role assignment that gender roles may manifest with millennials, not as active choices but as passive patterns that are barely noticed until they are already in place. I thought I would perhaps find that millennials were almost subconsciously adhering to gender roles in these more muted ways. But no,

172 *Gender and a Role-Less Marriage*

this did not appear to be the case. If anything, any pattern that appeared seemed to be random.

Travis, married 10 years, was asked how he had negotiated roles in his marriage with his wife. He acknowledged that he and his wife had regular responsibilities, but had this to say as he explained how they had figured out roles in his marriage:

> I don't think we've negotiated anything! I mean, we both live here, it's our house, we both need to take care of things. If she doesn't do something that needs to be done, I'll end up doing it and vice versa. If I don't do something that needs to be done, she'll do it.

Were roles really so haphazard in their marriage? Surely, they had had some conversations about tasks and roles. When pressed a bit more, he insisted that they rarely talked about roles, saying, "There's never actually any discussion about it. I mean, she'll ask me to do something sometime, like, 'Can you make coffee?' or 'Will you put the clothes in the dryer?' Things like that." The theme here was centered on requests. Rather than having clearly defined roles, millennials appear to rely heavily on the personal requests of their partners.

There is another strong theme of individualism in the assignments of tasks within me-marriage. While there was clearly a sense that tasks in the marriage and home were the responsibility of both partners, there was also a desire for each partner to still be largely maintaining their own personal schedule and life. Yes, these individual tasks may intersect (there was little sense that these millennials were doing laundry or cooking separately), but they seemed to remain *individual* tasks, even if they were for the larger family or partnership. If they needed help in their individual tasks, they asked for it. Let's return to Jose and Joselyn for an example of what could happen if a partner did not request help. Like many couples, they noted a similar pattern in their marriage when it came to role assignment. Joselyn was asked if assigning roles and tasks in a marriage was important. She explained,

> I don't know, I don't think it's super important because I feel like there's times of life where, like, I have a ton going on at work and I'm not gonna be at home as much. I'm going to be out of energy, so he picks up the slack. Or there are times when he has a lot going on or he's traveling or sick, so I pick up the slack. So it doesn't have to be equal all the time.

Joselyn was fine with this non-equal distribution of roles, but there was a point at which she felt this arrangement might become unfair: a situation where one partner could get overburdened but never request help from their partner. If she suddenly found herself with too much of the role burden in her marriage and never asked for her husband's help, her load might start to feel problematic. She noted that it was critical to express these frustrations or risk ending the marriage. As she put it, "I guess I'd be lying if I said that I'd be fine with doing all of it; I would not be fine with that at all." Her husband, Jose, took it a step further, explaining, "Yeah, I'd say a flexible structure is helpful 'cause I think it's a breeding ground for resentment if one person just always feels like they're doing all the things."

Achieving such an arrangement wasn't without difficulties, however. Such ambiguous roles are likely to lead to issues around unclear expectations and a higher probability of unfulfilled jobs. Let's turn back to Lucy, who noted that this role slippage was an issue in her marriage. Like her peers, she stated that what job you got done in marriage was mostly based on "energy levels and stress levels and frustration." But she noted that when one person failed to get a role done because they were tired or stressed, it became a burden on the other person. She explained that this might be frustrating and seemed to connect the frustration to timing—not getting a job done quickly enough if it needed to be done. She gave an example, explaining that one spouse might get angry at another if internal expectations were not met. She explained that anger might arise

> if we are expecting one thing and it's not done, and then we get home where you're expecting to have the dinner done and they only got one thing done and you expected them to get everything done because they had all day.

Travis' wife Isabella noted similar issues, explaining that "sometimes things don't get done, but that's sometimes kind of a miscommunication on timing." In the cases of both Lucy and Isabella, the primary concern appeared to be getting tasks done in a timely way. They both seemed to understand that, without clearly defined roles, this may not happen as much as they hoped. They also both seemed to accept this reality, with Isabella noting later in the discussion that, "It all gets done eventually, maybe just not right away."

Despite some potential difficulties, some millennials felt this role-less arrangement was superior to the more role-defined marriages of previous generations. When speaking to Aliyah, a millennial who worked at the same company as her husband, she noted how her and her husband's dual careers and joint sharing of roles made their marriage happier and healthier than their parents'. She noted that sharing tasks with her husband was critical because "we were not going to repeat their [their parents'] mistakes." What mistakes were these? For Aliya it was the strict adherence to traditional gender roles, especially what she felt was the oppressive nature of traditional female roles. She continued,

> For instance, both our moms were homemakers and stayed at home the whole day. So, from a very young age, I just wanted to go out and cry. Why is it that my father goes outside and my mom doesn't? That's why I'm working, and I think that leads us to not fighting as often as our parents used to, because they didn't have this great balance that we share.

This dynamic of a role-less marriage is interesting in that gender role assignment has been classically connected to power dynamics in relationships. Power (see Blood & Wolfe, 1960; Madden, 1987) refers to decision-making ability in a relationship. Relational scholars have noted that power imbalances can create unhealthy dynamics in relationships (Dunbar, 2004; Worley & Samp, 2016).

174 *Gender and a Role-Less Marriage*

Feminist scholarship has long connected such imbalances to male privilege and institutional inequalities in marriage that allow men to assume more decision-making ability (Rampage, 2002; Yoder & Kahn, 1992). Such findings have always made power dynamics an important component of the gendered scholarship on marriage.

Power imbalances were common in previous generations. If fact, we found one perfect example among our own interviews. Elise and Brandon served as an interesting illustration of these generational differences given their 20-year age gap. While Elise was in her mid-20s and espoused many of the millennial mindsets that have been discussed, her older husband, Brandon, was more of a product of the baby boomer generation. His views of gender roles were similar to a lot of his peers, stating, "Well, the way I run my household, and I'm the one who runs the household, is obviously as the sole provider." Notice his use of the term "my household" to describe his family. Brandon was adamant that, even though his wife did a lot of the jobs for the family, he, as the man, was ultimately in charge. He explained,

> Even though Elise is the female of the house, I still do a chunk of the work at home. I always made sure meals were done, the house was clean, the laundry was done. I made sure the bills were paid, I provided the money, all of our money together. We don't have two separate bank accounts. We have one bank account . . . . I take care of everything. Elise is a stay-at-home mom now. I still don't make her do everything around the house. I don't cook as much because I work a lot, so I'm not home as much to worry about that aspect. But she takes care of the laundry now. I'm the one who pretty much sweeps, mops, you know, takes care of everything else, and financially, we still do the same thing.

In Brandon's mind, Elise was lucky to have him. Brandon did admit that they did talk about decisions together as a partnership, stating, "When it comes to decisions, we both discuss what the decision is to be made." However, he quickly followed this up with this: "Ultimately, it comes down to my decision in the end. Same thing when we're raising the kids is, we discuss it and then I make the ultimate, final decision on what's gonna be done."

Brandon doesn't speak to what all baby-boomer marriages were like, but the concept of a male husband who is ultimately "in charge" of all aspects of "his" home was fairly common in previous generations. But if millennials are increasingly creating marriages that no longer have defined gender roles, how does power operate? Are gendered power imbalances becoming a thing of the past? In our U.S. sample of newlyweds, I did find significant differences between the millennials and the older married couples when it came to perceptions of power imbalances in their relationship. Millennials appeared to report significantly fewer power imbalances in their marriage compared to their older counterparts. These results held after controls for a range of demographic factors, like children, education, and previous marriages. Figure 9.1 shows the raw percentages of married men and women, split by generational cohort, based on whether or not they

Gender and a Role-Less Marriage 175

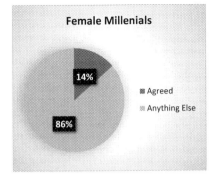
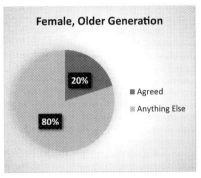
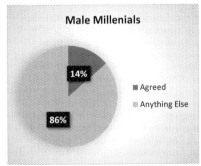
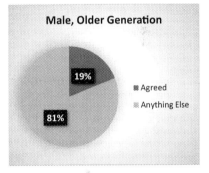

Figure 9.1 Percentage of Newlyweds Who Agreed That Their Marriages Had Power Imbalances, by Gender and Age Cohort.

self-reported or perceived a power imbalance in their marriage. You can see that, for both men and women, about 6% fewer millennials reported power imbalances in their new marriages. While this drop may not be as dramatic as some would expect, it certainly suggests movement in the direction of more perceived equality in decision-making.

Do Men and Women Need Each Other?

If marriage is now indeed becoming generally less role-oriented and specifically less tied to gender and traditional gender roles, how does gender impact millennial marriage? While it is possible that gender's impact on the daily roles of spouses may be diminishing, gender is still on millennials' minds. While it was infrequently mentioned in our conversations about roles and tasks within their marriages, gender did come up in most of the interviews we conducted. In particular, it seemed to be connected in participants' minds to the personal benefits on which me-marriages were centered. If marriage was about personal benefit, the gendered question for many millennials was whether men and women personally benefited differently from marriage. This is a question scholars have asked in the past, often finding that most people believe men benefit from marriage

176　*Gender and a Role-Less Marriage*

more than women (Dempsey, 2002; Kaufman & Goldscheider, 2007). Whereas very few of the millennials we spoke to had much to say when it came to gender and family roles, some had fairly strong opinions when it came to gender and the personal benefits of marriage. Monique was one such woman. She clearly thought that gender impacted the personal benefits derived from marriage. She seemed to have a rather negative view of her own gender as she noted, "Women are mean. They need men. They need men to just love 'em. Women just want so much to be loved." This was one of dozens and dozens of opinions that millennials offered regarding how men and women might benefit differently based on gender differences that millennials perceived. Where they were decidedly gender-neutral when it came to roles and tasks, they were decidedly gendered in this discussion.

Perhaps the most common theme we found was that each gender appeared to assume their own gender benefited the most. I suppose this is not surprising, given how much I have illustrated how me-marriage is very self-focused and that millennials often only marry if they perceive a personal benefit from such relationships. This may simply be another reflection of this me-marriage mindset. Jackson and MacKenzie illustrated this perfectly in their responses to the question, "Who benefits more in marriage, men or women?" They had been married for 7 years and had two young children. Jackson worked full-time and MacKenzie worked part-time from home while handling the majority of the childcare duties. Jackson was clear in his interview that men benefited more from marriage than did women. When asked if he had an opinion, he was direct:

> Men. Because women, in my experience, tend to be more selfless, and men tend to be more oblivious. To me, men don't realize all the things that are being done for them, so obviously if I don't realize, then I'm getting a lot of benefit out of it.

So, men benefited from marriage because Jackson felt it brought a lot of relational benefits to the forefront, perhaps becoming less easy to ignore.

His wife, MacKenzie, felt the opposite. She responded next, saying,

> That's interesting because my thought was women. Because women typically need more of a commitment than men, and marriage is all about commitment. If a woman isn't getting that commitment outside of a marriage, then she wouldn't have that commitment that marriage provides. It seems, like, to women, it would be more beneficial because you would receive confirmation that he really is here for me.

Perhaps there was a bit of projection on the part of both MacKenzie and Jackson when they spoke about men and women generally, but these thoughts—that men are ignorant and women seek commitment—were among the most gendered beliefs expressed during their interview. Many millennials were similar, sharing a variety of stereotypical beliefs about both genders as they discussed the various benefits of marriage.

Gender and a Role-Less Marriage 177

But if there was a pattern in our interviews when it came to the gendered nature of personal benefits to marriage, it seemed to be that slightly more millennials felt that men benefited from marriage more than women. Jess, a religious woman who had been married for 8 years, noted a common explanation for why men need both women and marriage: "People, maybe particularly men, behave better when they're married in ways that are better for society." Her husband, Kevin, agreed that men benefit more from marriage, explaining, "I think it gives men something to focus on besides themselves. That makes them make better choices with their lives." Kevin also had a personal connection to this gendered benefit. He went on to explain,

> For me, personally, it allows me to focus on my career in a way that I can be better focused at work because I can come home and the house is usually well cared for and I don't have to worry too much about it because I have a good spouse that takes care of a lot of the things at home that I would otherwise have to worry about.

Wait. Remember that just a few paragraphs ago I shared that Kevin and his wife, while having a traditional work–home gendered arrangement, claimed that their marriage was "role-less." Yet here, talking about the personal benefits of marriage for men, Kevin slipped into some very stereotypical language. He, as a husband, benefited from marriage because his wife took care of the home. He didn't have to "worry about" that part of his life, something he felt helped him focus on work-related activities. Yet notice the main benefit he described was not that this traditional balance of roles was a benefit to his family holistically or to his partnership with his wife (perhaps delegating different tasks so that collectively things ran more smoothly). No, this benefited, as he put it, "*my* career."

Carter and Aria both agreed that men probably benefited more from marriage because men "need" women. Aria explained, "It's just that, I know so many guys who need help from women, and usually the girls don't." Carter simply laughed in agreement, with Aria quickly adding, "I feel bad saying that." She may have felt bad, but this sentiment appeared somewhat common. Men needed women because men were perceived as a bit of a mess. This fits with current cultural standards regarding men and masculinity. Other researchers have noted both cultural messaging and growing individual perceptions that men are lazy and irresponsible (Bridges & Boyd, 2016; Edin & Kefalas, 2011; Hymowitz, 2011). Some of this cultural messaging has clearly slipped into the minds of millennials, and they have internalized it, as we can see in the ways they discuss the benefits of marriage for men.

While there is not much else to dig into here regarding these beliefs about gendered benefits (our interviews provided dozens of specific benefits for men and women and had little cohesion or connection across interviews), it is certainly worth noting that such gendered language suggests that gender is still a very important and viable construct in the marital lives of millennials, at least in some ways.

Happiness Check!

As I have already mentioned, this role-less marriage concept appears to be heavily intertwined with the personal fulfillment many millennials aspire to have in their marriages. Gender appears to have become less relevant, not because millennials are actively seeking to replace traditional gender roles, but because they simply want to be happy. Some roles, regardless of their traditional gender assignment, may simply detract from that happiness quota that so many millennials are hoping to reach.

It's worth digging a bit deeper into where this happiness comes from and how it connects to gender roles in a marriage. As I illustrated in previous sections, marital roles now appear to largely not be assigned based on skill ("I'm good with numbers") or time ("She has to work late, so I cook") for the millennials I spoke to, but rather happiness and enjoyment. This was a near-universal theme across interviews. In the case of Justin and Monique, one of our religious couples who had a very traditional gender role division, this happiness-based language still crept into the interview. Here's Justin explaining why he works and his wife stays home:

> I think we just are complimentary in the way that we just do what we enjoy. I don't cook out of obligation, I do it because I enjoy it. She takes care of the baby because, I don't know if it's enjoyable for her every day, but she does it based on what she wants to do. It's not because she feels like she has to [or] because she's in trouble if she doesn't.

Despite a traditional arrangement, Justin felt their decisions as a couple were based on enjoyment more than anything else.

Jose and Joselyn were very happy with their role assignments when my team spoke to them. They had clearly defined roles, more so than many of the couples we spoke to. However, yet again this assignment was based on mostly happiness and enjoyment. Joselyn felt they had probably fallen into these roles based on being lucky that their likes and dislikes complemented each other's. Joselyn explained that, "We kind of fell into some things, chore-wise, that we really didn't like to do and a bunch that we didn't mind doing, and I think they kind of lined up really well."

A sense of selfless service again arose among some couples I spoke to as they explained this happiness-driven task assignment. Tied into their overall desire for stress-free relationships, marriage was seen by some couples as a chance to free their partner up from the daily hassles and stress of life. Trevor noted that having an equal workload in a marriage "is very important. You don't want one person to be physically or mentally stressed out about home or work." Lanelle noted in her interview that she hated doing the dishes. The expectation, then, was that her spouse, Denzel, would pick up this task to help her avoid issues that she didn't desire to do. She explained,

> Certain things we don't expect from each other, like I don't wash dishes. Like, that is a thing for me. I knew I had to be with somebody who understood that I don't wash dishes, because I think it's really gross. So it just kind of works.

Gender and a Role-Less Marriage 179

Yet another millennial, Ava, explained that people shouldn't have to do chores they don't like, explaining, "If there's something I really don't like, or [my husband] really doesn't like, like getting gas or doing dishes, then the other just takes it on."

There were many more examples I could point to, but all showed the same theme. Like many aspects of me-marriage for millennials, gender appears to be less and less of a consideration when assigning tasks in marriage, instead being replaced by a strong focus on personal happiness and creating a relationship that helps minimize daily tasks that one dislikes.

Equal Merit Given to Separate Tasks

Of course, some millennials are still adhering to traditional gender roles. In our interviews, I found examples of this, often among the religious couples I spoke to. Even in a society that had made such arrangements more challenging, these traditional millennials seemed to long for the simpler times of the past. Cyrus and Heather, a Christian couple I've mentioned in previous chapters, had been struggling with money since Cyrus fell out of the mortgage business. With one young child at home and another on the way, they now relied mostly on Heather's full-time employment as a behavioral therapist for children. This non-traditional arrangement, with Cyrus functioning mostly as a stay-at-home dad, appeared to weigh on them during the interview. Cyrus explained that after losing his job, he and Heather were forced to decide if he would work a low-paying job and put their son in daycare. Heather needed to work her higher paying job to make sure the bills were covered. He noted that he felt forced into this decision, stating,

> Whatever job I'd have, most of that money would have gone towards paying for daycare. After reflecting on putting this little life in the hands of somebody else for so many hours throughout the week, I don't think I can do that.

So Cyrus decided to become a stay-at-home dad, although Heather chimed in and noted that they both believed "it would just be a temporary thing." But it hadn't been temporary, and Heather could see her husband struggling. She continued,

> It hurts him, you can tell, that he doesn't get to be the one that is providing. And it hurts me that I have to be the one that provides, but we just know that it's not a life-long thing and it is just a temporary thing. I have been very blessed that my type of work, I can consult and I can do 5 hours a week with one company and 10 hours at another, so I can easily go part-time when he gets that kind of money, and I can still be a stay-at-home mom. So, we're living off of the fact that we know that God is going to allow those roles to reverse at some point and, thankfully, he was good enough to agree to be a stay-at-home dad.

It was clear that both Cyrus and Heather were unhappy with their current roles, longing for traditional gender roles that they felt God would provide to them. What about our other more conservative and traditional couples? Did they

180   *Gender and a Role-Less Marriage*

all have similar views as Cyrus and Heather? To be fair, we did speak to several couples who did have very traditional gender roles in their marriages; many were rather religious and did in fact have similar views as Cyrus and Heather. But a role-less marriage was not simply the arrangement for non-traditional or non-religious couples. Even these more traditional couples we spoke to often expressed at least some desire for this new role-less configuration. Take Jess and Kevin for example. Deeply religious, Kevin was finishing dental school and Jess stayed home with their three children. On the surface, they had a very traditional marriage, especially when it came to gender roles. It was clear that they planned to continue this traditional gender arrangement, with Jess at home and Kevin working, well into the future. Yet Jess claimed that despite this current config-uration, each person wasn't really "in charge" of tasks in their marriage. She explained,

> At this point, and maybe it's just because our baby's barely been sleeping and I'm so tired, but I feel like we just have a lot of work and we just do it together. There isn't really a very clear division, it's just when he's at work he's working and I'm doing work here, and then when he's home we just work together with whatever needs to be done. And often, even when he's home he has things from work that he needs to get done and so that's his priority, but he helps with the children and the dishes and whatever needs [to be done]. We just both do whatever needs to be done really.

You can sense some paradox in the way Jess discusses the roles in her marriage. This was a marriage with what seemed like clearly defined roles when it came to nurturing and providing, yet it seemed clear that she did not feel like there were clear gendered lines in their roles, at least on other more mundane tasks, like cleaning and cooking. The feeling from Jess was that, at any given time, their roles might be reversed based on need or individual circumstance.

Syed and Marcy were similar. They were another deeply religious couple who had been married for 4 years when they were interviewed. They had a very trad-itional home when it came to gender roles, with Marcy taking care of the majority of household tasks, even though they didn't have children. They even labeled themselves as "traditional" when it came to gender roles. Yet Syed was very clear that this traditional arrangement could be altered at a moment's notice if it best served his wife's personal goals. He explained,

> but at the same time, if all of a sudden [our roles] had to change, it's not a problem for me. It's not a big issue if my wife had to work more or all of a sudden I had to stay home. We will just sit down again and talk about it and we'll make it happen. It won't be a "no."

Like Jess, Syed felt like his partnership's traditional gender roles were not set in stone or based on any underlying adherence to gender stereotypes. Marcy and Syed seemed desperate to be clear that if gender roles were reversed, they would be just fine with their new arrangement.

Gender and a Role-Less Marriage   181

In this sense, more traditional married millennials appear to be trying to blend the old with the new. They often hold to traditional gender roles, yet they express a clear openness to change and flexibility. Many millennial couples who have fairly traditional gender role divisions in their marriages also appear to be keen on making sure things appear "fair" to outsiders. Looking back to Monique, a fairly religious woman with a young baby who was mostly in charge of maintaining the home while her husband worked, we can see an example of this concern. While she didn't work, herself, she felt it was essential for women in modern marriages to have that capacity. She explained,

> I think, for women, you probably shouldn't get married until you have some way to provide for yourself—should you get divorced or become a widow. I don't think it is healthy for women to just jump into marriage if they want a more traditional household where the man is the breadwinner, but [they] have no skills or education themselves. I would probably object fast and hard to that. But if she has some kind of trade or education that she could provide for herself, then I'd be like, "Sure, whatever age you're at, if it's something that can pay the bills, then you're ready."

This blending of the old with the new continued into her discussion of her current decision-making process with her husband. Later in the interview she shared,

> When [my husband and I] started dating, we had this big thing when we were getting serious that we would never tally-keep with each other. Whether that's with favors or issues we've argued about, we don't bring up the past in a tally-keeping way. Right now I take care of the baby most of the time, especially with him working at night and school during the day. But Justin, he cooks more than I do, and we both share a lot of the domestic responsibilities pretty fairly. It's never something like, "Well, you do this, because I did this"—we volunteer a lot to do stuff for each other. Like, he'll take out the trash without being asked, and I'll put a new bag in without having to say it.

In Monique's example, you can see an interesting blend of new and old when it comes to gender roles. Even while having a more traditional gender role in her home, she was clear that most tasks around the home followed the role-less ideal of so many millennials.

Income Divide?

One final item related to gender and roles emerged in my work with millennial couples that is worth noting. There was some suggestion in my data that perhaps the new ideal of role-less marriage was facilitated by the privilege of class. Some of the couples I spoke to who, based on reported household income, were middle-class or lower had a slightly different perspective on splitting roles in a marriage. For example, Cole and Serenity, from earlier in the chapter, were both trying to

182 *Gender and a Role-Less Marriage*

make ends meet with fairly low-paying jobs. Cole worked long hours in a warehouse, sometimes pushing over 60 hours per week. This influenced how they viewed their roles. As Serenity explained,

> I think it's essential that you divide things equally so one person isn't carrying the brunt of everything. It depends on what's going on 'cause when he's working 80 hours a week and I'm not working, I'm going to carry more of the load of caregiving. Taking care of children and the house. But at the same time everyone needs to contribute something.

It was clear that Cole and Serenity didn't feel the same freedom that many of their peers did when it came to assigning roles. Serenity continued, "I think Cole is very good at sharing the load and he doesn't think that, 'the house and kids are yours cause you're the woman.' We don't have gender roles, we split everything fairly equally." Even here there were elements of a role-less marriage. As she later explained, she would prefer to just "split up who wants to, who wants what, you know?" Yet here was a heightened sense of fatigue in their interview that was not apparent in others. A sense that personal desire and happiness, which seemed like such important factors that had overtaken gender roles in so many cases, simply did not feel like options.

While my own data do not provide enough variation in class to fully explore some these differences, I do think they are worth noting for future exploration. Like so many other elements of our modern culture, perhaps the role-less, gender-neutral marriage that many millennials appear to be moving toward is a partially class-based movement.

References

Amato, P., & Booth, A. (1995). Changes in gender role attitudes and perceived marital quality. *American Sociological Review, 60*, 58–66.

Barber, J. S., & Axinn, W. G. (1998). Gender role attitudes and marriage among young women. *The Sociological Quarterly, 39*, 11–31.

Blood, R. O., & Wolfe, D. M. (1960). *Husbands and wives: The dynamics of modern living.* Macmillan.

Bradshaw, M., & Ellison, C. G. (2009). The nature-nurture debate is over, and both sides lost! Implications for understanding gender differences in religiosity. *Journal for the Scientific Study of Religion, 48*, 241–251.

Bridges, T., & Boyd, M. L. (2016). On the marriageability of men. *Sociology Compass, 10*, 48–64.

Chaplin, T. M., Cole, P. M., & Zahn-Waxler, C. (2005). Parental socialization of emotion expression: Gender differences and relations to child adjustment. *Emotion, 5*, 80–88.

Coltrane, S. (2000). Research on household labor: Modeling and measuring the social embeddedness of routine family work. *Journal of Marriage and Family, 62*(4), 1208–1233.

Dempsey, K. (2002). Who gets the best deal from marriage: Women or men? *Journal of Sociology, 38*(2), 91–110.

Dunbar, N. E. (2004). Dyadic power theory: Constructing a communication-based theory of relational power. *Journal of Family Communication, 4*, 235–248.

Eagly, A. H., & Wood, W. (2013). The nature–nurture debates: 25 years of challenges in understanding the psychology of gender. *Perspectives on Psychological Science, 8*(3), 340–357.

Edin, K., & Kefalas, M. (2011). *Promises I can keep: Why poor women put motherhood before marriage.* University of California Press.

Fausto-Sterling, A. (2005). The problem with sex/gender and nature/nurture. In G. Bendelow, L. Birke, & S. Williams (Eds.), *Debating biology* (pp. 133–142). Routledge.

Fredricks, J. A., & Eccles, J. S. (2005). Family socialization, gender, and sport motivation and involvement. *Journal of Sport and Exercise Psychology, 27*(1), 3–31.

Hymowitz, K. S. (2011). *Manning up: How the rise of women has turned men into boys.* Basic Books.

Jackson, E. F., & Bussey, K. (2020). Under pressure: Differentiating adolescents' expectations regarding stereotypic masculine and feminine behavior. *Sex Roles.* https://doi.org/10.1007/s11199-019-01113-0

Kaufman, G., & Goldscheider, F. (2007). Do men "need" a spouse more than women?: Perceptions of the importance of marriage for men and women. *The Sociological Quarterly, 48*(1), 29–46.

Knight, C. R., & Brinton, M. C. (2017). One egalitarianism or several? Two decades of gender-role attitude change in Europe. *American Journal of Sociology, 122*(5), 1485–1532.

Madden, M. E. (1987). Perceived control and power in marriage: A study of marital decision making and task performance. *Personality and Social Psychology Bulletin, 13*(1), 73–82.

Matsuno, E., & Budge, S. L. (2017). Non-binary/genderqueer identities: A critical review of the literature. *Current Sexual Health Reports, 9*(3), 116–120.

Mendelsohn, M. E., & Karas, R. H. (2005). Molecular and cellular basis of cardiovascular gender differences. *Science, 308*, 1583–1587.

Perry, D. G., Pauletti, R. E., & Cooper, P. J. (2019). Gender identity in childhood: A review of the literature. *International Journal of Behavioral Development, 43*(4), 289–304.

Rampage, C. (2002). Marriage in the 20th century: A feminist perspective. *Family Process, 41*(2), 261–268.

Thornton, A., & Young-DeMarco, L. (2001). Four decades of trends in attitudes toward family issues in the United States: The 1960s through the 1990s. *Journal of Marriage and Family, 63*(4), 1009–1037.

Worley, T. R., & Samp, J. A. (2016). Gendered associations of decision-making power, topic avoidance, and relational satisfaction: A differential influence model. *Communication Reports, 29*(1), 1–12.

Yoder, J. D., & Kahn, A. S. (1992). Toward a feminist understanding of women and power. *Psychology of Women Quarterly, 16*(4), 381–388.

10 Modern Diversity in Marriage

Most social science, by its very nature and methods, is about what most people do. We are drawn to the statistical mean, to what we think of and perceive as normal. This draw to be "like others" is at the very heart of culture and many of our human interactions. In the social sciences, our measures of central tendency, the focal point of most quantitative exploration, are designed to assist us in understanding what is typical within a certain population. Even when social scientists investigate diverse groups that fall outside the norm, we are often still interested in what is "normal" or "average" within that subpopulation. That's a long-winded way of saying that any social science endeavor naturally tends to make broad conclusions and assumptions. The optimist would say that this is because we, as social scientists, want to write things that impact as many people as possible. The cynic would say that we are perhaps also writing in a way that does not directly apply to anyone. All of us, to some extent, fall outside of the norm.

This exploration of millennial marriage has been no different. In my effort to capture the essence of what millennial marriage looks like and whether or not it benefits millennials, I have largely been exploring what it looks like for *most* millennials. As I mentioned early on in this book, this approach, while helpful in painting broad brushstrokes on the topic, has major limitations in that it provides little perspective on minority or underrepresented groups, and it may therefore have little relevance to them. But this diversity in marriage is important to acknowledge, not only because it can further contextualize the themes of the majority, but also because this recognition shines an important light on strengths and challenges within minority groups. These strengths and challenges open important lines of inquiry to any scholars looking to weave a full tapestry of millennial marriage based on some of the more mainline themes I have presented.

Exploring diversity is my goal in this final content chapter, before I end this book with a summary chapter outlining the themes and takeaways from this exploration into me-marriage. My hope here is not to somehow do justice to the diversity of millennial marriages in one short chapter. That would be selling the unique aspects of such diversity short: The issues of race, sexual orientation, and poverty could each easily fill their own chapter. No, my focus remains on the broad themes of millennial marriage. And so, instead of attempting to hit on all aspects of diversity, I will summarize and contextualize a few issues of diversity that I think are important avenues of future scholarship. I have selected these

Modern Diversity in Marriage   185

topics because I believe they do and will impact what is deemed "normative" in marriage for millennials. In that way, the focus here is not to explore the ins and outs of diverse millennial marriages but rather to note some of the unique themes across a few diverse groups and how these themes relate to some of the larger ones I have noted in previous parts of this book. I have decided to focus on three areas in this chapter. I start by first highlighting the growing research on same-sex relationships and discuss some of the challenges these millennials are facing as the first generation of sexual minorities with equal access to legal marriage. I then provide an overview of issues related to interracial and cross-cultural marital relationships, issues that millennials are increasingly likely to experience. I end the chapter by briefly highlighting the growing research on non-monogamy and marriage, a new area largely being driven and constructed by some millennials' unique approaches to relationships.

Same-Sex Relationships and Sexual Minorities

Perhaps no area of diversity has received as much attention in the last two decades as same-sex marriage. To say that this issue captured the attention of the general public would be vastly underselling the unique cultural touchpoint the topic has become over the last 20 years. In the United States alone, the amount of public policy and media attention dedicated to same-sex marriage has been enormous, especially in the years leading to the striking down of sections of the Defense of Marriage Act (DOMA) by the U.S. Supreme Court and the Court's decision in *Obergefell v. Hodges*, the case that legalized same-sex marriage in the United States. This mirrored similar policy trends in a variety of countries in both the eastern and western hemispheres (Perper, 2019; Pew Research Center, 2019). In many ways, it was *the* family and marriage issue that defined the first decade of the new millennium.

On the social science front, much of the focus (I might even say obsession, given the strong feelings and opinions tied to such research) was on differences between same-sex and opposite-sex couples (Joyner et al., 2019; Ketcham & Bennett, 2019; Roisman et al., 2008; Rosenfeld, 2014). To date, most of this research has yielded similar results—mostly that very few, if any, differences appear to exist between same-sex relationships and opposite-sex relationships. Joyner and colleagues (2019) found that same-sex relationships have similar levels of satisfaction, commitment, and emotional intimacy compared to those of other couples. Other studies have even suggested that same-sex relationships may be healthier in some ways than relationships of opposite-sex couples (Ellis & Davis, 2017; Garcia & Umberson, 2019). This may especially be the case for lesbian couples (Roisman et al., 2008). Research has also shown that sexual minorities experience many of the same marriage benefits that I have discussed at various points in this book (Solazzo et al., 2020). One possible exception to this rule may lie in stability. Some studies have suggested that same-sex relationships may be slightly less stable than those of opposite-sex couples (Lau, 2012; Manning et al., 2016). However, many scholars believe such differences may simply be due to the inaccessibility of legal marriage at the time that most of these data were

186 *Modern Diversity in Marriage*

collected (see Rosenfeld, 2014). With marriage now legal for same-sex couples, the assumption is that their marriage stability will rise to match the stability levels seen in heterosexual couples.

In other words, although scholars have acknowledged that relational processes likely differ based on the gender composition of couples, the general consensus is that sexual orientation does not appear to drastically influence much when it comes to how marriage operates or which outcomes are associated with it. Differences that do appear may be largely due to stigmas faced by sexual minorities, which have been linked to poorer relationship functioning (Doyle & Molix, 2015). It may be tempting, then, to think that this issue simply does not matter when it comes to discussing millennial marriage. If little difference exists based on sexual orientation, why bother making a point of discussing it? In my mind, there is a very important reason to focus some time on this issue: It will give us a better understanding of the unique place that millennials hold in history when it comes to the legalization and cultural acceptance of same-sex marriage.

Millennials grew up in the heart of this public debate, most of them young adults and dating when the most vicious and heated public deliberations on equal rights and equal love were occurring. In many ways, their dating lives were partially framed by this debate, regardless of their own sexual orientation. I remember teaching many undergraduate students during this time who were pondering the very meaning of love and the basic human yearning for connection and romance, largely due to these debates. For millennials who identified as a sexual minority, their relational trajectory was directly influenced by both the possibility of impending policy changes and the ambiguity of whether or not policy changes would ever occur. Many of these millennials dated in a period in which their marital options were limited and unclear. Yet, by the time most were of the age where they would typically be considering marriage, marriage was suddenly an option, one that none of their older peers had.

In this way, millennials in same-sex marriages are pioneers. They represent the first cohort to have access to marriage at roughly the normative age of marriage. So, what do their marriages look like? Are they still no different than heterosexual marriages? In the sample of newlywed millennial couples I have utilized throughout this book, same-sex married couples looked demographically very similar to other millennial couples. They were similarly educated and had similar family backgrounds. Same-sex couples tended to be a little older and were less likely to have children or to have been married previously (the latter likely due to the newly minted legal status of same-sex marriage when these data were collected). Scholars have noted that fertility patterns and other demographic markers are often different among same-sex couples (U.S. Census Bureau, 2017), so these differences were not surprising. But I was more interested in outcomes rather than demographics. So, in this sample of newlywed millennials, I explored differences between those in same-sex and opposite-sex marriages. Keep in mind, the sample of same-sex marriages in this particular dataset was small (N = 68), a constant problem for most research in this area. Due to this small size, comparisons should be interpreted with some caution.

Modern Diversity in Marriage 187

As in previous analyses in this book, I controlled for the usual demographic factors, even though there appeared to be no differences among the couples in this area. I first looked at some individual health outcomes and largely did not find any differences, as expected. The one exception was with men's depression. I did find that men in same-sex relationships were slightly more likely to report higher ($p = .04$) rates of depressive symptoms (same-sex estimated average $= 1.77$; opposite-sex estimated average $= 1.64$). In the result that is perhaps the most pertinent to the historical debate on this topic, I found no differences at all in relationship quality. Across stability, satisfaction, conflict, and sexual satisfaction, millennial married couples in same-sex and opposite-sex relationships looked essentially the same. In fact, the only relational process where I found differences was in sexual frequency. Here, opposite-sex partners reported significantly higher sexual frequency after controls ($p < .001$) than did same-sex partners.

Of course, this exploration is making some assumptions on sexual orientation differences based solely on the gender composition of the couple. As a robustness check, I also repeated the same analysis, this time not based on the gender of each partner, but on whether an individual reported anything other than a heterosexual orientation, regardless of gender. While I could not do this analysis with the newlywed sample, I could do this with the national sample of millennials in their early 30s. I did not have partner data for this sample, meaning I did not know if they were married to someone of the same gender or not. But I was able to split the married millennial sample into two groups based on whether they reported a heterosexual orientation or anything else. That gave me about 200 married millennials who reported a minority sexual orientation. Again, this does not assume their spouse was of the same gender. Looking at a similar slate of outcomes, and again with all the normal controls, I again found no differences in some areas, particularly in relationship quality, where heterosexuals and others did not differ on relationship satisfaction or stability. I also found no differences in health outcomes like BMI or satisfaction with overall health.

I did find some differences, however. Life satisfaction was significantly different across groups, with the minority sexual-orientation group reporting significantly ($p < .001$) lower (estimated mean: 2.72) life satisfaction than heterosexual married millennials (estimated mean: 2.94). Similar to the newlywed dataset, non-heterosexual married individuals also reported significantly higher depressive symptom rates (non-heterosexual estimated mean: $= 2.70$; heterosexual estimated mean: $= 2.40, p < .001$). I also found differences in sexual satisfaction (heterosexual estimated mean: $= 3.89$; non-heterosexual estimated mean: $= 3.68$, $p = .015$) and sexual frequency (heterosexual estimated mean: $= 4.00$; non-heterosexual estimated mean: $= 3.71, p = .005$), with heterosexual individuals reporting higher sexual frequency and better sexual satisfaction. These results mirror some of the differences I saw among newlyweds based on gender.

Overall, these data paint a picture where sexual orientation does not appear to be a major factor when it comes to millennials' marriage outcomes. However, a few small but consistent effects suggest some disadvantage to same-sex marriages and the individuals within them. Keep in mind, these effects do not mean that

188 *Modern Diversity in Marriage*

same-sex marriages or the individuals within them are necessarily weaker. Scholars have long noted that minority stress (Meyer, 2003) and other factors of discrimination may be the main causes of these outcomes. In addition, some of the outcomes seen in the national sample of individuals may simply be due to sexual-orientation minorities being in heterosexual marriages because of either religious or cultural pressures. Regardless, these results do suggest that these disadvantages remain a viable and important area of future study.

But let us get back to the main point here, about the pioneering aspect of same-sex marriage for millennials. With their distinctive historical situation, what are some of the unique aspects of same-sex marriage for millennials? While millennial same-sex couples can now enjoy the benefits of legal marriage, they still likely face unique challenges. This was clear in the few interviews my team conducted with couples where one or both partners identified as non-heterosexual. Whitney, married for several years to her female partner, noted that in her view, while she and her partner had access to marriage, it was an unequal marriage compared to other millennials. She stated,

> [Marriage] comes with a lot of protections and so that's helpful in a lot of ways. It's still not totally equal, because we have kids and in a same-sex marriage we still have to do other things like adoption that other parents don't have to do when they're legally married. So that's frustrating.

On the positive side, Whitney seemed fixated on the legal protections marriage gave her. She felt these legal protections and the legal status of their relationship in general created a different level of commitment than other unions. She continued in her interview, saying marriage mattered because

> it provides a lot of legal protections that people don't always think of. It makes it a little bit harder to end a relationship. You have to at least try a little bit when things get hard, even if it's just for the sake of not getting divorced, you still have to put forth a little effort.

Whitney's sense that all might not still be equal in me-marriage for same-sex couples is not unique. Those that fall outside of the normative heterosexual orientation of marriage still often feel marginalized by their status. Despite the legalization of same-sex marriage in the United States and other countries around the world, the recent history of these changes has not provided individuals with much in the way of clear role models or expectations. Remember, millennials have no older married cohorts to look to in order to help them figure out what a same-sex marriage even looks like. For some, marriage was simply a relic of a past that was no longer relevant, even if they partook of it.

Alexis, a millennial who identified as non-heterosexual but was married to a man, felt that marriage was still a very heteronormative relationship. She explained,

> When we first got married, I was fresh out of high school pretty much. We went from 18 to a marriage license being the ultimate declaration of love. We

Modern Diversity in Marriage   189

decided that we wanted to be together forever. And now, if anything were to happen between us, I don't know that I would ever do it again. When I look at marriage now, it's great for people who are in, like, a heteronormative relationship. But for everybody else, it's not the same.

Alexis did not elaborate much on which aspect of marriage was not meeting her expectations, but she alluded to the fact that it was related to expectations around gender roles. While probably not the best or even most appropriate analogy, Alexis launched into a comparison that helped make sense of this disparity in her head. She added, "Like, for disabled people. Based on certain circumstances, like disability checks or insurance reasons, they won't be able to get married without losing all of those benefits." Alexis noted that, given their unique situation, she was not sure if she would get married if she had to do it again. She shared, "It's nice to have the benefits of marriage. But at this point . . . I don't know if I would ever do it again." Her husband, Leo, likewise seemed to have a certain disdain for marriage, noting,

> You can get all the benefits you get from being married currently under another document, under another legally binding thing. It could change a lot of things for other people. Leave marriage to be something that people who are religious feel they have to do for their beliefs.

Among the non-heterosexual couples and individuals my team spoke to, there was a strong theme of feeling out of place and lost in marriage, even if it was legal. This was the case for Natalie and Lucas. Natalie and Lucas both identified as queer, and Natalie came out to her husband Lucas after several years of casually dating. She noted in her interview that when she was younger, she felt she might never end up in a committed or married relationship. She shared,

> [My husband and I] are both queer. So, when I came out [to my friends], I was like, there it goes, I might never be in a serious relationship because I didn't know any models for what that looked like. I was basically like, "who knows what is going to happen?"

Her partner, Lucas, felt much the same way growing up in terms of sensing a lack of mentors and examples. Later in their interview, talking about influences in his life on marriage, he shared, "Growing up a queer kid, I didn't know that I would ever get married. Marriage was never something that really played into my early years or my early conceptions of what I thought my life would be like."

This belief expressed by Natalie and Lucas was not unusual. I have spoken to many minority sexual-orientation young adults over the years who have expressed a similar belief in their lack of long-term relationship prospects for much the same reason as Natalie: they simply had never been exposed to legal and long-term relationships that looked like theirs. To be clear, this does not mean that long-term non-heterosexual relationships have not existed prior to the legalization of same-sex marriage. But without the societal stamp of marriage and with the general

190 *Modern Diversity in Marriage*

social stigma against same-sex relationships common throughout history, these relationships have often historically fallen into the background.

Natalie felt this lack of role models impacted another aspect of their relationship. When Natalie met Lucas, she felt their relationship quickly got stuck in neutral. Things were further complicated by the fact that they were not a typical same-sex relationship. They were an opposite-sex couple, but one in which they both considered their sexuality fluid. Because they were atypical, Natalie felt like they got trapped when it came to typical relationship rituals. For example, their engagement/proposal story was atypical and a challenge. As Natalie put it,

> Our relationship didn't progress [normally] because we didn't have expectations for what a relationship should do or looks like. When we got engaged, we were sitting on the couch. We were living in a studio apartment in New York City and I think we just looked at each other and said, "we wanted to do this for a long time," and then we decided to get married. So not very traditional I guess.

Engagement, one of the strongest relationship rituals we have, seemed foreign to Natalie and Lucas. Was this simply a heterosexual ritual? Was it something they should follow as well? Here is where the pioneering aspect of same-sex marriage is clearly seen among millennials. Lucas and Natalie had to blaze their own path and figure out what was "normal" in a culture where normal did not yet exist for couples like them.

This process of creating norms is not separated from the historical realities of the last decade. Marriage itself may still be associated with negative emotions among these non-heterosexual millennial couples, many of whom were in their early 20s when the battle over same-sex marriage was raging in the United States. Natalie and Lucas were honest that these memories still lingered for both of them, and one of the only reasons they were legally married was due to the legal protections and benefits that that step afforded them. Even though they could now be part of the club, they were still questioning whether they even wanted to join.

Because of a perceived lack of social support and resources created by these unique cultural and historical events, many non-heterosexual millennials also felt the need to seek out and actively cultivate their peer resources, even as married couples. Natalie talked about this in terms of her "created family": those with whom she had developed close, family-like relationships due to her feeling that her friends and family did not support her lifestyle. She said, "Because we're queer, we have a lot of chosen family. There are people who aren't biologically related to me who I consider my family." Natalie noted that these peers and social supports were vital to her in helping her through the normal ups and downs of her young marriage.

The story of marriage when it comes to sexual minorities is just now being written. Millennials are blazing a new path and are likely setting the norms and patterns that will become the benchmark for future generations. However, despite the legalization of same-sex marriage in most parts of the world, unique anxieties, stresses, and discrimination exist for these couples and individuals. In particular,

Modern Diversity in Marriage 191

the lack of social models for marriage has led many sexual-minority couples to lack a clear path forward to a successful marriage. Combined with some continued differences in individual and couple outcomes, it is clear that this remains an important topic of me-marriage, a topic that is only just beginning to be understood by both scholars and couples, themselves.

Cultural and Racial Issues

Like sexual-orientation minorities, ethnic and racial minorities also face some unique relational challenges when it comes to marriage. Suggestions that marriage and family formation differ based on racial or ethnic background have a long history in the social sciences (Hummer & Hamilton, 2010), and I have already touched on some of these issues in previous chapters. Historically, scholars have argued that racial-minority couples are at a disadvantage when it comes to satisfaction and relationship quality in long-term relationships (for an early example, see Renne, 1970). Today minority race status is still often viewed as a risk factor in terms of healthy marriage outcomes (Fu & Wolfinger, 2011). Like minority stress with same-sex couples, these disadvantages are mostly explained by non-racial issues, such as poverty and lower education, where minority individuals and couples often find themselves at a structural disadvantage compared to others. While some scholars have noted that relationship behaviors appear similar across racial and ethnic groups (Sanderson & Kurdek, 1993), other studies have at least hinted that some process differences exist. For example, Osborne and colleagues (2007) found that stability within relationships operated differently for white vs. minority couples, with marriage (as opposed to cohabitation) dramatically improving the stability of white couples' relationships. Such studies at least hint that marriage may not be an equal institution or provide the same benefits for all. Like other issues of diversity, issues of race and ethnicity are complex and are only becoming more intricate as our interconnected and international world expands (see De Guzman & Nishina, 2017).

My own data suggest that minorities still face some uphill battles when it comes to individual and relational health. I split the newlywed millennial data into two broad categories: those who reported a Caucasian or White race and those who reported a minority group (including multiracial or "other"). I controlled for the other demographics I have used in previous chapters and explored differences in individual and relational health. Figure 10.1 summarizes these findings. You can see that in some areas (relationship satisfaction, conflict, and depression), I found no differences between the two groups. However, in two areas—overall health and instability—I found significant differences. In both cases, minorities were at a disadvantage, reporting less overall health and more overall instability in their relationships. While much progress has been made in the last century when it comes to equality and reducing racism, millennial racial and ethnic minorities are still facing some unique challenges.

Some of these challenges are not new but are related to long-standing institutional racism still seen in many cultures. Like with non-heterosexual individuals my team spoke to, racial minorities also highlighted some of these challenges in

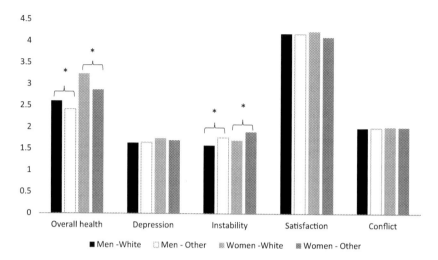

Figure 10.1 Estimated Means on Various Outcomes for Millennial Newlyweds, by Gender and Race.

Note: Stars represent significant differences between groups ($p < .05$).

their interviews. Vivian, who had some Latino heritage in her family and had what she called a "Hispanic-sounding name" prior to her marriage, noted that her marriage and acquisition of the last name "Richards" showed her some of this racism that she had been unaware of before. She shared, "I had a Hispanic-sounding last name and now that I don't have a Hispanic-sounding last name [after marriage], I can see the difference. Something as simple as LinkedIn contacts." She noted that after her marriage and name change, she experienced an uptick in job prospects and returned phone calls. As she put it, "I was able to sort of benefit [from marriage] in that sort of regard." Of course, Vivian's story of marriage "benefit" uncovers some difficulties that many ethnic minority couples deal with when it comes to attempting to achieve the personal happiness deemed so important in me-marriages. In a world where millennials are trying to pursue their dreams, minorities often still feel like some dreams are out of reach.

Cultural differences between partners, which are often tied to race and ethnicity but go beyond those issues related to being a cultural minority, create another wrinkle in the fabric of me-marriages. Cultural variations in expectations and values can swing millennials in and out of the various components of me-marriage that I have noted in previous chapters. Sometimes minority millennials can feel out of touch with their peers if their cultural heritage does not line up with the strong values of millennial culture. Akeem and Aliyah, a young married couple I reference in the previous chapter, both came to the United States from Pakistan. Akeem noted that their views and approach to marriage were likely different from those of their peers and that this was a major concern for him when he was in the dating market. Akeem noted,

Modern Diversity in Marriage 193

For me, [marriage] was kind of like a joint family culture, so our families live with us usually. For me, the person I was going to marry had to be caring and compassionate and supportive of everything that my culture represents. I mean, the thing was, since we were in a relationship for 5 years, I already knew that my wife could do all these things.

Akeem felt lucky. He knew that his strong collectivist family culture was at odds with some of the individualistic focus of most millennials. He found comfort in finding someone who shared his cultural background and values. Yet this cultural difference clearly altered his path to and through marriage.

As another example, Cameron, referenced throughout the previous chapters, noted that his extended-family-focused South American culture created some odd dynamics with his millennial peers. He said, "I come from Argentina, a place where many people stay at their parents' home for a long time. It is way different from the States, you know, where you normally leave home when you're 18." In his case, he said he had to fight this mentality while he was dating. He preferred the independence that millennials were given in the United States. Here, he was able to move in with his dating partner without the watchful and disapproving eyes of his parents. The move afforded them freedom and time alone together that he thought had ultimately benefited his marriage. He added, "I just have the feeling that people get used to having a partner [when they live together]. By the time they decide to get married, they've been together for, like, 5 to 10 years." He contrasted this experience with his old culture, where he felt couples were at a disadvantage because "suddenly they start living together and having all these responsibilities and stuff and they don't like it. They prefer to be under the parents' roof."

Another common diversity issue for millennials is related to interracial or cross-cultural relationships. Since most laws forbidding interracial marriages were abolished over a half-century ago, cultural attitudes toward such relationships have continued to improve. The vast majority of millennials are accepting of interracial relationships (De Los Santos et al., 2019). While the rates of interracial marriage are increasing across the board, social stigma still creates some barriers for such couples, and some racial pairings appear to be more common and culturally acceptable than others (Choi & Tienda, 2017). Many scholars assume that interracial marriages carry an increased risk of negative outcomes tied to institutional barriers and a lack of social acceptance of such relationships (Karney et al., 2005; Paterson et al., 2015)

It is no secret that millennials are a mobile generation. They move more for their education and career than any previous generation has. Because they are increasingly mobile when it comes to school and employment (which often coincides with the development of long-term relationships), many millennials may fall in love and establish relationships with those of a different race or culture. Because of these factors, scholars have noted that millennials will likely create a growing group of interracial marriages and relationships (De Guzman & Nishina, 2017).

As I continue to highlight, however, some unique challenges remain for such marriages. Historically, interracial couples tend to not report many of the

194 *Modern Diversity in Marriage*

benefits associated with marriage for majority groups. In fact, some research has suggested that such marriages create greater risk of negative outcomes. For example, some studies have suggested that interracial couples are at risk for negative health outcomes (Gabriel & Esposito, 2017; Yu & Zhang, 2017). Other studies have noted that interracial marriage may have less stability than other marriages (Fu & Wolfinger, 2011; Zhang & Van Hook, 2009). Studies have shown lower scores of overall relationship quality across a variety of factors within interracial relationships (Hohmann-Marriott & Amato, 2008). The picture painted by this research is concerning. I often challenge my students with such findings, baiting them into a conversation about whether it is "easier" to marry someone of their own race. Of course, this question is merely to get such students into a discussion of race and racism. But the fact remains that these couples are clearly having some unique struggles.

Yet perhaps millennials may be different. Perhaps in most ways, interracial and cross-cultural me-marriages will have the same strengths and weaknesses as the marriages that I have outlined in previous chapters. I began this project thinking this was likely. Why? Remember how I have highlighted that millennials who are married are focused on communication and negotiation of individual differences more than ever before? Because of their ability to negotiate differences and focus on finding ways to maximize the goals and needs of both partners, millennials may be uniquely suited to handle some of the challenges of cross-cultural or interracial marriages. Indeed, some research evidence has suggested that in the new culture of me-marriage, interracial relationships may, in some cases, be more likely to both transition to marriage and remain stable across time (Kuroki, 2017). Like in the case of same-sex marriage, millennials may be blazing a new trail—one that is creating stronger and more stable relationships than in the past.

My own data show that perhaps some of these historical trends may not be as strong or as consistent as previously thought. Figure 10.2 shows the estimated means for millennial newlyweds once other demographic controls are accounted for, comparing interracial couples to those who married within the same racial group. I found no differences based on overall health, depression, or any of the relationship-quality indicators I explored. Of course, this lack of difference could be because these were all newlyweds in the first few years of their marriage, and differences might not appear until later in their relationship. Another issue is that any differences based on interracial configuration could be due to other institutional and demographic inequalities, things I controlled for in my model. To explore that possibility, I ran the models again, leaving out all the controls. This raw look at the data returned no new differences between same- and different-race couples.

These data provide some hope for me—hope that millennials may be overcoming some of the historical disadvantages seen due to racial and ethnic status. But work remains to be done. Many of the couples my research team interviewed that were in interracial or cross-cultural marriages reported some unique frustrations in their relationships. Some of these were portrayed simply as cultural quirks, while others were discussed in more serious terms. Many of these

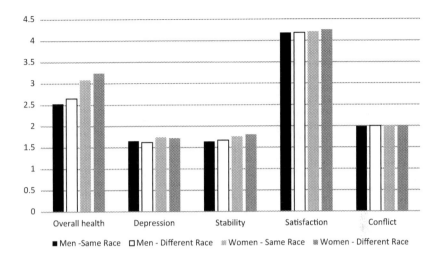

Figure 10.2 Estimated Means for Various Outcomes for Millennial Newlyweds by Gender and Racial Differences between Partners.

obstacles were logistical in nature, due to the inherent differences such couples found between partners in terms of background, language, and values. Carson and Brielle met online while Brielle was living in her home country of Vietnam. Carson is an African American man from the United States. They spent months talking to each other before Carson decided to visit Brielle in Vietnam. He noted some interesting obstacles their early relationship faced due to cultural differences. Many of these were related to language barriers. He shared that they had some challenges building their relationship early on "because [his wife] speaks another language. She can speak English, but she might not understand everything." After they married and Brielle moved to the United States, Carson had to take the lead in their relationship given Brielle's lack of familiarity with the United States and its customs. He added, "I have to communicate with her all the time and let her know what we're going to do today or tomorrow or what we're planning or if we have an arrangement for the future."

These differences in language also directly impacted their relationship. Remember, communication was seen by most millennials as a vital aspect of memarriage, needed to navigate the complexities of modern life. The language barrier between Carson and his wife made this process more difficult. Carson sensed that his wife became anxious when they had conflict or faced a difficult decision. Sometimes that led Carson to make the pragmatic decision that certain issues were not worth discussing at the moment, creating a protracted timetable for many of the decisions in their marriage. Carson reflected on this challenge:

> If I know that something's not going to make her feel good or feel comfortable, I'm not going to go on and make that decision. I just wait until she's completely comfortable. I won't make the move until she's comfortable.

196 *Modern Diversity in Marriage*

Another interracial couple I interviewed noted another issue, a lack of family support. Perhaps more so than any topic I have discussed in this book, interracial relationships among millennials have the highest potential to create intergenerational tensions. While widely accepted today, interracial marriages were largely taboo even one generation ago (Qian & Lichter, 2011). Julia and Dominic provided a good example of this issue. They met when Julia matched up with Dominic's brother on a dating app. When that relationship fizzled out, Julia was introduced to Dominic. Dominic was from the Philippines, something that did not bother Julia but seemed to be a deal breaker for her parents. She shared,

> Dominic is part Pilipino. My parents weren't too keen on the idea of me dating outside of my race. He is a quarter Pilipino. You can't even tell it looking at him. But they weren't too keen on that. And that's one of the reasons I pushed off the relationship to begin with. I was sort of waiting until I had the ability to be able to live on my own without my parents' financial assistance in any way. In case worst comes to worst and they kicked me out. So that was one of my biggest reasons for putting our relationship on the backburner. It wasn't him that I was trying to push off.

Interestingly, despite clearly dealing with the racism of her parents, Julia managed to reframe this problem in a unique millennial lens, saying that the extra time early in their relationship was good for her. In fact, she slowly began to change her tune later in the interview, eventually claiming that, despite her parents' reservations and her own admission of its impact, her delay in marrying Dominic was "more that I needed to be able to take care of myself." In fact, this was the reason she had given to Dominic at the time, never disclosing her parents' feelings. She admits now that this was probably a mistake. She added, "I didn't tell Dominic that [my parents disapproved]; I should've told him that. I told him later. I didn't want him to think, 'Oh, she's going with her family.' That kind of thing."

Mirroring some of the examples I shared earlier from non-heterosexual millennials, Syed, an African American man, noted that he had few clear examples of good marriages in his life. His marriage mentor instead came from television, where he found his passion for marriage and an example to emulate in a popular but dated sitcom. As he put it,

> My inspiration was from watching The Cosby Show. I don't think that I would have wanted to get married if it weren't for The Cosby Show. I was like, "dang I want a Clair Huxtable one day too." I want to be like them, it was just, like, a fantasy dream.

This lack of examples came up again later in the interview, when Syed spoke about examples in his life when it came to marriage. He shared,

> I didn't have no examples in my family. Honestly, like I said, Cosby was the biggest thing for me. That's kind of what I want. My mom was a single mom,

so I didn't have no pictures of successful marriages in my life. It was literally just me seeing something and feeling, like, that feels right.

The common denominator in these examples is increased stress and a lack of resources. As Julia illustrated, and like same-sex couples, racial-minority couples often lack strong social resources to support their relationships. Given that some research (Tomás, 2020) suggests that interracial marriage and relationships might have a component of intergenerational transmission—meaning that as one generation does it, the next is more likely to as well—such marriages and their unique hurdles will only increase in the future.

The Changing Norm of Monogamy

While I believe sexual orientation and racial/ethnic issues remain the most pressing diversity issues for millennials, before we move on and conclude this analysis of me-marriage, a short note on monogamy is warranted. Why? Because issues of monogamy are quickly becoming a hot topic in the relational sciences, spurred on by the fact that the gold standard of monogamy appears to be eroding in younger couples. The concept of partners agreeing to bring in multiple outside sexual partners has generated a flurry of new research centered on what scholars call consensual non-monogamy (Sheff & Tesene, 2015). Much of this newer research has been focused on understanding differences between couples who practice non-monogamy and those who do not. This research is still new and prone to methodological problems (Sizemore & Olmstead, 2017), but the need to understand this changing relational dynamic is critical. Sizemore and Olmstead (2018) reported that roughly a quarter of their emerging-adult sample was open to engaging in a non-monogamous relationship. When exploring outcomes between monogamous and non-monogamous couples, scholars often find few to no differences between such couples (Mitchell et al., 2020; Mogilski et al., 2017), and some scholars have suggested that the increased communication needed to maintain multiple partners may lead to better overall communication and conflict-resolution skills among non-monogamous partners (see Mogilski et al., 2017; Moors et al., 2017).

In my own data, non-monogamy was not frequently reported by millennials, but it certainly existed. Among the married millennials in the national dataset of those in their early 30s, 12% of the sample reported having at least some sexual exchange with someone other than their spouse while they were married. I would assume some underreporting is happening with this type of question, so the actual percentage is likely higher. This group was much more likely to be male (62%) and slightly less likely be heterosexual. Other demographics were roughly the same. Of course, these data did not provide enough detail on whether this non-monogamy was consensual or not, so the details of it are essentially unknown. But, taken with the latest research suggesting an uptick in consensual non-monogamous relationships, millennials in such marital arrangements may be on the bleeding edge of a new and emerging marital option.

While monogamy is certainly still the clear norm and expectation among millennials, the tide may be turning away from viewing monogamy as the only

198 *Modern Diversity in Marriage*

arrangement that could make a relationship work. Natalie and Lucas, the queer couple I mentioned earlier in this chapter, also touched on monogamy in their interview. They labeled their relationship as "casual" for the first several years and were clear with each other that they held no expectations of monogamy at that time. Even when their dating became more serious and they decided to become monogamous, they both noted that they would be open (slight pun intended) to expanding their physical relationship to others if one or both of them decided they wanted to explore additional partners. Natalie put it this way:

> We got married in my parents' backyard; we had a bunch of people; we had a ceremony; it was really fun. But we weren't legally married at that point, but then we got legally married a year later. It was totally logistical; we did it on Lucas's lunch break. We went to City Hall. We were monogamous when we got married; we weren't when we started dating, but then we became monogamous. But if we don't want to be monogamous anymore, we can talk about that; we didn't say that's what marriage is. Just because we are married doesn't mean we can't do that.

It is interesting that, in Natalie's mind, marriage did not necessarily equate to monogamy.

Alexis, also mentioned earlier in this chapter, identifies as queer and noted that her gender has been fluid in her marriage. Alexis and her husband were also the one couple I spoke to who talked openly about consensual non-monogamy in their marriage. Alexis and Leo opened their relationship a few years prior to speaking with us. They noted that this decision both created difficulty and strengthened their relationship. On the positive side, they both observed that having an open relationship had forced them to deal with some poor communication patterns that had plagued their marriage early on. As Alexis explained,

> Three or four years back, we decided to open our relationship. It's been the past four years, I think. We did a lot of research into how to make relationships like that work. And with that, we discovered that the main thing that we were lacking before in our relationship was clear, open, honest communication. We would do this beat-around-the-bush thing or kind of expect the other to know what we wanted at that point in time, things like that.

The couple faced other challenges, and jealousy was a tough hurdle for them both to get over. As Alexis noted later in the interview, "Our first relationships outside of the marriage, neither one of them worked out well. It was catastrophic." But she again felt that the overall benefit outweighed the negative, adding, "We're not seeing anybody else right now, but the biggest benefit we did get was being able to talk to each other about anything, and we do, and we don't ever hold anything back." Leo acknowledged some of the pain he had experienced when they opened their relationship but also agreed it had helped their overall relationship. He felt he could now say things he meant or felt, even if it might cause discomfort and pain for his partner. He added, "Even if it hurts, and we know it's gonna hurt,

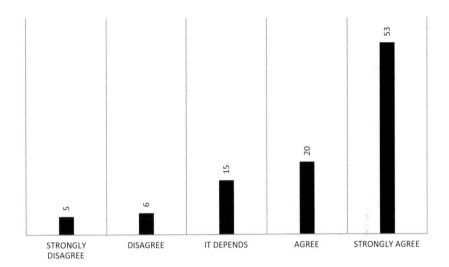

Figures 10.3 Percentage of 20-22 Year Olds Who Agreed With the Statement, "Intimacy With Another Person Is Never Okay in a Relationship."

it's better to be up-front and honest with each other instead of letting it sit and stew and become something bigger than it actually is."

All of these data and examples suggest that the issue of monogamy may be one of the aspects of marriage to keep a close eye on. I am currently overseeing a project exploring young adults' development through their 20s. As a part of that project, we are collecting data on their attitudes and views toward a variety of relationship topics, including non-monogamy. The data we have collected so far suggest that, while millennials have largely held tight to the standard of monogamy, the next generation may be quickly creating a different path. Figures 10.3 and 10.4 show some initial data from that project, taken from participants who were roughly 21 years old when these data were collected. In Figure 10.3, you can see that the majority (53%) still strongly agree that it is not okay to engage in intimacy with another person while in a relationship. But that means almost half of the sample were, on some level, lukewarm (or even opposed) to that notion. In fact, over a quarter of the sample said they either disagreed with this statement or that "it depends." Figure 10.4 is more telling as it measures more general acceptance of non-monogamy. Here, over 50% of the sample agreed or said "it depends" to the question asking if a non-monogamous relationship would be just as strong as a monogamous one. Clearly the rising generation is shifting away from believing that monogamy is the only way to do relationships correctly. Whether this mindset is mostly exclusive to the rising generation, or if it is also beginning to influence millennial marriages in the next decade, has yet to be seen.

These three issues of diversity are critical to fully understanding me-marriages. While most millennials in the United States and other parts of the world continue to engage in monogamous and heterosexual marriages within their same

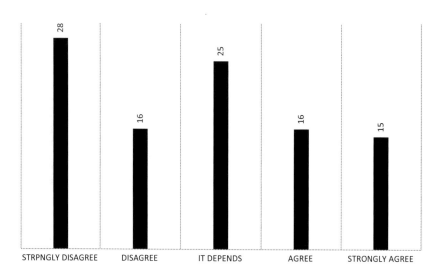

Figure 10.4 Percentage of 20–22 Year Olds Who Agreed With the Statement, "Relationships With More Than Two People Can Be Just As Strong."

race or ethnic group, diverse forms of marriage are becoming both more accepted and abundant. Minorities of all kinds face unique challenges as they strive toward many of the same me-marriage goals as other millennials. Such challenges should never disappear from our radar. In the interconnected world of millennials, minorities have more avenues and power to influence the majority than ever before and will likely continue to have an impact on the trajectory of millennial marriage in the future.

References

Choi, K. H., & Tienda, M. (2017). Boundary crossing in first marriage and remarriage. *Social Science Research, 62*, 305–316.

de Guzman, N. S., & Nishina, A. (2017). 50 years of loving: Interracial romantic relationships and recommendations for future research. *Journal of Family Theory & Review, 9*, 557–571.

De Los Santos, A., Turner, B., Gaye, F., & Kenne, M. (2019). Yesterday, today, and before tomorrow: How have attitudes towards interracial relationships changed from baby boomers to millennials. *Iowa State Conference on Race and Ethnicity, 20*(1).

Doyle, D. M., & Molix, L. (2015). Social stigma and sexual minorities' romantic relationship functioning: A meta-analytic review. *Personality and Social Psychology Bulletin, 41*, 1363–1381.

Ellis, L., & Davis, M. (2017). Intimate partner support: A comparison of gay, lesbian, and heterosexual relationships. *Personal Relationships, 24*, 350–369.

Fu, V. K., & Wolfinger, N. H. (2011). Broken boundaries or broken marriages? Racial intermarriage and divorce in the United States. *Social Science Quarterly, 92*, 1096–1117.

Gabriel, R., & Esposito, M. H. (2017, April). Interracial couples and the association among marriage and health. Paper presented at the Population Association of America 2017 Annual Meeting, Chicago, IL.

Garcia, M. A., & Umberson, D. (2019). Marital strain and psychological distress in same-sex and different-sex couples. *Journal of Marriage and Family*, *81*, 1253–1268.

Hohmann-Marriott, B. E., & Amato, P. (2008). Relationship quality in interethnic marriages and cohabitations. *Social Forces*, *87*, 825–855.

Hummer, R. A., & Hamilton, E. R. (2010). Race and ethnicity in fragile families. *The Future of Children*, *20*, 113–131.

Joyner, K., Manning, W., & Prince, B. (2019). The qualities of same-sex and different-sex couples in young adulthood. *Journal of Marriage and Family*, *81*, 487–505.

Karney, B. R., Story, L. B., & Bradbury, T. N. (2005). *Marriages in context: Interactions between chronic and acute stress among newlyweds*. In T. A. Revenson, K. Kayser, & S. Bodenmann (Eds.), *Emerging perspectives on couples' coping with stress* (pp. 13–32). American Psychological Association.

Ketcham, E., & Bennett, N. G. (2019). Comparative couple stability: Same-sex and male-female unions in the United States. *Socius*, *5*, 1–15.

Kuroki, M. (2017). Marital dissolution and formation for interracial couples: Evidence from parents of biracial children. *Race and Social Problems*, *9*, 255–261.

Lau, C. Q. (2012). The stability of same-sex cohabitation, different-sex cohabitation, and marriage. *Journal of Marriage and Family*, *74*, 973–988.

Manning, W. D., Brown, S. L., & Stykes, J. B. (2016). Same-sex and different-sex cohabiting couple relationship stability. *Demography*, *53*, 937–953.

Meyer, I. H. (2003). Prejudice, social stress, and mental health in lesbian, gay, and bisexual populations: Conceptual issues and research evidence. *Psychological Bulletin*, *129*, 674.

Mitchell, V. E., Mogilski, J. K., Donaldson, S. H., Nicolas, S. C. A., & Welling, L. L. (2020). Sexual motivation and satisfaction among consensually non-monogamous and monogamous individuals. *Journal of Sexual Medicine*. www.sciencedirect.com/science/article/abs/pii/S1743609520301223

Mogilski, J. K., Memering, S. L., Welling, L. L., & Shackelford, T. K. (2017). Monogamy versus consensual non-monogamy: Alternative approaches to pursuing a strategically pluralistic mating strategy. *Archives of Sexual Behavior*, *46*, 407–417.

Moors, A. C., Matsick, J. L., & Schechinger, H. A. (2017). Unique and shared relationship benefits of consensually non-monogamous and monogamous relationships. *European Psychologist*, *22*, 55–71.

Osborne, C., Manning, W. D., & Smock, P. J. (2007). Married and cohabiting parents' relationship stability: A focus on race and ethnicity. *Journal of Marriage and Family*, *69*, 1345–1366.

Paterson, J. L., Turner, R. N., & Conner, M. T. (2015). Extended contact through cross-group romantic relationships. *Journal of Applied Social Psychology*, *45*, 489–497.

Perper, R. (2019, June 12). *The 28 countries around the world where same-sex marriage is legal. Business Insider*. www.businessinsider.com/where-is-same-sex-marriage-legal-world-2017-11

Pew Research Center. (2019, October 28). *Same-sex marriage around the world*. Pew Research Center. www.pewforum.org/fact-sheet/gay-marriage-around-the-world/

Qian, Z., & Lichter, D. T. (2011). Changing patterns of interracial marriage in a multiracial society. *Journal of Marriage and Family*, *73*, 1065–1084.

Renne, K. S. (1970). Correlates of dissatisfaction in marriage. *Journal of Marriage and the Family*, *32*, 54–67.

Roisman, G. I., Clausell, E., Holland, A., Fortuna, K., & Elieff, C. (2008). Adult romantic relationships as contexts of human development: A multimethod comparison of same-sex couples with opposite-sex dating, engaged, and married dyads. *Developmental Psychology*, *44*, 91–101.

202 *Modern Diversity in Marriage*

Rosenfeld, M. J. (2014). Couple longevity in the era of same-sex marriage in the United States. *Journal of Marriage and Family, 76*, 905–918.

Sanderson, B., & Kurdek, L. A. (1993). Race and gender as moderator variables in predicting relationship satisfaction and relationship commitment in a sample of dating heterosexual couples. *Family Relations, 42,* 263–267.

Sheff, E., & Tesene, M. M. (2015). Consensual non-monogamies in industrialized nations. In J. DeLamater & R. F. Plante (Eds.), *Handbook of the sociology of sexualities* (pp. 223–241). Springer.

Sizemore, K. M., & Olmstead, S. B. (2017). A systematic review of research on attitudes towards and willingness to engage in consensual non-monogamy among emerging adults: Methodological issues considered. *Psychology & Sexuality, 8,* 4–23.

Sizemore, K. M., & Olmstead, S. B. (2018). Willingness of emerging adults to engage in consensual non-monogamy: A mixed-methods analysis. *Archives of Sexual Behavior, 47,* 1423–1438.

Solazzo, A., Gorman, B., & Denney, J. (2020). Does sexual orientation complicate the relationship between marital status and gender with self-rated health and cardiovascular disease? *Demography, 57,* 599–626.

Tomás, M. C. (2020). Parent's and child's interracial marriage in Brazil: An analysis of intermarriage as an intergenerational transmission process. *Population Review, 59,* 26–55.

U.S. Census Bureau. (2017). *Household characteristics of same-sex couple households by relationship type: 2017.* U.S. Census Bureau. www.census.gov/content/census/en/data/tables/time-series/demo/same-sex-couples/ssc-house-characteristics.html

Yu, Y. L., & Zhang, Z. (2017). Interracial marriage and self-reported health of whites and blacks in the United States. *Population Research and Policy Review, 36,* 851–870.

Zhang, Y., & Van Hook, J. (2009). Marital dissolution among interracial couples. *Journal of Marriage and Family, 71,* 95–107.

11 A New Case for Marriage

In the early spring of 2019, singer/songwriter Ben Platt released the song "Grow as We Go." It was a song that was so decidedly millennial in its message, it struck a chord with many of them. With almost 13 million views on YouTube as of this writing and countless imitator videos on various social media platforms, many from millennials themselves, the message of the song resonated with several of the themes I have outlined in this book. What was that message? While the details of the song's origin are still mostly ambiguous, Ben shared this on social media regarding his inspiration for the lyrics. He tweeted, "I wrote 'Grow As We Go' about how desperately I wanted a very special relationship to work despite knowing how much personal growth we both still needed."

The marriages of millennials are a unique blend of this personal desire for growth and individualism that have been the hallmarks of the millennial generation with the older norms and structure that marriage brought from generations past. These "me-marriages," as I have labeled them, are unique in their strengths, challenges, and processes. Millennials are struggling with transforming an institution that was not designed with their generation's unique perspective in mind. While cultural constraints of generations past may have made it difficult if not impossible to reform large social institutions like marriage, the deinstitutionalization of many aspects of modern culture that I have referenced in earlier chapters have allowed millennials to create marriage in their own image.

Of course, the question I posed at the beginning of this book was still lingering among scholars who knew that the foundations of marriage had been altering for the last few decades. Was marriage still "good" for millennials? Was there still a case for marriage to be made, or had millennials changed the nature of the marital relationship so much that the research and scholarship accumulated over the last few decades may no longer be relevant? Or, had the nature of society and culture shifted in ways that made marriage more meaningless or irrelevant when it came to individual outcomes, regardless of what millennials did or did not do?

In attempting to answer these questions, I have reviewed the uniqueness of me-marriage and what it entails, hoping to provide you with some context for what makes the millennial generation unique when it comes to marriage. I have also highlighted many areas and outcomes that have traditionally been associated with the "case for marriage," examining relationship outcomes, educational trajectories, and health outcomes, all in an attempt to see if married millennials are different

204 *A New Case for Marriage*

than those who, by choice or circumstance, never married. While doing that, I have also noted the potential for generational differences, comparing newlyweds of two different generations to see if their marital and individual outcomes appear to differ. Finally, I examined important contextual factors where, again, unique millennial shifts in behavior and attitudes have created differing marital processes than those of generations past. Millennials clearly approach some aspects of their life, like gender roles and religion, in ways that are almost foreign to those even one generation ago. These shifts in cultural norms provide further important and unique context to the me-marriages of millennials.

So, what is the answer to the question of if there is indeed a case for marriage among millennials? While a good social scientist should probably always answer with "it depends," I will attempt to not leave you in such an ambiguous place in regard to my own personal opinions about what the data I have presented show. In my mind, the simple and straightforward answer to this question appears to be *yes*, there is still a case for marriage. Regardless of a thousand caveats and contextual factors that probably should add a cascade of asterisks to the end of that answer, the individual and interpersonal benefits of marriage appear consistently robust across the variety of outcomes I have explored. Yes, it is probably safe to say that not all the historical benefits of marriage have transferred to the millennial generation, but it appears many of them remain. Married millennials, like generations past, do appear to be happier and healthier than their single and never-married peers.

Of course, the equally important secondary question here is simple yet perhaps infinitely more complex: Why is what appears to be a dying institution still beneficial? That is the topic of an entirely different book. I have hinted at and reviewed several theories that exist in the scholarship regarding the benefits of marriage. They cast myriad options that fall into the two most basic of social science camps, selection and causation. For me, these questions are important, yet secondary. Remember, my personal journey into millennial marriage began with the assumption, largely based on my personal biases and from my interactions with my scholarly peers, that millennials were likely messing up marriage forever. That does not appear to be the case, as me-marriages appear healthy and thriving—at least on average. Of course, there are other important summary points to be made that go beyond the answer to the core question at the foundation of this book. In this final chapter, I take one last opportunity to take a step back and summarize what I feel are the most important take-aways of this exploration given the information I have outlined in the previous chapters on me-marriage. By way of summary, I think there is both subjective good and bad to be taken from the data I have reviewed. Why don't we start with the good?

The Good

I will be honest here as I reflect on the best way to summarize what all the themes, data points, and trends I have outlined over the course of the last ten chapters mean. As I said, I went into this project assuming the worst about millennials. As I shared at the beginning of the book, I had spent many years hearing several, if not most, of my colleagues speak about the problematic relationships of millennials during their late teens and early 20s. I had my doubts that this generation would be able to create and sustain the type of thriving marriages that had for so long been linked to positive individual, couple, and family well-being. Yet as I look back at what I learned through my study of millennial marriages over the last two years of this project, it became increasingly clear to me that there was much good in the marriages of millennials.

As I have already mentioned, and central to one of the key questions of this entire project, it appears that there is indeed still a "case for marriage." My attempt to explore if Waite and Gallagher's arguments from 20 years ago still held true a generation later has some compelling points to it. Focusing just on the relational side of things, my own analyses suggested that millennials who marry have healthier and more stable relationships than those who do not. These effects, while small, were consistent. Married millennials, after factoring in several controls, had more satisfying and stable relationships than their non-married counterparts. I also found that married millennials were more stable than cohabiting millennials, a key question for many relational scholars who suspect that cohabitation may be replacing marriage. And in perhaps one of the most surprising findings for me, I found that newlywed millennials were more satisfied with their relationship and reported less overall disagreements than older newlyweds. Millennial men also reported significantly less relational aggression in their relationships than older married men.

These positive effects related to marriage are not restricted to relational benefits. They appear to extend to several aspects of life for millennials. Like generations past, some of the clearest benefits to marriage are centered on economic well-being. Married millennials in my data are wealthier, more educated, and more content in their careers than those who never married. In fact, this may have been the most consistent finding of my research. Married millennials, on essentially every outcome I assessed, looked better financially than never-married millennials. As I noted in the chapter on education, many of these outcomes may be related to increasing selection into marriage among the educated (Kalmijn, 2013). I even noted that education appeared to be a strong predictor of marriage in my own data. Yet many of these differences persisted in my analyses, even when controlling for things like educational attainment.

Despite their relative youth, I also found consistent differences in health outcomes, with married millennials being more likely to be satisfied with their overall health and—perhaps most importantly in our current culture of increasing awareness of mental health problems among young adults—I found married millennials were significantly less likely to report high levels of depressive symptoms compared to never-married millennials. As I noted in the chapter on health, most health differences may not even fully appear until later in life, but there is already evidence of a growing health divide between millennials based on marital status.

Taken together, it would appear that many of the "traditional" benefits of marriage remain intact for millennials. Previous scholars have noted that married individuals appear happier (Lee & Ono, 2012; Stack & Esleman, 1998), healthier (Zheng & Thomas, 2013), richer (Ludwig & Brüderl, 2018), and create a more stable environment for children (Björklund et al., 2007; Fomby & Cherlin, 2007).

206   *A New Case for Marriage*

Regardless of the methodological holes any good social researcher can likely poke in my admittedly rather simple comparisons, I think it's important to note that I did not find any consistent advantages to being single or in a committed, non-marital relationship across my many comparisons. In social science we are often looking for trends, hoping to not get too caught up in a single finding or statistic. Here, the trend seems clear: if marriage is doing anything for millennials, it's certainly leading them in a positive direction. In addition, any marriage-like alternative union is providing no clear advantages to millennials.

But there is more to the positive story here about millennial marriage than simply a continuation of previous trends. There are new wrinkles to marriage that are uniquely millennial in nature that could be viewed as enhancements to the institution of marriage. As just one example, millennials' more flexible role assignments would appear to not only be appealing but potentially beneficial to work–family balance. Work–family scholars have long advocated for flexibility in the workplace due to growing complexity in family arrangements (Allen et al., 2013; Shockley & Allen, 2007), with some even calling for an ideal "dual-part-time" arrangement where both partners work around 30 hours per week (Hill et al., 2006). Millennials appear to be pushing in that direction. While not perfect, these progressions have the potential to open more flexible and manageable marital processes.

As I highlighted several times across various chapters, millennials are navigating an increasingly complex world. They seem more willing and excited to navigate this complexity than previous generations and more willing to negotiate with a spouse. Gender roles and other static features of marriage appear to be eroding and replaced by a more customizable and personalized type of marriage. From this perspective, me-marriage is an improvement on an outdated model. Millennials are having their cake and eating it too. They are retaining many, if not most, of the benefits of marriage, while transforming it into something that fits their modern and relativist reality.

The Bad?

Despite the continued benefits that appear to accompany married life and the new and potentially strengthening paths that millennials are creating in their marriages, there remain potential roadblocks and pitfalls in the road toward marital bliss. Some are related to the data I explored. The benefits of marriage were not universal. For example, sexual and intimacy-related outcomes were consistently no different between married and never-married millennials. Across a variety of outcomes, marriage appeared to provide no sex-related benefit to millennials (and in some cases, I found evidence of a disadvantage). But most of this potential "bad news" came in the form of some uniquely millennial marital problems that I am not sure have fully manifested yet. They are less quantitative and more hypothetical and conceptual, things that I think may happen but have yet to materialize. After all, the quantitative data appear to paint a rather rosy picture of me-marriages. Yet my interviews sometimes uncovered some stumbles and struggles along the way. Often these were the flipside of issues that could also be considered strengths.

For example, I already mentioned how the role-less marital arrangements of millennials may give such couples more flexibility and nimbleness in a world that is increasingly complex. But I also noted when I discussed such arrangements that millennials were also reporting some difficulty in implementing these arrangements in an effective way. This may lie in their motivations, which often seemed to be more individualistic than altruistic. Rather than creating flexibility for the purpose of benefiting the relationship and their family, many millennials appeared to engage in role-less me-marriages for the main purpose of avoiding tasks they did not care for. What happens when these families becoming increasingly complex (more children, older children) and such a laid-back approach to roles begins to fundamentally undermine the equilibrium of the family system? I see some small cracks developing for many millennials in this area, cracks that have the potential to start shaking the foundation of some of these relationships in the future.

It also seems clear that millennials are struggling with the age-old balance between one's career and one's family life. While not a new concern, millennials seem to be facing increased tension between their career and family identities. The unique stresses of the modern workplace and their increased desire for individual fulfillment and career advancement make balancing career trajectories and married life a constant struggle for millennials. In my interview data, I could consistently sense this tension as millennials tried to have the best of both worlds, a happy married life and a thriving individual career. Despite work–family scholars who have offered numerous potential solutions to this problem, the consumer and profit-driven nature of most professions has made progress in this area slow. Millennials often feel like they must choose between their career and their families, a dilemma that is causing increased tension and anxiety in a lot of millennial marriages. Whether millennials shift priorities as they age to find more personal balance across these roles has yet to be seen.

Parenting is another area of concern. As I noted, my own data and the general lack of older children among millennials did not allow me to dive deep into any potential child outcome differences that may exist due to the changes millennials have made to their marital relationships. How children will fare in me-marriages as they develop and grow remains an unanswered question. But I wonder if there is potential cause for concern here too. While two adults who are both committed to each other and their own individual pursuits of individual happiness may work in a vacuum, I wonder how children may change this dynamic. I noted in my parenting chapter that many of the millennials with children were struggling with prioritizing not only their relationship, but also many of these individual goals. There was a weariness in many of those interviews, some of which might be expected, but I wonder if there might be a uniquely millennial reframing of the benefits of parenting as many millennials hear about and see these struggles with their peers. Given the historical drops in fertility rate we see around the world, I wonder what the case for marriage might look like for the children of millennials who will be raised in very different families than those of their parents.

Then, of course, is the entire issue at the heart of me-marriage. I will admit that I was surprised that the individuality and self-focused marriages of millennials appeared just as healthy, if not healthier, than those of generations past. I will also

208　*A New Case for Marriage*

admit that, as a relational scholar, I still have my doubts about whether or not this healthy relational outlook can last. Decades of relational science have suggested that self-less and virtuous relational behavior tied to sacrifice and commitment lie at the heart of long-term and healthy marriages (Fincham et al., 2007; Jeffries, 2000). Much of what I heard coming from millennial married couples appeared at odds with this scholarship. Perhaps millennials will create a new normal in the next few decades, a marriage of 20 or 30 years that looks nothing like what we currently have. But the scientist in me is still waiting for the other shoe to drop, wondering if perhaps a follow-up volume in another decade might reveal some cracks in the protective shell of millennial marriage.

The Uncertain Future

Did you think I was going to label the last section "the ugly"? I really do not believe there is anything truly ugly happening with millennials and me-marriage. However, I do believe there is an uncertain future for these marriages, as I just described. As I already noted, there are some things to be concerned about when it comes to the future of these marriages. I also think there are some important issues that need to be addressed by scholars, practitioners, educators, and millennials themselves; items that I think will likely determine if and how marriages on the whole succeed or fail in the future. In an effort to keep these concerns and recommendations brief, I highlight two critical features from my data that I believe will be important factors in how me-marriages look in the future, both for millennials and for the next generation.

The Need for Clear Expectations

One thing that became apparent during our interviews with millennials is the need for clear and healthy expectations about marriage. Millennials have been able to create marriages with more flexibility and more equality than in the past, largely because of the disintegration of many of the social norms traditionally tied to marriage. The continued trend toward the deinstitutionalization of marital norms (Cherlin, 2004) has created a large, often scary, open playing field when it comes to forming and maintaining marriages. While this creates some unique freedoms, I also believe it creates some unique challenges that must be addressed for millennials to succeed in their marriages.

For example, I already mentioned some of the potential issues that role-less marriages were creating for millennials. While some couples naturally fell into a system that worked for them, others were clearly becoming frustrated with experimenting with a seemingly endless number of options. Similarly, in the areas of career development and education, many millennial couples struggled to know if they were making the best decision in terms of career paths, promotions, and relocations. Social norms have always created a sense of what is "right" or "correct," and without them, millennials face a lot of anxiety about potentially picking the wrong path through life with little guidance beyond what they might glean from their family, friends, or the internet.

While I am not advocating for a return to rigid social norms, I do believe in the importance of clear expectations. If they do not come from culture, I think it is pivotal that millennials communicate clearly the expectations they have for each other. Marital transitions have always been challenging for previous (Waite, 1981) and modern (Ogolsky et al., 2019) generations. Married millennials recognize it. As Katie and Jeremy, married for 6 years, noted, the struggles they had early in their marriage took them a bit by surprise. Katie explained, "It's [being married] definitely been ten times harder than I thought it would be." Jeremy jumped in and added, "Right? Yeah." His wife added,

> Everyone makes it sound like, "It's so easy being married!" No! It's really difficult. It's hard. It is work to stay married, it is work to be in a relationship. You don't just fall in love and magically stay that way! No, you really have to work at it!

I believe this work involves millennials having honest and open conversations about their individual and family goals. They must find clarity where there is often little to be found. In truly millennial fashion, they must articulate "their truth" when it comes to marriage. What do they want out of life? How can they accomplish it together? While I have noted that many millennials have become adept at this type of negotiation, I also believe many millennials are not having these conversations. Modern technology is making such vulnerable and sometimes difficult conversations easier to avoid. Rather than attempting to construct or rebuild the social norms of the past, I believe encouraging and educating millennials on the importance of creating openness and clarity around family and personal goals is and will be a key to happy me-marriages in the future.

The Need for Marriage Mentors

The second issue I think is critical to the success of me-marriages is related to the pressing need to give millennials access to marriage mentors in their lives. Tied to the issue of unclear and ambiguous expectations, as more millennials experience instability in their families of origin and as media examples of stable relationships become fewer, there is a growing need for clear marital examples that can help create moments of healthy socialization for millennial couples. I noted in my previous book, *The Marriage Paradox* (Willoughby & James, 2017), that one of the most important things young adults desiring a healthy marriage needed was a strong network of marriage mentors. I believe this is still the case, if not more so, for our growing and young cohort of married millennials. As noted by Monique, someone I have often referred to throughout this book, these mentors can create critical turning points in the lives of millennials seeking guidance. Monique had seen the power of these mentors in her own life. She shared:

> I had two mentors growing up who were women who had phenomenal marriages. I was like, "They can do it." If I were to be super honest when it comes to marriage and influences, I see a lot of bad marriages and I used to

210   *A New Case for Marriage*

be like, "I'm not going to be them." Because of my mentors, I told myself that I'm going to work even harder.

Her husband, Justin, also talked about an important mentor in his life. After his wife was done, he shared this:

> There's a guy that I worked for all throughout high school, mowed lawns, chopped wood for him and everything. He had a unique situation in his marriage because he was a widower and she was a widow, but seeing how much it worked for them and how much they loved each other, that was really what I wanted. I didn't want marriage if it didn't look like that.

Owen, married 7 years, noted the important role marriage mentors had played in his life. He shared how the examples around him had been critical to how he approached marriage. He said,

> Just being around men who loved their wives, that was something that really encouraged me to want to exemplify that in my life, just in the way that they talked to their wives, treated their wives. When they make mistakes, to be open and honest and being willing to tell your wife that you're sorry. Just seeing a lot of great men who did that helped to encourage me to want to implement those in my own life.

What stands out to me about these examples is that they did not occur in formal settings. These were not church leaders or relationship educators. They were not even family members. They were just people who had a sphere of influence and used part of that influence to share details of their married life—details that made a difference in the motivations of several young millennials who did not have a lot of proximate examples of good marriages. Millennials need, more than ever, examples of good marriages in their life. While our personal romantic lives are often something we tend to keep private, these examples speak to the importance of sharing both successes and struggles with the younger generation.

The Intentional Marriage

With those final recommendations out of the way, I finally come to my parting thoughts. I have thought for many months about what the central take-away message of this study into millennial marriage has been. As I researched and wrote over the last year, I had many students and colleagues ask one similar question at various conferences or in the hallways outside my office: "What is the big take-away?" For many months, I was not certain what the answer to that question was. Eventually, I could add a few thoughts on some specific summary points, many of which I have included for you above. But that never felt like it got at the heart of the question. What did this all mean? What was the biggest thing I learned? As I began preparing the final chapters of this book, as I pondered over the data, both survey and interview, and considered what the central theme of all these data might be, it finally came to me. I remembered again where I started, with the assumption that perhaps millennials and their marriages would look decidedly less healthy than in the past. I then was left to wonder why I was not finding this, why marriage for millennials looked in many ways not only just as healthy as in generations past, but also—in some select areas—even better. These millennials were saying and doing things that countered decades of established relational science regarding what they should be saying and doing if they wanted healthy and long-standing relationships. Perhaps you, as a reader, have been left shaking your head across these chapters at some of the things these millennials have said about their marriages and about their spouses.

Yet healthy they remained. Their relationships looked generally strong and their outcomes were positive. Why? What was happening? The epiphany happened as I turned to one of the central themes of my academic research. My doctoral dissertation was focused on how teenagers thought about marriage and how those perceptions and beliefs predicted their actual marital behavior. I have written several reviews on this area of scholarship (Willoughby & Carroll, 2015; Willoughby et al., 2015) and it was the focus of my previous book (Willoughby & James, 2017). In short, much of this research suggests that millennials who think positively about marriage are a dwindling number. When young, single adults do have positive thoughts and attitudes about marriage, they tend to both get married at higher rates and have healthier relationships. How is this related to millennials who have already chosen to marry? The more I thought about it, I realized that millennials who are married are a more selective group than perhaps ever before in modern human history. With the social norms around most aspects of family life eroding, millennials have been afforded more choice and freedom in their lives than any previous generation. Yes, this increased choice has led to increased anxiety and fear, but it has also provided them with almost endless possibilities. Relationally, the story is no different. There is less stigma today for individuals who would rather spend their life engaging in causal relationships, open relationships, no relationships, or relationships of an almost endless variety and flavor. When viewed through that lens, millennials who select into marriage are likely becoming an increasingly unique group. And it is in that one uniform aspect of me-marriage that I think perhaps the answer to the paradox of millennial thinking and outcomes lie. You may disagree with their methods or with their relational approach, but almost all of them were intentional in their decision to marry. Whether it is for love, similar interests, or children, millennials who choose the path to marriage are increasingly doing so based on a commitment to the symbolic power of marriage and what it represents to them—a relationship of life-long commitment and personal happiness.

With this intentional mindset, many millennials understand that marriage will take work. Carter, a millennial reflecting on the difficulties of marriage, perhaps said it best when he explained what marriage meant to him. Carter shared, "Marriage is hard . . . . You have to put effort into it. A lot of people don't think about that. We have hard days, but marriage is awesome." Marriage was awesome to most millennials I spoke to. Millennials understand that effort will likely be required to navigate and balance marriage with the many other things they hope

212   *A New Case for Marriage*

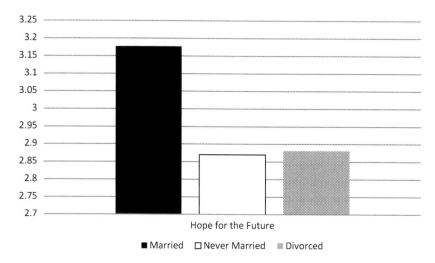

Figure 11.1 Estimated Mean for Millennials In Their Early 30s on a 4-Point Scale, by Marital Status.

to achieve in life. They entered marriage not only hoping for the best, but often believing that marriage was the right choice for them. Figure 11.1 shows how much agreement millennials had in my data with the statement that they had "hope for their future." This was measured on a 4-point scale ("none of the time" to "all of the time"). In our sample of 5,000 older millennials in their early 30s, and after controlling for a range of background factors, the married millennials were more likely to express hope about their future than their single or divorced counterparts. Millennials in me-marriages are a hopeful bunch. I believe this mindset, what I have begun to call the *intentional marriages of millennials*, is perhaps why there is still a case for marriage.

And so, with that, I leave you my thanks for undertaking this journey with me into me-marriage and all that it entails. I hope this book has given you some insight into the married lives of millennials and the successes and challenges they face. Whether you are of the older generation looking for ways to support millennials, a millennial trying to make sense of your own life, or a younger individual or couple wondering what the future will bring, I hope this book has brought to you some perspective on how marriage has and will continue to evolve. For the scholars out there, I hope this book has both answered some fundamental questions about marriage while also creating a host of other questions that you will be inspired to follow-up on. In my mind, the best scholarship is the type that generates new ideas and new questions, and I hope I have done that to some degree for some of you. Like anything in the social sciences, marriage is an evolving and changing institution. For now, millennials are largely reaping the benefits of this institution. But the last page of this journey has yet to be written, and the diverging paths forward into adulthood will only increase the nuance of trying to understand this generation that has captured so much of our cultural attention.

References

Allen, T. D., Johnson, R. C., Kiburz, K. M., & Shockley, K. M. (2013). Work–family conflict and flexible work arrangements: Deconstructing flexibility. *Personnel Psychology, 66,* 345–376.

Björklund, A., Ginther, D. K., & Sundström, M. (2007). Family structure and child outcomes in the USA and Sweden. *Journal of Population Economics, 20,* 183–201.

Cherlin, A. J. (2004). The deinstitutionalization of American marriage. *Journal of Marriage and Family, 66,* 848–861.

Fincham, F. D., Stanley, S. M., & Beach, S. R. (2007). Transformative processes in marriage: An analysis of emerging trends. *Journal of Marriage and Family, 69,* 275–292.

Fomby, P., & Cherlin, A. J. (2007). Family instability and child well-being. *American Sociological Review, 72,* 181–204.

Hill, E. J., Mead, N. T., Dean, L. R., Hafen, D. M., Gadd, R., Palmer, A. A., & Ferris, M. S. (2006). Researching the 60-hour dual-earner workweek: An alternative to the "opt-out revolution". *American Behavioral Scientist, 49,* 1184–1203.

Jeffries, V. (2000). Virtue and marital conflict: A theoretical formulation and research agenda. *Sociological Perspectives, 43,* 231–246.

Kalmijn, M. (2013). The educational gradient in marriage: A comparison of 25 European countries. *Demography, 50,* 1499–1520.

Lee, K. S., & Ono, H. (2012). Marriage, cohabitation, and happiness: A cross-national analysis of 27 countries. *Journal of Marriage and Family, 74,* 953–972.

Ludwig, V., & Brüderl, J. (2018). Is there a male marital wage premium? New evidence from the United States. *American Sociological Review, 83,* 744–770.

Ogolsky, B. G., Monk, J. K., Rice, T. M., & Oswald, R. F. (2019). Personal well-being across the transition to marriage equality: A longitudinal analysis. *Journal of Family Psychology, 33,* 422–423.

Shockley, K. M., & Allen, T. D. (2007). When flexibility helps: Another look at the availability of flexible work arrangements and work–family conflict. *Journal of Vocational Behavior, 71*(3), 479–493.

Stack, S., & Eshleman, J. R. (1998). Marital status and happiness: A 17-nation study. *Journal of Marriage and the Family, 60,* 527–536.

Waite, L. J. (1981). Young women's transition to marriage. *Demography, 18,* 681–694.

Willoughby, B. J., & Carroll, J. S. (2015). On the horizon: Marriage timing, beliefs, and consequences in emerging adulthood. *The Oxford handbook of emerging adulthood,* 280–295.

Willoughby, B. J., Hall, S. S., & Luczak, H. P. (2015). Marital paradigms: A conceptual framework for marital attitudes, values, and beliefs. *Journal of Family Issues, 36,* 188–211.

Willoughby, B. J., & James, S. L. (2017). *The marriage paradox: Why emerging adults love marriage yet push it aside.* Oxford University Press.

Zheng, H., & Thomas, P. A. (2013). Marital status, self-rated health, and mortality: overestimation of health or diminishing protection of marriage? *Journal of Health and Social Behavior, 54,* 128–143.

Appendix

Three datasets were used for this book. Two were large national survey datasets involving data from the United States. These were used for all quantitative analyses in the book (with one exception noted in Chapter 10). One smaller dataset was used for all the qualitative data presented throughout the book. Data collection procedure details for each dataset are presented below.

National U.S. Data on Millennials in their Early 30s (Project READY)

Data for this project came from Project READY (Researching Emerging Adults' Developmental Years). The study was approved by all appropriate IRB bodies. As part of several data collection efforts for this project, data were gathered from a nationally representative sample of 30–35-year-old millennials in the United States to obtain retroactive data on their 20s. These data were collected in 2016 through YouGov, a data collection firm. YouGov interviewed 5,215 respondents who were then matched down to a sample of 5,000 to produce the final dataset. The respondents were matched to a sampling frame on gender, age, race, education, party identification, ideology, and political interest. The frame was constructed by stratified sampling from the full 2010 American Community Survey (ACS) sample with selection within strata by weighted sampling with replacements (using the person weights on the public use file). Data on voter registration status and turnout were matched to this frame using the November 2010 Current Population Survey. Data on interest in politics and party identification were then matched to this frame from the 2007 Pew Religious Life Survey. The matched cases were weighted to the sampling frame using propensity scores. The matched cases and the frame were combined, and a logistic regression was estimated for inclusion in the frame. The propensity score function included age, gender, race/ethnicity, years of education, voter registration status, non-identification with a major party, census region, and ideology. The propensity scores were grouped into deciles of the estimated propensity score in the frame and post-stratified according to these deciles. The final weights were post-stratified to match a full stratification of 4-category age, 4-category race, gender, and 4-category education.

The analytic sample for this project was 59% female. The majority of the sample reported their race as White (69%). Other common racial categories were Black

Appendix 215

(12%), Hispanic (10%), Asian (4%), and mixed (3%). Eighty-seven percent of the sample reported a heterosexual orientation and 76% reported at least some college education. Of the total sample, 48% had completed at least a 4-year college degree. At the time of data collection, 54% of the sample reported full-time employment, while 7% reported being a full-time student. Sixty-one percent of the sample reported at least one biological child (M = 1.33). Fifty-four percent of the sample reported being married. For all analyses reported in the book, millennials who were currently married were compared to those who were divorced (but not currently married) or never married. Those who reported being widowed were removed from analyses.

National U.S. Data on Newlyweds (CREATE)

Participants for this study were respondents in the Couple Relationships and Transition Experiences (CREATE) study. The CREATE study is a nationally representative survey of newly married couples. The study was approved by all appropriate IRB bodies. Participants for the study were recruited using a two-stage cluster stratification sample design, with the first stage involving a sample of counties, and the second involving a sample of recent marriages within those selected counties. Counties were selected based on a probability proportion to size (PPS) design. Selection was based on county population size, marriage, divorce, and poverty rates, and the racial/ethnic distribution of the county. The number of marriages selected per county ranged from 40 to 280, depending on these five characteristics. This design yielded a sampling frame of 11,960 marriages across 239 counties. Ten counties did not have at least 40 marriages during the sampling period, leaving the final sampling frame at 11,889 marriages.

In the second stage, marriage record information was used, with assistance from publicly available databases, to locate couples and invite them to participate. To be included in the sample, respondents had to (a) be married and selected into the sample frame (since some marriage applicants did not end up marrying), (b) have at least one partner between 18 and 36 years of age at the start of the study, (c) be a first marriage for at least one of the partners in the dyad, and (d) be living within the U.S. The majority of couples in the study were married during 2014 (90%), with the remainder in 2013 (4%) and 2015 (6%).

Based on the Dillman survey method, potential participants were first contacted by mailed letters that contained a $2.00 bill with an invitation to participate and instructions on how to enroll in the study. For those who did not respond to the initial invitation, follow-up postal mailings, e-mail invitations, and phone calls were made. As is common with online surveys, participants were asked to read and then acknowledge consent to participate in the study. Participating couples were given a $50.00 Visa gift card upon completion of the survey.

Among the 11,889 couples contacted, 8,140 declined participation by either not answering or responding, and 1,220 did not meet inclusion criteria. A total of 2,187 marriages were recruited into the study, drawing a raw response rate of 18.24% (2,187/11,889). After dropping ineligible couples, the adjusted response rate was 20.50% (2,187/10,669). Of the 2,187 marriages, data from both members

216 *Appendix*

of the dyad were received in 1,889 (86%) cases, and data from one member of the dyad were received in the remaining 298 (14%) cases.

Additional information gained in the recruiting process allowed us to estimate a more accurate response rate, in accordance with the standards set by prominent survey research organizations. To calculate this, we first estimated the percentage of marriages known to be ineligible (i.e., the percentage of people who responded but who were not eligible to participate). In total, the proportion of known marriages that were ineligible for participation was .48. If we assume that the proportion of ineligibles among those who either refused or did not respond (the unknowns) was similar, then there were an estimated 5,147 couples who were ineligible for our survey. When subtracting these from the original 11,889, we get an estimated total response rate among eligible households of 32.43% (2,187/ 11,889–5,147).

Among the unweighted dataset, husbands and wives were generally in their late 20s (husband M = 29.82, wife M = 28.03). The most common racial category was White (husband = 65.4%, wife = 65.5%), followed by Latinx (husband = 12.8%, wife = 13.2%). About half of all participants (husband = 46.0%, wife = 55.5%) reported some type of post-secondary degree. The most common religious denomination was Protestant (husband = 48.3%, wife = 49.7%) followed by none (husband = 24.4%, wife = 22.1%). For most comparisons reported in the book, millennial couples were those who were under the age of 35 while "older" couples were those where both partners reported an age over 35.

Me-Marriage Project

Interview data for this project were taken from the Me-Marriage Project. The study was approved by all appropriate IRB bodies. For this project, 101 married couples were interviewed from across the United States. Couples were identified through two mechanisms. First, a mailing list of married couples between the ages of 25 and 35 was obtained and emails were sent to 2,491 couples. This initial data collection effort resulted in very low response so an alternative recruitment method was employed. Targeted recruitment ads on Facebook were posted to couples between the ages of 25 and 35 in targeted states aimed at collecting data from a diverse geographic area in the United States. Potential couples were sent to a screening survey where they were asked about their relationship history, willingness to be interviewed for the study, and basic information about their relationship status. The number of couples screened was 918, of which 468 were found to qualify for the study. Those potential couples were contacted and formally invited to the study. The number of couples who responded to this invitation and joined the study was 101 (21.5%).

Once couples were enrolled in the study, they took a 10-minute survey asking for additional background information and information related to their relationship. They then scheduled either a phone or video interview with the project team. Couples were given the option to be interviewed together or separately and this did not change the format of the interview or the questions asked. Interviews were semi-structured, with trained interviewers or the principal investigator asking a

Appendix 217

series of central questions and then letting the couple dedicate the course and content of the interview. Couples who were interviewed together were encouraged to both share their thoughts and opinions, but the interviewer did not require or encourage a certain amount of engagement from either partner. Questions centered on understanding the nature and processes within each marriage ("How have you negotiated roles in your marriage?") and their general thoughts about marriage ("How would you rank marriage compared to other life priorities?").

All interviews were recorded and transcribed by a team of research assistants. After transcriptions were completed, the research team read through every transcript and began to discuss themes that stood out related to marriage and marital process. After each interview, the transcripts were initially coded using both Values coding (Gable & Wolf, 1993) and In Vivo coding (Charmaz, 2014). Values coding aims at exploring the underlying values, attitudes, and beliefs expressed by the participants. In Vivo coding seeks to code interviews based on retaining the participant's own voice and words.

References

Charmaz, K. (2014). Constructing grounded theory. Sage.

Gable, R. K. & Wolf, M. B. (1993). Instrument Development in the Affective Domain: Measuring Attitudes and Values in the Business and School Setting (pp: 275.). Kluwer Academic Publishers, Boston.

Index

abuse 113, 115–16
addiction 99–100
advice: relationship 64–7
aggression: relational 57–8, 128, 205
alternative seeking 72–3
altruism 38–9
ambition *see* goals
anxiety 9, 46–7, 190–1, 195, 207–8, 211;
    see also health
argument *see* conflict

baby boomers 4, 44–5, 147, 174
balance: of career and marriage 62, 76–8,
    84, 90–2; struggles with 85–9, 122, 133;
    see also priorities
benefits of marriage *see under* marriage

career: balancing 31; gendered 90–1, 171;
    limited 94–6; loss of 179; and marriage 63,
    76–9, 82, 85–94, 95–7, 207; as a priority
    42–5, 76–7, 85–6, 88–93, 141–2
children: and marriage *see* parenthood
choice *see* options
Christianity *see* religion
cohabitation 12, 20–3, 27, 52–5, 58–9, 205;
    backlash against 13; and parenthood 123
comfort 117
commitment 24–26, 68, 99, 150, 154–57,
    160, 188; avoiding 31; constraint 26, 70
communication 56–7, 60–6, 71–2, 194–5,
    197–9, 209; and mental health 110
community 159–62
companionship 32, 114–16, 157–8
comparison 72–3
compromise 39, 88, 90–1, 110–11, 158
conflict: in marriage 50–1, 56–7, 58, 99, 113;
    parenthood and 128, 134; priority 84, 88;
    resolution of 61–2
confrontation 65; *see also* conflict
counseling *see* therapy

courtship *see* dating
cross-cultural relationships 193–6
cultural differences 192–3, 203
    see also cross-cultural relationships

dating 27, 121, 145, 151–4, 165, 192;
    priorities 16–18, 152
debt 81–2
dependency 99
diversity 184–5, 199–200; *see also* same-sex
    relationships *and* racial minorities *and*
    monogamy
divorce 12, 13, 36–7, 60–1, 66–72, 80, **212;**
    attitude toward 67, 69–71, 155–6, 188;
    mental health and 102–3, 105–6
dreams *see* goals
drugs *see under* health
dual-income household *see under* income

economic benefits of marriage 78–82, 97,
    205; *see also* income
education 30, 76–8; gendered 85, 95–6; about
    marriage 160–62; marriage and 78, 82–5,
    89–90, 94–6, 205; minorities and 191;
    parenthood and 127, 130
empathy 124
engagement 8, 190
equality 186, 191–2, 208; gender 167–8
ethnic minorities *see* racial minorities
examples of positive marriages *see* mentoring
exercise *see under* health
extended family 115

faith *see* religion *and* spirituality
family *see* parenthood
fertility 123, 129, 135, 142, 186, 207
finances *see* income *and* economic benefits of
    marriage
flexibility 41, 117, 198, 206, 208
focus: on self 9

Index 219

fostering 131
fulfillment *see* happiness

gender roles 124, 145; antiquated 165, 174; fluid 166, 169–73, 180–1, 206–7; frustration with 168–9, 172–3, 189; impact on marriage 167, 173, 175–9; me-marriage and 167–9, 171–2, 175–6, 178; neutrality in 167; traditional 165–9, 173–4, 177–81; *see also* roles
goals: career 88–94, 97; personal 63, 87, 121, 136, 142; relationship 85, 121; *see also* priorities
growth: personal 34–5, 39, 47, 68, 135, 203

happiness 178–9; and marriage 12–13, 33–41, 52, 60, 205; personal 41–8, 51, 79, 141–2, 154, 192, 211; *see also* individualism; in jeopardy 68; sacrificing 158
health: drugs and 104–5; emotional 110–14; and exercise 103–4; gendered 101–2; mental 46, 64–8, 100–106, 108–17, 123–24, 187, 205; marriage improving 101–2, 114–18; and me-marriage 109–15, 117–18; and parenthood 121–24, 126–7; physical 99–100, 103–5, 107–9, 117; relationship 51–2, 59, 73, 84, 191, 205, 207–8, 211; satisfaction with 104–7, 205
homeowning 31, 82
honesty 63, 71–2, 150, 198–9
housework *see* gender roles

income 78–82, 93, 205; dual-income households 78–9, 181–2, 206
incompatibility 71
independence 30–1
individualism 3–5, 17, 32–3, 59, 193, 203, 207–8; and parenting 122, 207
infidelity 54–5, 70, 110; *see also* alternative seeking
interracial relationships *see* cross-cultural relationships
intimacy: physical 152; *see also* sex
investment: in marriage 50–1

legal implications of marriage *see under* marriage
lesbian couples *see* same-sex relationships
life satisfaction **36**, 36–9
location: as determined by career 89, 93
loneliness 102
love: unconditional 150, 157

male privilege 173–4
marriage: age and 13–14; *see also* maturity; anxiety about *see* anxiety; apathy about 18–19, 25; benefits of 6, 9–10, 26, 32–4, 39–40, 52–5, 78–80, 176–7, 204–6; build up to *see* courtship *and* cohabitation; careers and *see under* career; children and *see* parenthood; delayed 79, 83, 85–6, 196; drawbacks of 50–1; education and *see under* education; expectations of 11–12, 15–16, 167, 173, 208–9; importance of 23–4; individualized *see* individualism; as an institution 18–19, 33, 35–6, 52, 68–9, 150, 203; legal implications 14–15, 25, 99, 131–2, 185–6, 188–90; long-term implications of 18, 52; perceived value of 13, 23–5, 40, 46; preparation for 160; *see also* dating *and* therapy; as a priority *see under* priorities; quality of 50–3, 58–60, 62, 103, 123; readiness for 19–20; rejection of 16, 25; religion and *see under* religion; strength of 5, 51; struggles 62, 64–5, 70; *see also* conflict; success of 23, 41, 50, 52, 60–2, 67, 160, 211–12; symbolic meaning of 15, 23–5, 132, 211; timing of *see* timing; *see also* me-marriage *and* tool mentality
maturity: and marriage 13–14, 20
media: portrayal of millennials 1, 4, 32
me-marriage 24, 30, 32–6, 40–2, 45–8, 154; benefits of 90, 205–6, 211–12; careers and *see under* career; challenges of 59–60, 72, 94, 200, 203, 206–7; *see also under* health; and divorce 71–2; future of 208–9; quality of 51–4, 59
mental health *see under* health
mentors 161–2, 189–91, 196–7, 209–10
minority groups *see* diversity *and* same-sex relationships *and* racial minorities *and* monogamy
momentum: in relationships 111–12, 118
monogamy: erosion of 197–200
mortality 150; marriage affecting 102; *see also* religion *and* spirituality

narcissism 32
nature versus nurture 167
needs, individual 62–5, 71, 116, 138, 141

older married couples 38; *see also* baby boomers
online dating 30, 86, 99, 110, 121, 195
opportunity: cost 42–3; lost 94–6
optimism 43, 51, 107
options: for careers 85–6; for relationships 12–16

220   Index

parenthood 9, 42, 47, 90–1, 100, 112;
  balancing marriage and 129, 133–4, 137–8,
  141–2; challenges with 121–25, 136–9,
  141–3, 207; factors indicating 127, 130;
  fear of 133–4, 136–7, 142; intentionality of
  124, 127; marriage before 129–32;
  me-marriage and 121–22, 128–30, 133,
  138–41; non-marital 123–5, 129;
  relationship satisfaction *see under*
  relationship; religion *see under* religion;
  timing of *see under* timing; transition to
  123–7, 134, 136–7, 139; *see also under* roles
partners 30, 45–6; selection of 16–18
peers: as resources 66–7
perception of marriage 24–5, 113–14;
  gendered 175–6
personal discovery 90, 114
poverty 43, 62, 114, 191
power dynamics 173–5
pragmatism 16–18, 21–2, 67–8, 132, 152
pregnancy 135; *see also* parenthood
priorities: balancing 76, 86, 93, 207; career as
  a *see under* career; challenges with 138–9,
  207; marriage and 31–2, 41–4, 66, 122,
  138–42, 154–5, 158–161; parenthood and
  136–42, 207; personal 39, 41–8; religious
  146, 159; shifting 42, 44, 91; 136–42
problem solving 62
purpose, fulfillment of 15

racial minorities 191–7
racism 191–2, 194, 196
readiness for marriage *see under* marriage
relationship: aggression *see* aggression; length
  53; satisfaction 53–58, 103, 123–8, 142,
  185–7, 194, 205; success 12, 16–17, 23–4
relativism 14, 18–19, 147
religion: dating and 145–6, 151–3, 162, 165;
  as a deal breaker 162–3; individualized
  149–51, 163; *see also* spirituality; marriage
  and 26, 92, 112, 146–9, 151–9, 160;
  me-marriage and 149–50, 157–8, 163;
  organized 147–50; parenthood and 150,
  159; as a priority *see under* priorities; as a
  resource *see under* resources; retreat from
  147–9, 162; return to 148–9; *see also*
  sanctification
resentment 94, 137, 172–3
resources 43–5, 64–7, 82–4, 111–12, 124, 190,
  197; drains on 109–10, 139–40; emotional
  113–18; online 66; for parenting 137,
  139–42; religious 146, 159–61; unhelpful
  64; *see also* time *and* economic benefits of
  marriage
risk-taking 101

role models *see* mentors
roles: absence of 169, 172–3, 177, 180–1, 208;
  expectations of 173, 179–80, 189, 208;
  in marriage 155, 165–6; and parenthood
  124, 134, 136–8, 171, 179–80; shared
  166–7, 170–73; shifting 167–72; *see also*
  gender roles

sacrifice 42–4, 51, 77, 133, 157–9, 178, 208;
  of career trajectory 87–94, 97; fear of 39,
  94; as parents 140, 142–3; of time 87
same-sex relationships 185–91; challenges
  with 187–8
sanctification 155
satisfaction: life 126–7, 141, 187; sexual
  124–5, 140, 185, 187; *see also under*
  relationship
security 90
selection effect 82, 85, 93, 101, 104–6,
  204–5
self-worth 41
sex 54–5, 187; *see also under* satisfaction
single, being 206: advantages of 9–10, 12,
  95
"sliding" relationships 18
social media 32, 63, 65–6, 73
social norms 15–16, 133, 184–5, 188–91,
  197–8, 203, 208–9; erosion of 23–7,
  33, 110, 130; pressure to conform to
  188–9; 193
social status: as tied to marriage 25–6
soul mate 152–3
spirituality 146–7, 149–51, 160; loss of
  162–3
stability: emotional 115; familial 209; financial
  15; lack of 65; relationship 53–59, 125–33,
  142, 185–7, 191, 194, 205; societal 15, 177
stay-at-home parent *see* roles
stress 46–8, 123–4, 169, 182, 188, 190–1, 197;
  see also health *and under* parenthood
substance abuse *see* addiction
success: career 82; *see also* career; global 41–3;
  in marriage *see under* marriage
support: emotional 115–17, 169, 190; in a
  marriage 46–8, 63, 103, 190; from peers 71

taboo: marital problems as 64
teamwork 77
technology: as a marriage resource 64
therapy 50–1, 57, 64–8, 111, 159
time: as a limited resource 42–4, 50, 68, 86,
  124, 140–1
timing 86–7; of marriage 13, 76–77, 100,
  133–5, 151–2; of parenthood 124–5,
  131–36, 142–3

tool mentality 11–16, 27, 39, 69
transitions: interdomain 42
transparency 63–4; *see also* honesty
two-parent household 131

unity 170

values: shared 77, 100, 121, 153–54, 192–3

weddings 82, 132, 151, 160

Printed in the United States
By Bookmasters